THROUGH WITH KINGS AND ARMIES

Through with Kings and Armies

The Marriage of George and Jean Edwards

Rhonda Mawhood Lee

CASCADE *Books* • Eugene, Oregon

THROUGH WITH KINGS AND ARMIES
The Marriage of George and Jean Edwards

Copyright © 2012 Rhonda Mawhood Lee. All rights reserved. Except for brief quotations in critical publications or reviews, no part of this book may be reproduced in any manner without prior written permission from the publisher. Write: Permissions, Wipf and Stock Publishers, 199 W. 8th Ave., Suite 3, Eugene, OR 97401.

Cascade Books
An Imprint of Wipf and Stock Publishers
199 W. 8th Ave., Suite 3
Eugene, OR 97401

www.wipfandstock.com

ISBN 13: 978-1-61097-270-3

Cataloging-in-Publication data:

Lee, Rhonda Mawhood.

   Through with kings and armies : the marriage of George and Jean Edwards / Rhonda Mawhood Lee.

   x + 178 p. ; 23 cm. —Includes bibliographical references.

   ISBN 13: 978-1-61097-270-3

   1. Pacifists—United States—Biography. I. Title.

JZ5540 .L44 2012

Manufactured in the U.S.A.

Contents

List of Illustrations · vi
Acknowledgments · vii

Introduction: "I Knew that We Would Never, Ever Argue about Pacifism" · 1

1 "We Really Needed to Start a New Way of Thinking": George and Jean's Early Years · 9

2 "At Least We Make a Witness": Anti-Communism and the Vietnam War · 43

3 "When People Become Peacemakers, This Is Their Vocation": The Founding of the Louisville Fellowship of Reconciliation · 82

4 "Praying for Peace and Paying for War Are Inconsistent": Radicalism in Retirement · 120

Epilogue—"Through with Kings and Armies": The Legacy of George and Jean Edwards · 157

Questions and Topics for Discussion · 163

Bibliography · 167
Illustrations · 175

Illustrations

1. "Buddy" Edwards at a Presbyterian youth gathering, circa 1941 (Courtesy of Jean Edwards) · 177

2. George and Jean Edwards in front of Louisville Presbyterian Theological Seminary, January 1948 (Courtesy of Jean Edwards) · 177

3. Riley, Virginia, and Johnny Edwards with their Sunday school class, Peace Presbyterian Church, circa 1961 (Courtesy of Jean Edwards) · 178

4. George Edwards in the classroom, circa 1975 (Courtesy of Louisville Presbyterian Theological Seminary) · 178

5. Jim Flynn at the Louisville airport with Central American refugees, circa 1983 (Courtesy of the Louisville Fellowship of Reconciliation—LFOR) · 179

6. Jean and George Edwards celebrating the twentieth anniversary of the Louisville Fellowship of Reconciliation, 1995 (Courtesy of the LFOR) · 179

7. Cover page, LFOR newsletter, March 1988 (Courtesy of the LFOR) · 180

Acknowledgments

MANY FRIENDS, TEACHERS, AND benefactors have helped bring this book into being. It gives me joy to thank them here, hoping that they will understand how very grateful I am.

I was fortunate to be awarded a Sabbatical Grant for Researchers from the Louisville Institute that allowed me to spend a year working full time on *Through with Kings and Armies*. I am grateful to the Institute, to the Lilly Endowment that funds it, and especially to the Institute's executive director, Jim Lewis, and his administrative assistant, Suzanne Case, for their generosity and kindness. I would never have begun working on the book without the prior guidance and encouragement of my professors at Duke, William H. Chafe, Peter H. Wood, Raymond Gavins, and Susan Thorne, and at Louisville Seminary, Kathryn L. Johnson and Dale C. Andrews. Amy Plantinga Pauw offered information about Presbyterian heritage. Rick Nutt and Steven J. Taylor generously shared their work on conscientious objectors and peace activists, while Gerhard L. Weinberg showed gracious interest in my work and shared his knowledge of sources about dissenters from war. Tracy K'Meyer introduced me to George and Jean Edwards and shared the hours of interviews she conducted with them in 1996, along with her encyclopedic knowledge of Southern history. A. Glenn Crothers was a thoughtful conversation partner about faith and pacifism, and provided technical assistance with several of the photos that illustrate this book. None of these scholars should be held responsible for any of my errors, including those that an Episcopalian will make when discussing Reformed theology and Presbyterian polity. For connecting me to Cascade Books, I thank Stanley Hauerwas, and at

Cascade, I am grateful for my editor, Charlie Collier, and for Christian Amondson and their whole staff.

Historians could not work without archivists and librarians. I am particularly grateful to Greta Boers, Lauren Crowell, Carson Holloway, Kelley Lawton, Danette Pachtner, Lee Sorensen, Yunyi Wang, and Ken Wetherington, all with Duke's Lilly Library, who provided assistance on an almost daily basis for months. My archival research was graciously facilitated by Wendy E. Chmielewski of the Swarthmore College Peace Collection; Carrie Daniels and Tom Owen of the University of Louisville; Elizabeth Gates of Rhodes College; the late Marcia Hertzman of The Temple (Congregation Adath Israel Brith Sholom); Maureen Hill of the National Archives in Atlanta; Lisa Jacobson of the Presbyterian Historical Society; Angela Morris of Louisville Seminary; and Judy Williams of Belmont University. For access to privately held church records, I owe a debt to the clergy, staff, and people of Blacknall Presbyterian Church, Durham, North Carolina; Central Presbyterian Church, Louisville, Kentucky; Christ Church Cathedral, Louisville; Church of the Epiphany, Louisville; and Pittsboro Presbyterian Church, Pittsboro, North Carolina. For sharing their memories and organizational records, I thank Mark Baridon; Eileen Blanton; David Brown Kinloch; John Cumbler; Bob Cunningham; Johnny Edwards; Virginia Edwards-Menz; Riley Edwards-Raudonat; Jim Flynn; Pat Geier; David Horvath; Paula Jackson; Mattie Jones; the staff of the Kentucky Civil Liberties Union; Joe Sigur; Malcolm H. Squires, III; Glen Stassen; and Terry Weiss.

I am blessed with a large circle of friends who supported my work on this book, just as they have accompanied me in so many other endeavors. Among them are Rich, Hannah, and Marika Ball-Damberg; Emily Burrill and Erik Anderson; Dirk Bönker, who shared not only his friendship but also his knowledge of German history, and Kate Moran; David and Leslie Carter; Kat Charron; David and Shelley Cline; my bishop, Michael B. Curry; Éric Darier; Kirsten Delegard and James Eli Shiffer; Maria Doerfler; Kathleen DuVal and Marty Smith; Deborah Finkel; Marjorie George and Mark Straubel; Christine Gilsenan and Vincent Masciotra; Cheri, Michael, and Clara Harper; Lisa Hazirjian and Michelle Kaiser; Ralph Hirsbrunner; Michael and Meg Buerkel Hunn; Jonah and Caty Kendall; Dwayne, Nancy, and Krista Lee; Adriane Lentz-Smith and Christian Lentz; Jehangir Malegam and Kathryn Mathers; Gordon Mantler; Danielle McGuire; Malissa McLeod and Brett Whalen; Towns Middleton; Colin and Lisa Miller; Tim Moody; the late Ned Reiter; Gwen Schulman, Carl Mulvey, and

Acknowledgments

Dylan Mulvey-Schulman; Jake Selwood; Mark Sheftall; Maggie and Andy Silton; Travis K. Smith; Phil and Kim Stern; Tim Tyson, for his support of my application to the Louisville Institute, and Perri Morgan; Fr. Anthony Vinson, OSB; and Sister Joanna Walsh, FCJ, and my fellow students in the FCJ Sisters' training program for the ministry of spiritual direction. Three friends—Sarah Ball-Damberg, Ann Claycombe, and Craig Werner—provided support, editing, and brainstorming on a nearly daily basis. I'm grateful that they continue to answer my calls and e-mails.

When I met Wayne E. Lee in 1992, I wasn't interested in getting to know a man with whom I thought I had only the Persian Gulf War in common: I had protested against it in my home city of Montréal, while he, a U.S. Army Engineer, had fought in it. We soon became friends, however, after he informed me with a smile that I was not the first to spurn him as (here he quoted *Doonesbury*, among others) a "running dog of the imperialist order." We have both grown a lot in twenty years of sharing our lives and our vocations, and we hope that our marriage testifies to the value of practicing faith, hope, and love while staying in conversation about war and peace. I'm grateful for Wayne's daily support, for his editor's eye, and for his military history library, so useful to a student of peace.

My greatest debt is to George and Jean Edwards. At our first meeting in 2005, I thought I was simply considering the possibility of writing about the Louisville Fellowship of Reconciliation, but Jean's cheery greeting sealed my fate: "I'm just delighted you're going to write about the LFOR!" Never before had I encountered such a combination of tenacity and grace, and now I am grateful for it. Jean and George welcomed me into their home on a weekly basis for months as I worked with the LFOR records, answering my questions as best they could while respecting my need as a scholar to write about the group as I understood it. George kindly and firmly corrected a number of errors that unfortunately remained in the final version of my dissertation, so that they would not be reproduced elsewhere. After his death in 2010, as I was writing what Jean insisted on calling "your book about George," she generously offered documents and photos from her personal collection. I pray that this story of George and Jean's witness for peace will testify to their commitment, and be a blessing and a spur to others.

For any errors of fact or interpretation, I hope that only I will be held accountable, and then forgiven.

Introduction

"I Knew that We Would Never, Ever Argue about Pacifism"

GEORGE RILEY EDWARDS AND Jean Branch Maney got engaged in the late fall of 1947, on a Saturday night that stretched from a church conference in Memphis to Jean's parents' home in Nashville. George had just returned from an eighteen-month sojourn in Italy rebuilding war-destroyed houses with the American Friends Service Committee, and was due to enroll at Louisville Presbyterian Theological Seminary in January; Jean was the director of Christian Education at a Nashville church. Meeting by chance at the conference after years apart, the childhood friends discovered, in Jean's words, that they "had a lot to catch up on." Neither wanted their conversation to end. As time passed and Jean observed that she needed to be at church for worship the next morning, George postponed a speaking engagement to drive her and one of her youth group members the more than two hundred miles back to Nashville. When he and Jean found themselves back at the house where she lived with her parents, she later remembered, "We talked and we talked that night, and it was getting very, very late . . . Then he decided he'd ask me if I would go to Louisville with him." Jean said she would. They attended church together the next morning before George returned to Memphis; by the end of December they were married and on their way to Louisville.[1]

---

1. Jean M. Edwards interview with K'Meyer, 15–16. Jean remembered the conference as taking place in either October or November.

Their whirlwind courtship was years in the making. Although Jean had grown up in Nashville and George in Memphis, they had become friends in the 1930s as teenagers who regularly attended the camps and youth conferences of the Presbyterian Church (US).[2] George was already a charismatic speaker, capturing Jean's attention as he addressed his peers on such subjects as the dangers of gambling and alcohol, and, as war loomed in Europe, the Christian call to nonviolence. But his sweet voice won her heart. A trained singer, George often performed solos during the camp worship services. One afternoon, as Jean rested in her cabin, the sound of his rehearsal floated across the grounds. As she listened to his baritone singing "I Walked Today Where Jesus Walked" and "Deep River," Jean later recalled, "That was when I fell madly in love with his voice, and also with him!" The constant presence of George's steady girlfriend, Tommie Jean Haywood, kept his interactions with Jean from going beyond group discussions and sing-alongs, but the church continued to bring the two together.[3] By 1939, when George was nineteen and Jean eighteen, both had been elected to the council (or governing committee) of their synod (the regional PCUS body), which held its annual summer meetings at the Montreat church conference center in the North Carolina mountains, three hundred miles east of Nashville. George would drive from Memphis with a group of friends who would all spend the night at the Maney home and then "squeeze [Jean] in for the rest of the journey."[4]

War soon separated the friends. In his senior year of college, George renounced his draft deferment as a pre-divinity student, registered as a conscientious objector, and entered a Civilian Public Service camp, while Jean married a soldier, Jim Gregory, after she graduated from college. When Jean and George met again that night in 1947 as a veteran conscientious objector and a war widow, the old spark reignited, but this time their connection was grounded, not in adolescent attraction, but in a deeper love, inseparable from the faith they shared. Fifty years later,

---

2. The Presbyterian Church (US) was the southern branch of a church that, like most of its white Protestant counterparts in the United States, split before the Civil War over the question of whether or not faithful Christians could own slaves. For a discussion of how these divisions reflected and contributed to the nation's division, see Goens, *Broken Churches, Broken Nation*. The northern and southern Presbyterian churches reunited in 1983 to form the Presbyterian Church (USA).

3. Jean Edwards e-mail to Rhonda Mawhood Lee, November 21, 2006. George was later elected president of the Young People's League of the Tennessee Synod; *Sou'wester*, December 5, 1941.

4. Jean Edwards e-mail to Rhonda Mawhood Lee, November 21, 2006.

Introduction

Jean summed up the reason why she trusted her partnership with George would last: from the night they got engaged, she said, "I knew that we would never, ever argue about pacifism."[5]

In their journey from adolescence to adulthood, both George and Jean had deepened their conviction that Jesus Christ commanded his followers to renounce war and violence, and that complicity with white supremacy and militarism had warped American Christianity into a poor—although powerful in worldly terms—substitute for the gospel. In his eighties, George summed up the belief that had stood at the center of his faith for decades: "The confession of Christ, to me, means that you are through with kings and armies."[6] While most of the Edwardses' Christian compatriots assumed that loyalty to Christ and to the United States overlapped, or were identical, the couple proclaimed that not only was patriotism often incompatible with Christianity, but the church's own beliefs and practices could betray the gospel. For sixty-three years, until George's death in 2010, the Edwardses' marriage was the foundation for a witness against war that placed them at odds with both church and state in an era when the spirit of anti-Communism led most Americans to place their trust in weapons.

For most of their life together, Jean and George carried out their witness in one city, Louisville, Kentucky, whose charms and flaws they grew to know well as George taught at Louisville Presbyterian Theological Seminary. Over the years, they bore with the city and challenged it in ways—always nonviolent—that were particular to that place, while keeping faith with the larger prophetic movements calling for peace and justice within America's borders and beyond. Jean and George's testimony raised the hackles of many, as they challenged established definitions of patriotism and the norm of white supremacy, and, in their later years, extended civil disobedience so far as to withhold payment of tax funds earmarked for military purposes. Others found that the Edwardses' example inspired them to deeper faith and more consistent practice, particularly after Jean and George cofounded the Louisville Fellowship of Reconciliation (LFOR), a chapter of the country's oldest and largest pacifist organization, in 1975. That group offered them the allies they needed to persist in their witness as a tiny but motivated minority.

---

5. Jean Edwards interview with K'Meyer, 28.
6. George and Jean Edwards interview with Lee.

George and Jean Edwards' experience is exceptional in many ways, but it is not idiosyncratic. The story of their life together poses questions every Christian should consider, even those whose vision of the faithful life differs significantly from the Edwardses'. What does it mean to live daily as a disciple of Jesus Christ, knowing that obedience can be costly in a world that is—today as in his earthly lifetime—governed by power rooted in violence? When our duties as citizens of an earthly nation conflict with our obligations as inhabitants of God's present and future kingdom, how do we express our ultimate loyalty? Most importantly, how can we build communities of witnesses to discern faithful responses to those questions, and to sustain each other through the challenges inherent in this lifelong journey?

For over six decades, George and Jean explored and answered those questions together, and for that reason, their story invites reflection on the nature and purposes of marriage. At a time when both church and state are wrestling with questions about the forms that marriage may take, and who may live within it, the church must work together to discern just what we might be defending or expanding. What is marriage for? How can a vocation to marriage combine with the other vocations to which Christians may be called? How does marriage relate to the great commandment to love God fully, and one's neighbor as oneself? Jean and George's life together is a love story, but not one that fits the romantic ideal that defines love for so many people, both inside and outside the church.[7] Theirs offers another, more authentic vision of Christian marriage: as a community rooted in the church that joins with other households to form disciples who will testify to their faith with their lives. Before Jean and George were spouses, they were friends, and brother and sister in Christ; after they married, their covenant with each other was inseparable from their commitment to live as members of a peacemaking community, within and without the walls of their home. Working within the traditional gender roles of their time, they supported each other's vocations: as leaders in the church, as parents to three children born just over three years apart, and as public advocates for peace. Their relationship had its tensions: the couple were known equally well for their squabbles about small matters—Jean's lack of punctuality and George's tendency toward long-windedness—as for their unwavering agreement on the blasphemy and futility of war. Seen in the context of their enduring union, however,

---

7. For historical background on the development of the romantic ideal of marriage, see Coontz, *Marriage, A History*.

those daily disagreements simply affirm the truth of theologian Stanley Hauerwas's comment that Christian marriage is "the practice of fidelity over a lifetime in which you can look back upon the marriage and call it love. It is a hard discipline over many years."[8]

As the physical, spiritual, emotional, and economic union of two persons, Christian marriage is intensely personal and intimate, but it is not private. Secular American law also defines marriage as public: a legal contract that confers status and enforceable rights and obligations.[9] Despite the secular law's partial roots in Christian teaching, however, the church's claims about the public nature of marriage run far deeper.[10] Marriage is a covenant within which disciples can offer each other daily mutual support, express their sexuality, and nurture children. But Christians have also historically proclaimed that the desire spouses feel for one another, and the sexual expression they reserve for each other, offers a glimpse of God's passionate, noncoercive love for humankind. The community that married persons form, then, is inseparable from the divine kingdom to which their common life—and the life of the whole church—points. As such, marriage is a necessarily public commitment that fosters, and requires the support of, the broader community of disciples. It is a spiritual practice, a rule of life jointly and freely undertaken, rooted in nonviolence and the daily practice of hospitality and forgiveness, that both depends on and cultivates the fruit of the Spirit: love, joy, peace, patience, kindness, generosity, faithfulness, gentleness, and self-control. Rodney Clapp put it succinctly when he wrote that Christians "get married because this is the key way they participate as sexual beings in an adventure far surpassing the potentials of any aphrodisiac, the adventure of witnessing to and building up God's kingdom on earth."[11] Jean and George Edwards shared in that adventure together for over six decades.

Through with Kings and Armies focuses on George and Jean's public witness, exploring the challenges facing those who would testify with

---

8. "Faith Fires Back."

9. Cott, *Public Vows* is a detailed exploration of the state's regulation of marriage in the United States.

10. The other primary influence on American marriage law is Enlightenment ideas about the freedom of autonomous individuals to make contracts. Witte, Jr., *From Sacrament to Contract* offers a detailed historical discussion of marriage in the Roman Catholic, Lutheran, Calvinist, Anglican, and Enlightenment traditions.

11. Clapp, "From Family Values to Family Virtues," 199. Clapp elaborates his theology of the Christian family, including the particular witness of unmarried Christians, in his *Families at the Crossroads*.

their lives about the heresy of militarism and the sinfulness of war. In the support Jean and George offered each other and found in their family and friends, and in the ways in which their collective witness fell short—as all witness does—this book suggests what might be necessary to create a peacemaking community. The Edwardses' greatest challenge, as pacifists in a just war church and as dissidents from white supremacy and other forms of violence, was to connect with others who understood the gospel as they did, to create the network of households they needed for mutual support and accountability.[12] The Edwardses' cooperation with fellow Christians, their attempts to build interfaith alliances, and their work with secular activists invite reflection about the extent to which the church is called to focus on a distinctively Christian witness, or to work with people of different beliefs who share the same goals, and how to do either with integrity.

I am not a disinterested observer of George and Jean Edwards' work for peace. We met while I was studying at the Louisville Presbyterian Theological Seminary, where George had taught for years (retiring long before I arrived), and I have written and spoken about the work of the Louisville Fellowship of Reconciliation. While I have disagreed at times with their positions on particular issues or with their tactics, I affirm the faith claim that was the bedrock of their life together: that the God Christians worship does not bless war. Jean and George stood tenaciously by that simple confession in a world, and a church, where it is considered radical and at times even heretical, because they understood another message of Jesus: that his followers could expect to be misunderstood, maligned, and even persecuted for following his nonviolent way.

The memory of George and Jean's tenacity sustained me when I became the vicar of St. Joseph's Episcopal Church in Durham, North Carolina, in 2006. St. Joseph's had split because of disagreements about human sexuality the previous Easter, when the rector and most of the congregation had left the Episcopal Church to form a new church in another branch of the Anglican tradition. After an interim period of several months, I arrived to pastor a church of about a dozen deeply faithful but exhausted souls. They held a variety of different beliefs about sexuality and Christian marriage, but they shared one deep desire: to follow Jesus Christ by worshipping God and loving their neighbors inside and

---

12. David Matzko McCarthy offers a vision of Christian families as members of interdependent networks of households, within the community of the church, in his *Sex and Love in the Home.*

outside the church walls. The church was soon challenged to define what form that love would take. On its grounds lived a community of homeless men—and the occasional woman—who had gathered there because the church property was virtually the only noncommercial space in the neighborhood. The presence of our homeless neighbors quickly became a source of controversy. A few church members wanted me to have the police evict the men, while the rest debated how best to live in community with them. The owners of neighboring businesses and the police warned that the church was abetting crime and hurting business by allowing homeless people to gather on our property. Because that property was private, however, they could only suggest, not require, that I have our homeless neighbors arrested for trespassing.

Although George and Jean Edwards did not know it, they were present in our discussions about hospitality, because at the time, I was writing my doctoral dissertation about the LFOR. If I had been tempted to use the armed power of the state to remove the poor from God's house, their flawed yet faithful example would have shamed me into reconsidering. Call it accountability to the communion of saints, or call it the well-grounded fear of a fierce little old lady and a grumpy old man: violence was not an option. Our allegiance to Jesus Christ, who himself was homeless and who died at the hands of the state, trumped our concern for the comfort of our merchant neighbors, and our respect for the police who sought to make our corner of Durham safe. Rooted in that conviction, the church grew over time into a community of prayer, fellowship, and hospitality, seeking to live nonviolently with all, and frequently arguing about how best to do that. The friendships that developed led members of the church to open a house of hospitality in the neighborhood: a home for several of its formerly homeless neighbors, and a space where everyone is welcome to break bread, worship, and spend time together. I am no longer the vicar of St. Joseph's, but the church's discussions and discernment about its fellowship ministry are ongoing. George and Jean Edwards never visited St. Joseph's, but their story contributed to its resurrection by providing a contemporary example of gospel faith lived by disciples as fallible as the rest of us. It is my hope that reading George and Jean's story will lead other Christians to reflect on what it means to live together as citizens of God's kingdom.

This rest of this book is divided into four chapters, a conclusion, and questions for discussion. Chapter 1 follows George and Jean from the beginning of their relationship through their wartime experiences, the birth of their children, George's seminary and doctoral studies, and their arrival in Louisville in 1955. Chapter 2 focuses on the years of the Vietnam War, when George became known as a pillar of the city's anti-war movement and was targeted by pro-war members of his own church. George's academic tenure provided some protection, but he and Jean both sacrificed prestige and professional advancement for their faith. Chapters 3 and 4 move from 1975, when the Edwardses founded the Louisville Fellowship of Reconciliation, through the mid-1990s. This was the period when they were most active in forming an ecumenical community devoted to peacemaking, in the absence of a significant peace witness among the churches to which most LFOR members belonged. In the 1980s, George and Jean and other members of the LFOR became increasingly involved in civil disobedience, raising questions about the kinds of relationships that are necessary to practice consistent Christian witness against state violence. Later, although subverting white supremacy was a lifelong concern for George and Jean, the LFOR was challenged to consider whether its witness for peace was compromised by the fact that virtually all its members were white. The conclusion will offer the couple's reflections on their life together, and point to some questions raised for Christian discipleship by their work with allies inside and outside the church. I hope that the discussion questions will be used in a variety of settings, not only by reading groups but also in premarital counseling, to guide church retreats and conferences, and in interfaith groups seeking ways to practice nonviolence and to build peace together.

1

"We Really Needed to Start a New Way of Thinking"

George and Jean's Early Years

NO ONE COULD HAVE predicted that two scions of Southern Presbyterianism would grow into such rebels against church and state. Born in Nashville in 1921 to Virginia Branch Maney and Lawrence Maney, Jean was one of four children in a family that taught virtues she would embrace her whole life, along with others she would soon reject. In what Jean remembered as "a very happy home," there was a lot of laughter around the dinner table, where the children loved to hear the stories their father brought back from his road trips selling Duck Head overalls.[1] The household included Jean's great-aunt as well as her maternal grandparents, both deaf due to childhood infections. Her grandparents' presence taught Jean compassion and communication skills. She learned sign language early—the only hearing person in her household, besides her mother, to do so—conversing with her grandmother as they did housework together, and helping her grandparents communicate with the hearing world. Having been taught by her parents to see facilitating her

---

1. Jean Edwards interview with K'Meyer, 27.

grandparents' contacts with the hearing world as "normal," Jean would accompany her grandmother on the streetcar to visit family and friends across town. "It was a sad experience in a way," she later remembered, but ultimately an enriching one: "It certainly did help me to become more aware of people with disabilities, and I'm certain it helped me all of my life to have some compassion."[2]

As Jean grew older, she learned that racism trumped compassion in the segregationist order that governed relationships inside and outside her household, and by her senior year of high school she was beginning to look at the world through a more critical lens than her parents had offered. Her mother, the state treasurer of the Daughters of the American Revolution, had taught Jean "to salute the flag, and to value the flag very highly," but that same involvement raised Jean's awareness of racism. Shocked in 1939 to hear that the DAR had refused to bend its policy of segregation so that opera singer Marian Anderson could perform at its Constitution Hall in Washington, DC, Jean was more scandalized to learn that the incident did not disturb her mother. That was the moment, as Jean later said, when she knew "that we had serious difficulties."[3] Around the same time, her family's African-American cook did not arrive to work on Christmas morning, precipitating a household crisis "because Mother had to make all this big Christmas dinner, with nine people." That incident was a revelation for Jean, precipitating her quiet, lifelong quest to see beyond the blinders of white supremacy. Whereas before "it never had occurred to me that she might not want to come," that year, she realized simply that the cook "wanted to be with her own family and take care of her own children on Christmas Day."[4] Jean was starting to realize that these power struggles extended far beyond her own family, in a city that enjoyed a reputation as being relatively liberal on racial matters, but where segregation was firmly entrenched, and that would later become a battleground of the freedom movement.

As Jean's critical faculties developed, she realized that her elders would not encourage debate and argument about political or theological issues. Reflecting on her mother's response to the Marian Anderson incident, Jean remembered that she first learned of the DAR's action through

2. Jean Edwards interview with K'Meyer, 4.

3. Ibid., 3. The story of the DAR's refusal, Anderson's subsequent outdoor concert at the Lincoln Memorial, and her performance at Constitution Hall in October 1964 after the passage of the Civil Rights Act, is told in Arsenault, *The Sound of Freedom*.

4. Jean Edwards interview with K'Meyer, 20.

"We Really Needed to Start a New Way of Thinking"

the newspaper; although her mother "had been thinking and talking about it a lot," she hadn't spoken of the matter in front of her children. In her daughter's eyes a person who "was just always avoiding controversy," Virginia Maney offered a practical explanation for not wanting to discuss the matter: "She said it was not her decision, and she didn't worry about it anymore." "I'm sure," Jean added dryly, "that she was aware that we had a difference of opinion."[5] At the same time, Jean remembered her mother's consistent refusal to argue as a positive influence that taught Jean "to be a reconciler."[6] For Jean, however, "reconciliation" later came to mean risking offending others for the sake of the gospel as she knew it, rather than staying silent to avoid conflict. As she went about that work, her greatest asset was a cheerfully fierce tenacity that assumed the other person's goodwill and openness to conversion, rather than the head-on approach her future husband would adopt. In that sense Jean was her mother's daughter.

Born in Memphis a year earlier than Jean, George Edwards had similar experiences: first learning to question white supremacy by looking around his own home, and initiating discussions his elders would have preferred to avoid. Like Jean, he grew up in a lower-middle-class family, and he also came to the beginnings of critical consciousness as a teenager. That was when he realized the relative domestic freedom his mother, Analee Hall Edwards, had enjoyed as a piano teacher and accompanist during his childhood depended upon the labor of the African-American women, themselves mothers, who had cared for George (known as Buddy) and his older brother John (called Jack).[7] As George became aware of the lack of recreational facilities for black children in North Memphis, a couple of miles from his family home, he set up his own leisure program for them, "organizing" them to "play games and tell them Bible stories and things like that."[8] George had been "taught religiously that racism was wrong," but when he decided, one day, to bring the children over to play on a piece of vacant property in his own neighborhood, he ran up against the limits of his community's Christian faith. As the property belonged to George's church, Evergreen Presbyterian, its elders deputized

---

5. Jean Edwards interview with K'Meyer, 3.

6. Ibid., 27.

7. George's mother's official given name was Rachel, her father's preferred name for her, but she was always known as Analee, her mother's choice. George Edwards interview with K'Meyer, 4–5.

8. George Edwards interview with K'Meyer, 15.

one of their number to forbid the teenager from bringing the children back to church property. Much later, George remembered that although he had initially been "very attracted" to his pastor at Evergreen, W. J. (John) Millard, after this incident he came to believe that Millard "was a chicken on the race issue," who knew that "part of his ministerial status depended on his being a sort of a closet segregationist."[9] The church leaders' preemptive move to reinforce racial boundaries only furthered George's developing critique of white supremacy. As he later reflected, "You have to learn someway what it's all about. That's segregation."[10] As an adult, George remembered Memphis as "a wicked city" for its entrenched white supremacy. Although he felt "estranged" from Memphis after moving away, he reflected, "That's a little childish on my part, I think," recognizing that he had had "excellent educational opportunities there" far surpassing what had been available to earlier generations of his family.[11]

Like Jean, George grew to appreciate the character traits he had inherited from each of his parents. He remembered his father, John Thompson Edwards, a hardware store clerk and later manager with an eighth-grade education, as a "rational" man of little faith who didn't appreciate the "emotions" of the Baptist worship favored by his wife, an "ebullient and very outgoing" woman. The family joined Evergreen Presbyterian Church as a "compromise," his father attending, George later speculated, mainly because of his "great attachment" to his children and his suspicion that, for their sake, "it was better if he went with us to church rather than to play golf," his preferred Sunday morning activity.[12] George came to believe that he had inherited both his father's "rationality" and his mother's faith. As he entered adulthood, his Christian faith gave him a theological context for his growing consciousness of "the injustice of segregation," a conviction deepened by subsequent years of study.[13] The gift that most defined George's relationship with his mother, however, was music. She taught him and his brother to read music and secured skilled voice teachers, like Louis Thurston Nicholas, who went on to a distinguished career in music education, to cultivate George's baritone

---

9. George Edwards interview with K'Meyer, 19, 21.
10. Ibid., 15–16.
11. Ibid., 9, 17.
12. Ibid., 10; the description of George's mother comes from 18.
13. George Edwards interview with K'Meyer, 14.

"We Really Needed to Start a New Way of Thinking"

and Jack's bass.[14] Not only would George's singing voice capture Jean Maney's heart one summer at camp, but their shared love of music would be a thread running through their shared ministry and their family for decades after they married.

Music was one of the passions that sustained George when he entered the Presbyterian-affiliated Southwestern (now Rhodes) College in 1938 on a scholarship designated for men pursuing ordination. Although Southwestern was located only a mile from George's family home and just blocks from their church, he felt like something of an outsider there as an "extremely religious" young man who had committed himself to Jesus Christ at a church youth conference years before. Although he later came to critique the "very personalistic" style of religion he grew up with, in which faith was "highly a matter of individual decision" rather than an identity rooted in community, he never regretted the decision to "give [his] heart to Christ."[15] His adolescent social life had revolved around the church, and at Southwestern he held himself apart from the "elitist" fraternities and sororities that dominated the campus, despite the fact that most of his friends and his brother were fraternity members.[16] Upon reflection years later, George believed that his desire "to make a virtue out of a vice" may have colored his view of fraternities, remarking, "If you're timid," as he was, "then you can be morally aloof to the people who like to go to parties."[17]

George was an intellectual from the beginning of his time at Southwestern. In his sophomore year, George responded bluntly to an informal poll by the student newspaper, *The Sou'wester*, about whether the college spent too much on sports: "I think that when the athletics department reaches the size that it requires as much money to run it as the scholastic department then the athletics are exaggerated."[18] He got involved in campus life in other ways: through the Southwestern Ministerial Club, which performed service at the Crippled Adults' Hospital;[19] as one of nine students participating in a radio discussion in November 1940 of the question, "Should the United States promote and participate in an

14. Ibid., 9.
15. Ibid., 21–22.
16. Ibid., 22.
17. Ibid.
18. *The Sou'wester*, October 6, 1939.
19. Ibid., January 20, 1939.

international federation of democracies?"; and in music.[20] In October 1940, George gave a voice recital at the Memphis College of Music, presenting fourteen pieces in English, French, and German, including what *The Sou'wester* called "the high point of the performance," "Avant de quitter ces lieux"—the emotional farewell of a young soldier—from *Faust*.[21]

Most importantly for the later course of George's life, college was the time when he began to read the pacifist writings that were widely circulated during the period between the world wars. Although the United States had fought the Great War for only a year and a half, the conflict's devastation had marked a generation. George remembered his mother's "emotional" abhorrence of war, the result of having seen her brother suffer the physical and psychological aftereffects of a gas attack.[22] In American Protestant circles, that revulsion was channeled into what George later called a "popular pacifism of sorts" in the interwar period. Americans joined ecumenical organizations like the Fellowship of Reconciliation (FOR) and the Women's International League for Peace and Freedom (WILPF), both founded in 1915, as well as the War Resisters League (WRL), established in 1923 as a secular alternative to the largely Protestant FOR.[23] The number of people willing to publicly declare their pacifism was small, however: the largest of the peace groups, the Fellowship of Reconciliation, had only six thousand members in 1928, growing to almost nine thousand by 1937.[24] Several churches, including the Northern Presbyterian Church (PCUSA), the Methodist Episcopal Church, and the Disciples of Christ, took official stands against war; other bodies, like the General Council of the Congregational and Christian Churches and the House of Bishops of the Episcopal Church, affirmed that when cross and flag conflicted, it was the duty of Christians to uphold the cross.[25] George's own Presbyterian Church (US) passed a

20. Ibid., November 8, 1940. The starting point for the discussion was the recent book, Streit, *Union Now*, which blamed the nationalism or isolationism of the League of Nations' members for that organization's ineffectiveness in confronting totalitarianism.

21. *The Sou'wester*, October 11, 1940. The story noted that George had studied under Louis Nicholas "for the past several years."

22. George Edwards interview with K'Meyer, 12.

23. Ibid., 27. The growth in pacifism in the United States at this time is extensively treated in Appelbaum, *Kingdom to Commune*.

24. Kosek, *Acts of Conscience*, 50, 146.

25. Appelbaum, *Kingdom to Commune*, 25.

resolution against war in 1929, but its wording betrayed a limited sense of the church's mission: its "historic position," the PCUS General Assembly resolved, "is that the function of the Church is purely spiritual." The resolution further stated that "the Church should never again bless a war, or be used as an instrument in the promotion of war," but its definition of a "purely spiritual" role for the church offered little guidance about what to do when "spiritual" and "temporal" loyalties came into conflict.[26] In practice, as George and Jean found, the church muzzled itself, reflecting the white supremacy and militarism of the surrounding culture, with few traces of the risky political witness on which Christianity had been founded.[27]

As George, the future conscientious objector, looked around the world with increasingly critical eyes, the signs looked no better for his generation than they had for his parents': the international crisis of capitalism had spawned not only the New Deal but also fascism; white supremacy reigned around the globe, as its opponents gathered strength for a long and costly struggle; and the Spanish Civil War looked like a dress rehearsal for another world conflict. For every young American man subject to the draft after it was reinstated in the fall of 1940, the question of whether or not to participate in war was by definition both personal and political. For George, it was inseparable from his growing faith, and as he wrestled with the issue, he heeded the voices proclaiming that war was not only futile, as each conflict sowed the seeds of the next, but contrary to Christianity. Those voices included leaders of the Social Gospel movement like liberal New York pastors George Buttrick and Harry Emerson Fosdick, known for having opposed the nascent fundamentalist movement in the 1920s; the prominent Disciples of Christ pacifist Kirby Page; and the English Fellowship of Reconciliation organizer Muriel Lester, an associate of Gandhi. Lester's influence on George was particularly strong, coming at a time when he was seeking a theological foundation for his multifaceted aversion to war, and finding no support for that quest in his home church. Lester's pacifism rested on two core principles: the kinship of humanity that Christianity proclaimed, and Jesus' example of self-sacrificial nonviolence. She summarized these in the final chapter of her autobiography: "Unless God meant the human race to be actually

26. Quoted in Nutt, *Toward Peacemaking*, 21.
27. For a chilling exploration of the evil that can result when the church separates the "spiritual" and the "temporal" or "political" in this way, see Cavanaugh, *Torture and Eucharist*.

one family, we have no right to the phrase 'Our Father.' Unless Jesus was misinterpreting God, we cannot overcome evil with evil, or gain security by armies and navies, or defend ourselves by preparing to kill potential enemies."[28] Lester gave a chapel address, which George remembered well, at Southwestern in the fall of his sophomore year.[29] At the time, he was also beginning to read Fosdick and Buttrick, who, along with Lester, initially seemed like "people from outer space because . . . I was not raised on those kinds of ideas."[30] Lester's words at Southwestern, George later remembered, "impressed my mind indelibly"; she gave a "tough interpretation of the Sermon on the Mount" as the centerpiece of her "no-holds-barred [address] on Christian pacifism."[31]

Closer to home, George had already been introduced to radical ideas by Nelle Morton, a member of both WILPF and the FOR, who served on the PCUS Board of Christian Education before and during the war. George remembered Morton speaking to his and Jean's youth group at Montreat, making an impression on him as "a very radical person, for us, at that age." While at first George "couldn't relate to her"—as he said, "She was so far out for me"—he found that as he listened, "I could relate to her pacifism."[32] That connection became the basis of a lifelong association. When the United States entered the war, Morton became the PCUS liaison to its few conscientious objectors, remaining in touch with George for years afterward. Morton offered an early example of a faith that would not dance to war's insistent drumbeat: pressured by the church to buy war bonds, she instead contributed "an equal percentage of [her] salary directly to peace organizations"—a forerunner of the war tax resistance George and Jean would later practice together. She left church administration in 1945 to become the general secretary of the Fellowship of Southern Churchmen (FSC), an interracial group founded in 1934 to, in Morton's words, "act out the social and political dimensions of faith."[33] Previously, she had invited members of the FSC to conferences at Montreat, introducing

---

28. Lester, *It Occurred to Me*, 278.
29. *The Sou'wester*, October 13, 1939; George Edwards interview with K'Meyer, 24.
30. George and Jean Edwards interview with K'Meyer, March 12, 1996, Tape 1, 2.
31. George R. Edwards, undated autobiographical notes, Jean Edwards papers.
32. George Edwards interview with K'Meyer, 24–25.
33. Morton, *The Journey Is Home*, 188. For more about Morton's generation of Southern dissidents from the theology and politics of white supremacy, see Egerton, *Speak Now against the Day*, and K'Meyer, *Interracialism and Christian Community in the Postwar South*.

their theology to the generation that included George and Jean.[34] Morton worked to include young African-Americans in youth conferences at the center in the 1930s and early 1940s, with the result that the young people were allowed on the premises as employees, attending workshops "if work permitted." Dissatisfied with that outcome, Morton noted in her memoir that "in the light of what was said in our materials about faith, it was hard for the young people and youth leaders to understand the restrictions."[35]

George was one of the young people who had a hard time understanding the church's restrictions on human fellowship, but as war approached, he focused on the choice the Selective Service required him to make. He had fulfilled his high school requirement of two years of junior ROTC, finding that "at that time, although I didn't like it, I couldn't articulate why I didn't like it."[36] In college, focusing his reflections on the Sermon on the Mount, George came to believe that participation in war was incompatible with Christian faith.[37] In this, although he agreed with Morton, Page, and others, he differed from most Christians. Nonviolence was central to the confession and practice of the "historic peace churches"—Mennonites, Brethren, and the Society of Friends—but other Protestants, and Catholics, fell under the umbrella of "just war churches," which taught that Christians' participation in war could be justified in some circumstances. In the fifth century, Augustine of Hippo had limited those circumstances to three: for "the revenging of injuries"; when it was the only way "to constrain a city or a nation which has not wished to punish an evil action committed by its citizens"; or "to restore that which has been taken unjustly."[38] Even under those conditions, war was not required, but should be waged only as a last resort; if the expected good would outweigh the evil done (the principle of proportionality); and, once war was declared, taking care to protect noncombatants (the principle of discrimination).[39] Given that Hitler had invaded more than one European country in the 1930s, and that the government and citizens of Germany had persecuted Jews and others, fighting the Second World War could be justified by Augustinian standards. The stricture against

---

34. George Edwards interview with K'Meyer, 25.
35. Morton, *The Journey Is Home*, 187.
36. George and Jean Edwards interview with K'Meyer, March 26, 1996, 17.
37. Ibid., March 12, 1996, Tape 1, 3.
38. Quoted in Johnson, *Just War Tradition*, 153.
39. Ibid., 123.

targeting civilians, however, would be repeatedly violated by all sides over the course of the conflict, as would Augustine's requirement to value the lives of enemies and allies equally when calculating the expected good and evil outcomes of the war.

After the attack on Pearl Harbor in December 1941, all but the peace churches in the United States put aside their calls for members to abstain from war, declaring nonviolence an unattainable ideal in the face of fascism. In so doing, they followed the guidance of the theologian known for his elaboration of "Christian realism," Reinhold Niebuhr, a former pacifist who had left the Fellowship of Reconciliation in 1934 when the FOR refused to recognize the right of striking workers to use violence in self-defense. Niebuhr's theology emphasized "the full seriousness of sin as a permanent factor in human history," an incontrovertible reality that meant all human choices were necessarily compromised.[40] A decision for nonviolence, even if intended as a positive witness, could allow evil to abound. As American churches gave their approval to the government's declaration of war, they tended to identify sin and evil with the Axis side, rather than seeing them as human traits that Jesus Christ's life, death, and resurrection had equipped the church to resist nonviolently. In 1942, despite its resolution of a decade earlier, the General Assembly of the Presbyterian Church (US) came as close as possible to blessing the United States' participation in the war without using those words, stating that "our hopes for a just world order, the continuance of the Democratic [sic] way of life, and the very freedom of the Church to continue her world mission are definitely at stake in this conflict."[41] Most Americans agreed: although the FOR's membership increased by almost 50 percent over the course of the war, as historian Joseph Kip Kosek has pointed out, this growth is "highly deceptive," measuring not the conversion of just war advocates into pacifists, but the incorporation into the FOR of "the few remaining absolutists still unwavering in the face of an unprecedented national consensus."[42] Outside the historic peace churches, conscientious objectors found little support. A 1942 report of the PCUS Permanent Committee on Moral and Social Welfare made it clear that the onus was on COs to prove they weren't shirking their patriotic duty, emphasizing that the conscientious objector must recognize "that he

---

40. Niebuhr, "Why the Christian Church Is Not Pacifist," 3.
41. Quoted in Nutt, *Toward Peacemaking*, 27.
42. Kosek, *Acts of Conscience*, 146.

"We Really Needed to Start a New Way of Thinking"

does owe an obligation to his government." He could fulfill that obligation nonviolently, but only "as he seeks to perform that service with the same sacrificial devotion as the man who lays down his life on the field of battle, can the position of the pacifist be justified by his brethren."[43] The historic Christian bias against killing had become a bias against those who refused to kill. Compared to general public sentiment, however, even such strongly qualified support for conscientious objectors may have seemed generous. A Gallup poll taken in 1940, well before the attack on Pearl Harbor, found that 13 percent of Americans thought COs should be exempt from military service; 37 percent thought they should be required to perform noncombatant military duty; and 14 percent had no opinion. The remaining third of respondents thought COs should be forced to do regular military service, be imprisoned, or be put to death.[44]

Grounding his actions in what he saw as the core of Christian faith, rather than in church resolutions or patriotic exhortations, George registered with the Selective Service Administration as a conscientious objector in the summer of 1941.[45] In doing so, he became one of only three men in the half-million-member Southern Presbyterian Church who served through the war as conscientious objectors.[46] George's action was all the more remarkable because it was legally unnecessary: as a student who had already been identified by his local Presbyterian authority as a

---

43. Quoted in Nutt, *Toward Peacemaking*, 27.

44. Goossen, *Women against the Good War*, 17.

45. Selective Service Administration Records, Order Number S-2940, George Riley Edwards Registration Card, National Archives and Records Administration Southeast (Atlanta).

46. The other two were Asa Watkins (who left the PCUS for the Society of Friends) and Robert Swink. The PCUS membership figure comes from Bullock Jr., "Critical Period," 75. There has been some confusion about the number of PCUS COs in World War II. According to Taylor, *Acts of Conscience*, 400, there were five PCUS conscientious objectors. My research shows, however, that one, Malcolm H. Squires Jr., left the Civilian Public Service (CPS) camp in August 1942 to serve as a medic to US forces in Europe; National Interreligious Service Board for Conscientious Objectors, *1996 Directory of Civilian Public Service*, 377, and Malcolm H. Squires III e-mail to Rhonda Mawhood Lee, October 24, 2010. A fifth Presbyterian drafted from the South, Henry J. Buckner of Maryville, Tennessee, may have been a member of a Northern Presbyterian church, of which there were eight in his town, or he may have ended the war doing noncombatant or armed service with the military, as he left CPS in August 1943; e-mail to Rhonda Mawhood Lee by Lisa Jacobson of the Presbyterian Historical Society, October 22, 2010, and *1996 Directory of Civilian Public Service*, 47. Nelle Morton, the PCUS liaison to its COs, states that "only three Southern Presbyterians" "persisted as conscientious objectors" throughout the war; *The Journey Is Home*, 188.

candidate for ordination, he was entitled to a ministerial exemption from the draft. He could have spent the war years finishing his undergraduate and seminary education and graduated in time for V-E Day, ready to seek a church that would reward his intellect, musical training, and gift for preaching. Instead, he declared himself a "conscientious objector opposed to both combatant and noncombatant training and service," required by law to perform alternative public service.[47] As George later remembered, he "didn't want an educational exemption. I felt that I should face up to what the war meant to me, morally, and I should declare myself an objector . . . I had biblical reasons and I had theological reasons and moral reasons that were to me all religious."[48]

George's stand became public when he returned to Southwestern for the fall 1941 semester. There, most assumed that the United States must join the effort to halt the territorial advances of Nazi Germany and imperial Japan. George remembered faculty members "rejoicing" in chapel over the fact that Germany had invaded the Soviet Union that summer, because "These two monsters were killing each other on the eastern front." He didn't share in the general jubilation, remarking, "I don't know how I resisted it, but I did."[49] Even his friends who were also preparing for ordination "didn't approve" of his becoming a conscientious objector, instead taking what George later called a "Niebuhrian" position that war was a lesser evil than a fascist victory.[50] His only "defenders" on campus were those few who "did not agree with my position, but had respect for the fact that I was willing to take a position."[51] George's witness against war also caused some distress in his personal life. Although his mother had a visceral opposition to war, she feared for her son's future after a member of the Shelby County draft board erroneously told her that claiming CO status was "a virtual criminal act" and that her son would spend the war in a POW camp. The board member may have been misinformed about George's legal obligation, since in the First World War the only legal options available to conscientious objectors had been to

---

47. Selective Service Administration Records, Order Number S-2940, George Riley Edwards Registration Card, National Archives and Records Administration Southeast (Atlanta).

48. George and Jean Edwards interview with K'Meyer, March 12, 1996, Tape 1, 6.

49. George Edwards interview with K'Meyer, 23.

50. George and Jean Edwards interview with K'Meyer, March 12, 1996, Tape 1, 7.

51. George Edwards interview with K'Meyer, 25.

perform noncombatant service in the armed forces or go to prison.[52] Others shared his ignorance. At a meeting of George's presbytery after he became a CO, an announcement was made, as George later remembered, "that this candidate for the ministry (and leader of youth in the presbytery) had been taken away to a concentration camp for refusing to comply with Selective Service." George's minister, John Millard, corrected the speaker, informing the assembly that George was, in fact, performing alternative service.[53] George and his mother reconciled before long, and his father never criticized his decision.[54] The war, however, ended George's long-standing romantic relationship with Tommie Jean Haygood, which their college newspaper had, a couple of years earlier, called "one of our campus' most consistent."[55] They parted ways when George left Southwestern in early 1942.[56]

In later years, George did not regret having taken a stand against the Second World War, noting that the principal argument used to deem it "the Good War," that Hitler's defeat had ended the Holocaust, had been made in retrospect. Citing the experience of the *St. Louis*, a ship carrying German Jews that was turned away from Cuba, the United States, and Canada in 1939 before finally being allowed to dock in Belgium, George argued, "We never let those people in. We didn't fight the war to save them." The *St. Louis*' passengers became another casualty of war and genocide: dispersed to several countries, many died in concentration camps.[57] Writing twenty-five years after the war, George noted that over its course, all sides had violated the just war principle of discrimination, using "saturation bombing [and] gigantic incendiary raids" to target civilians for "destruction and death."[58] For pacifists like George, the use of atomic weapons to end the war in the Pacific only reinforced their convic-

52. On the experience of American conscientious objectors before the Second World War, see Chambers II, "Conscientious Objectors and the American State."

53. George R. Edwards, "George Riley Edwards, A Biographical Summary" (n.d., after 1980), Jean Edwards papers.

54. George Edwards interview with K'Meyer, 12.

55. *The Sou'wester*, October 6, 1939.

56. George served in CPS from March 16, 1942 to January 25, 1946; *1996 Directory of Civilian Public Service*, 96.

57. George and Jean Edwards interview with K'Meyer, March 12, 1996, Tape 1, 9–10. George made this argument in *Jesus and the Politics of Violence*, 123–24, citing Morse, *While Six Million Died*. The voyage of the *St. Louis* and the fates of its passengers are discussed in, among others, Ogilvie and Miller, *Refuge Denied*.

58. Edwards, *Jesus and the Politics of Violence*, 123.

tion that calculations about the ethics of war were more often apologies for human brutality. He retained little faith in the church's commitment to expose those apologies, noting sardonically in the midst of the Vietnam War that "by the time Hiroshima and Nagasaki were atom-bombed in 1945, it is possible that some Christian moralists far removed from the decision-making processes of government had begun to question whether the limits of just war had been transgressed."[59]

Given his church's lack of commitment to nonviolence, and its grudging acceptance of conscientious objection, George made his decision to enter Civilian Public Service (CPS) in isolation from any local faith community, fortified only by the knowledge that in the broader church he was not alone. In the camps he found the fellowship he had been seeking, where his theology could develop in community and in conversation with his fellow COs. When George entered CPS in March 1942, the pacifist beliefs that would shape the rest of his life were deeply held, but open to refinement. The CPS camp served as a seminary of sorts where, despite the diversity of theologies represented, everyone agreed that God forbade killing. George would emerge from that community with two convictions at his core: that confessing Christ as Lord meant renouncing violence, and that this confession must be public, challenging both governments that relied on force to resolve disputes and churches that refused to call Christians to account for their participation in state violence. Most of his fellow COs were members of the historic peace churches: of the almost twelve thousand men who served through CPS, a majority were Mennonites, Brethren, and Friends, but Methodists, Baptists, Episcopalians and a variety of other traditions were also represented.[60] His time in CPS was George's first "real contact" with Quakers, and their time together marked the rest of his life. Later he reflected that "I call myself very often a Quaker Presbyterian because I grew to love those men," whom he remembered as "very gracious people."[61] In his first CPS placement, a lumber camp administered by the American Friends Service Committee

59. Ibid.

60. Taylor, *Acts of Conscience*, 1. Taylor's Appendix A lists the number of CPS participants from faith groups that had three or more men in the system. About twenty-five thousand men performed noncombatant service in the military, while about six thousand (three-quarters of them Jehovah's Witnesses) went to prison rather than cooperate in any way with Selective Service. Frazer and O'Sullivan, *We Have Just Begun to Not Fight*, xiii. A total of more than thirty-four million men registered for the World War II draft; Keim, *CPS Story*, 8.

61. George and Jean Edwards interview with K'Meyer, March 12, 1996, Tape 1, 17.

(AFSC) in Marion, North Carolina, George worshipped at the Friends' silent meetings early on Sunday mornings, before attending Presbyterian services in town. Although his CPS service and his postwar work with the AFSC in Italy gave him a lifelong appreciation for the Society of Friends, he always remained a Presbyterian, grounded in Scripture and in the skepticism about humanity's capacity for perfection that, ironically, he shared with Reinhold Niebuhr.

The core belief George shared with other Christian conscientious objectors was that Jesus Christ called his disciples to peaceful, self-sacrificial acts: to be less afraid of suffering physical harm themselves than of inflicting it on others. George's response was embodied in his wartime work: first in Marion, breaking rocks to build trails through the lumber camp, before moving on to even more physically and emotionally demanding work at Eastern State Mental Hospital in Williamsburg, Virginia, and then volunteering as a malaria test subject. All COs were aware that their service could be unfavorably compared to the risks that members of the military faced, and George was soon faced with that reality. On Sunday mornings in Marion, George would go from the early morning Quaker meeting to "the little old Presbyterian church" in town, where his singing voice soon gained attention. When asked to join the choir, he hesitated "very much," but sang with the group "two or three Sundays." When the choir director, whom George remembered as "naive about politics," asked him to sing a solo on Easter Sunday, he hesitated further, "not only because I was timid about trying to sing a solo, but because I really didn't know whether those people would accept it or not." His suspicions were well placed: on Easter morning a delegation of church elders met him to say that "the deal was off. They didn't mind me coming to their church and sitting in the congregation, but I should avoid getting up front for any reason." He understood the feeling behind that directive: "Heck, I realized that a lot of people, their boys were over there... and some of them were killed." At first disinclined to return to the church, George then told himself, "Well, that's chicken. That just shows you haven't got the nerve to face them or face yourself." His courage was rewarded by an invitation to supper at the home of two church members, a married couple who, despite that fact that their son was serving in the Army in Europe, "did not approve of what the church had done about me singing in the choir." George realized "that these were very generous people, because they really didn't believe what I believed, but they still felt that this was the wrong thing to do." In contrast, George thought of the church's pastor as "a chicken from the ground up," who "didn't stand for anything as far as I'm concerned."⁶²

From the lumber camp, George moved on in search of work more meaningful than breaking rocks. He served over two years as a ward attendant at Eastern State Mental Hospital after a CPS unit opened there in the summer of 1942 under the direction of the American Friends Service Committee. The hospital needed the labor supplied by conscientious objectors: attendants who hadn't been drafted had moved to higher-paying jobs in defense industries, leaving the hospital severely understaffed, with perhaps one ward attendant on duty to care for sixty to seventy patients.⁶³ George later remembered the job's demands: working eighty hours a week for $25 a month, a shared room, and board.⁶⁴ More disturbing were the conditions under which inmates were forced to live: as George later wrote, "Understaffed and underfunded, the hospital was a vivid example of what liberation writers would call institutional violence."⁶⁵ Eastern State was the first American mental hospital to be the subject of a CO-initiated investigation, in 1943. After the war, informed by CPS workers' stories, *Life* magazine published an exposé of the nightmarish conditions in the nation's mental institutions.⁶⁶ One violent incident at Eastern State remained a vivid memory for George years later: running to respond to a warning that "somebody was gettin' mauled," he discovered one patient, John, beating senseless an older inmate, an amputee named Cecil. When George intervened, pushing John away from Cecil and "demanding a reason for his brutal conduct," he learned that John had discovered Cecil, whom he called "a goddamned queer," in what George termed "the act of fellatio with another male patient."⁶⁷ The violence of John's attack on Cecil made a deep impression on George; his awareness of the abuse inflicted on homosexual persons was a key factor in his commitment, years later, to advocate for the full inclusion of gays and lesbians in the life of the church.

62. George and Jean Edwards interview with K'Meyer, March 12, 1996, Tape 1, 19–21.

63. Recalled in Edwards, *Gay/Lesbian Liberation*, 119.

64. George and Jean Edwards interview with K'Meyer, March 12, 1996, Tape 1, 15. George's memory of his working hours is corroborated in Taylor, *Acts of Conscience*, 197.

65. Edwards, *Gay/Lesbian Liberation*, 119.

66. The investigation of Eastern State is discussed in Taylor, *Acts of Conscience*, 237–43; the magazine article is Maisel, "Bedlam 1946."

67. Edwards, *Gay/Lesbian Liberation*, 119–20.

"We Really Needed to Start a New Way of Thinking"

In the midst of the ugliness at Eastern State, music continued to be a source of beauty and comfort for George and those who heard him sing. A fellow hospital worker, Benjamin Reid, later remembered "Buddy" Edwards as "a handsome, brown-skinned young man with a powerful body and a strong, well-trained voice," who "gave us all a moment of glory" performing the bass solo in Handel's *Messiah* at a church in Williamsburg.[68]

Later in the war, George joined the conscientious objectors who volunteered for projects that might demonstrate that their refusal of military service was not motivated by any lack of physical courage. He applied to participate in a twenty-week starvation experiment conducted by the University of Minnesota physiologist Ancel Keys (inventor of the boring but balanced military diet known as "K-rations"), who used thirty-six uncompensated CPS volunteers in order to understand, and find treatments for, the effects of malnutrition.[69] Turned down for the starvation study, George volunteered as a test subject in experiments to improve treatments for malaria, conducted at a hospital on Welfare Island in New York City. George remembered the experiment as straightforward: "They brought these little mosquitoes into our room . . . South Pacific mosquitoes, I think . . . They had a little wire cage and they put it on your bare chest like that for a few minutes. One or two of them would bite you; that was enough." Shortly afterward, the symptoms would start—"the high fever, and chills, and all those spells"—whereupon various drugs would be administered and their effects measured. After recovering from the tests, George worked as an attendant in the hospital for a year, his last CPS assignment.[70] On his Sundays off, George would attend George Buttrick's Madison Avenue Presbyterian Church, where he heard both the pacifist preacher and Reinhold Niebuhr, who often filled the pulpit when Buttrick was away (and whose sister, Hulda Niebuhr, served as director of religious education at the church). George described the preaching rotation as "almost comical": "Buttrick would preach against the war, and when he felt like it, he'd really haul off," while Niebuhr would visit and "tell them that the war was okay and we had to do it."[71] While he was in New York, not yet knowing that he would eventually end up in Louisville, George met Olof Anderson, a pacifist Presbyterian pastor from that city

---

68. Reid, *First Acts*, 217.

69. Tucker, *The Great Starvation Experiment*.

70. George and Jean Edwards interview with K'Meyer, March 12, 1996, Tape 1, 26–27.

71. Ibid., 28–29.

who, in New York on other business, called on George to offer his support for his stand against war. Anderson was the only PCUS clergyman to visit George during his years of service, a kindness George "appreciated... very much."[72] Anderson and George had convictions in common: the pastor had tried to register as a CO, telling his draft board he would set aside his ordination to do so, but the point became moot when draft eligibility was lowered below his age of forty-one.[73]

When he was released from alternative service in January 1946, George worked in Italy for eighteen months on a project led by the American Friends Service Committee and the United Nations, reconstructing homes bombed during the war. He prepared for that service at Pendle Hill study center in Pennsylvania, after a brief stop in Richmond, Virginia, to visit friends from his prewar youth group. Those friends included Jean, by now a widow in graduate school there—their first meeting since he was drafted and their last until the Memphis conference in 1947.[74] George was one of 155 AFSC volunteers who passed through Pendle Hill in 1946, the peak year in a busy decade for the center.[75] As George's group studied Italian and attended lectures by experienced relief workers, they sought to embody communal Christian living, sharing the work of running the center and, once a week, further limiting their already simple diet to send the money saved to the AFSC food relief program for Europe.[76]

George's time in Italy left him with indelible impressions of the human capacity for both creativity and destruction, as he encountered "the historical treasure of the nation on the one hand, and the unbearable task of recovery and reconstruction on the other." That was especially true of George's experience in Cassino, between Naples and Rome.[77] The Allied victory there in the spring of 1944 had allowed them to occupy Rome in June, but the battle took a heavy toll. Tens of thousands of lives were lost, including those of civilians seeking refuge in the sixth-century Abbey of Monte Cassino; bombing reduced the abbey and most other

72. George and Jean Edwards interview with K'Meyer, March 12, 1996, Tape 2, 18; George Edwards interview with K'Meyer, 33.

73. Nutt, *Toward Peacemaking*, 51.

74. Jean Edwards interview with K'Meyer, 14–15.

75. Mather, *Pendle Hill*, 47.

76. Ibid.; George and Jean Edwards interview with K'Meyer, March 12, 1996, Tape 1, 29.

77. George R. Edwards letter to Italian historian Massimo Rubboli, May 23, 1996, in author's possession.

buildings in the area to rubble.[78] Later, working in the Abruzzi region on the Adriatic Sea, George saw the human and physical devastation that German forces had wrought as they retreated.[79] The scale of the devastation, and the AFSC project's limited resources, meant that George and his colleagues could provide only modest aid: they had no cash assistance to offer, but simply sought to "find things we could do to help people in the very minimal one-on-one level." The project's truck hauled construction materials for Italians lacking transportation, while its members did hands-on work, moving the rubble of destroyed homes for reuse and learning carpentry on the job.[80] George later believed that he had gained much from his relief work, making connections with Italians, including one man whose name he eventually forgot, but with whom he became friends on their frequent hikes into the mountains. The man told George that he was a member of the Italian Communist Party, leading George to reflect years later that "where I grew up, as far as I knew, there were no Communists, so this was a first for me, and a very pleasant one at that!"[81] The project drew George out of his shell to some extent, helping him to be less timid, "except that I still wasn't as sociable as I think I could and should have been."[82]

George's lack of sociability would be compensated in future years by his wife's extroverted nature, one of several complementary traits that served them well in a life of ministry together. While George always strove to articulate the theological and biblical reasons for his beliefs, Jean's testimony was grounded in a strong sense of the ultimate senselessness of war. Although she shared George's faith, personal experiences were decisive for her: the words of a teacher, a controversy at her church, and early widowhood. Like George, Jean deepened her study of war and other social conflicts as a student. She enrolled in 1939 at the two-year Ward-Belmont College for women in Nashville (now coeducational Belmont University), which lay within walking distance of the Maney home, then finished her degree at Converse College in Spartanburg, South Carolina. While at Ward-Belmont, Jean was known for her friendliness,

---

78. Weinberg, *A World at Arms*, 661.
79. George and Jean Edwards interview with K'Meyer, March 12, 1996, Tape 1, 30.
80. Ibid., 30–31.
81. George R. Edwards letter to Rubboli.
82. George and Jean Edwards interview with K'Meyer, March 12, 1996, Tape 1, 32.

joining the Ariston Social Club and the bowling team.[83] After graduation, the strong music program at Converse College drew her to finish her degree there. Studying sociology, religion, and English as well as music, Jean gained a broader perspective on incidents like the Christmas Day absence of her family's cook a few years earlier. Jean shared George's admiration for Nelle Morton, the pacifist employee of the PCUS, who lectured at Converse while Jean was there. The critical viewpoint Morton offered on racial segregation made a strong impression on Jean, who later remembered, "She was powerful, and she really did stir our thoughts."[84] Another woman, a "Yankee" history professor whom Jean remembered as a Quaker, had already influenced Jean: when the United States entered the war during Jean's first semester at Ward-Belmont, the professor told her class, "We are going to have wars until the young men just decide not to go." For Jean, that statement was "the first I'd ever heard about being a conscientious objector."[85]

Jean heard more about the church's role in war when a controversy shook Nashville's First Presbyterian Church, where she had grown up. For Jean, the church was a community in which her teachers "nurtured me very beautifully," where she learned to sing in the choir, and whose pastor, Thomas C. Barr, had taught Jean's communicants' class when she was twelve years old and "ready to unite with the church."[86] In a few years, the church would repudiate Barr, after he preached in the spring of 1941 against the United States entering the war. Although he later stated that he supported neither pacifism nor fascism, Barr was condemned for espousing the PCUS position that "the Church should never again bless a war, or be used as an instrument in the promotion of war."[87] Jean later remembered her pastor having been tagged a pacifist, remarking, "Boy, that was a word that was ready to stir up a hornet's nest." Barr had grown up in South Carolina, and according to Jean, some parishioners believed that "he got these ideas because his wife [was] from the North."[88] The

83. *Milestones* 1940, 67; Ibid. 1941, 74, 89.

84. Jean Edwards interview with K'Meyer, 20, 22.

85. Ibid., 9; the term "Yankee" comes from Jean Edwards e-mail to Rhonda Mawhood Lee, January 3, 2011. Although Jean couldn't remember the professor's name, she was likely Vera L. Hay, the only Northerner who taught history at Ward-Belmont during Jean's time there; *Milestones* 1939, 15.

86. Jean Edwards interview with K'Meyer, 8.

87. Nutt, *Toward Peacemaking*, 29.

88. Jean Edwards interview with K'Meyer, 9.

"We Really Needed to Start a New Way of Thinking"

pastor, however, had received his own exposure to "northern" ideas during his theological education at New York's Union Seminary, which had steeped him in the teachings of Henry Sloane Coffin and Henry Emerson Fosdick.[89]

As the controversy at First Presbyterian played out over more than a year, Barr never took a stand on whether or not the church was called to nonviolence; rather, he invoked his pastoral freedom to preach the truth as he understood it. Laypersons, however, did not place a high value on pulpit freedom, at his church or elsewhere. A Gallup poll of American Christians in late 1941 found that 55 percent believed "preachers and priests" should not "discuss from the pulpit the question of American participation in the war," and only 5 percent believed that preachers "should say frankly and openly whatever they believe."[90] Barr had been too frank and open; his detractors criticized him for, in his words, "not being evangelistic, for not being patriotic, and for preaching on problems of race, economics and politics instead of preaching the gospel." In September 1942, the Nashville Presbytery removed Barr as pastor, declaring that there was no "hope for a united church under his leadership."[91] Barr appealed the presbytery's decision to the next higher church authority, the synod, which found in his favor. Once vindicated, Barr resigned his pastorate, founding Trinity Presbyterian Church two months later.[92] Its 275 charter members included many who had moved from First Church, but not Jean's family. Although Jean wanted her parents to move to Trinity, she was away at Converse and knew that "it was [my mother's] decision, and my father would do whatever she said to." In the end, although her parents liked Barr, they stayed at the church they knew.[93] For Jean, the conflict was not about pulpit freedom; instead, it exposed a deep contradiction in the church's teaching about nonviolence. From childhood, she had had "so many teachers, wonderful teachers" who led her in studying the Bible and "were always teaching me, 'Thou shalt not kill.'" That, she remembered, "was really a puzzle when the big split came in the church."[94]

89. Weems, *Family Faith Stories*, 90–91. Weems is Barr's daughter.

90. "Pulpit Liberty Denied by Poll," *Christian Century*, December 10, 1941, 1557.

91. "Dr. Barr Is Removed as Pastor of First Presbyterian Church," *The Nashville Tennessean*, September 14, 1942.

92. Weems, *Family Faith Stories*, 108; First Presbyterian Church, "The History of First Church."

93. Jean Edwards interview with K'Meyer, 19.

94. Ibid., 26.

Personal tragedy crystallized Jean's conviction against war. While finishing her undergraduate degree, she sang in Spartanburg's First Presbyterian Church choir with a young soldier, Jim Gregory, who was based at the Army camp just outside town. Besides their shared love of music, Jim and Jean had their faith in common; his father was a Presbyterian minister in East Aurora, New York. Jim's views about the war differed from Jean's growing suspicions: she later remembered that "he was not, in any sense of the word, a pacifist," believing that "the war was very important."[95] Jim visited Jean on campus from time to time, and the two corresponded after she graduated in 1943, returning to Nashville to work as a secretary in the Tennessee adjutant general's office, a job her mother's DAR connections helped secure for her. "Working in the state capitol with all those politicians," Jean recalled, was an education: "I really did get my eyes opened."[96] Jim and Jean soon "decided we wanted to get married," and they did, the day after Christmas 1943. They lived together for six months in Florida, Jim's next post, before he received orders to go overseas in June 1944 and Jean returned to wait out the war with her family in Nashville.

Although Jim was a motor pool mechanic, he was pressed into armed service at the end of that year, in the massive Allied effort known as the Battle of the Bulge. Taken to the front from the hospital where he had been ill with an infection, Jim was killed on his and Jean's first wedding anniversary.[97] Although some of Jim's fellow soldiers wrote to Jean to tell her that "he had done such great work" that day, Jim's death was the final experience that made Jean a pacifist for life. "I was just stunned," she later recalled. "I guess I wasn't prepared. I didn't read the newspapers a lot. I hardly even knew what was going on." What horrified her most "was not so much that he was killed, but that both of these nations had sent all of their young people. A whole generation of young men went out there, and shot and killed each other! I thought it was just so ridiculous." Her new sense of the futility and cyclic nature of war led her to resolve that "we really needed to start a new way of thinking. To stop that. We all knew what had happened in the First World War, and we all knew—what's to prevent us from having the next one, if they all keep on going

---

95. Ibid., 10–11.
96. Ibid., 12.
97. Ibid., 12–14.

"We Really Needed to Start a New Way of Thinking"

like this? I felt very called to do something about it."[98] That conviction led Jean to a change of vocation. College had equipped her to teach high school English while living in Gainesville with Jim, but now, as a twenty-three-year-old widow, she decided she wanted to focus her energies on younger children, to school them early in the ways of nonviolence. That new call led her to complete a master's degree at the Presbyterian School of Christian Education in Richmond, Virginia, and to take a job as director of Christian education at Westminster Presbyterian Church in Nashville in 1946.[99]

George and Jean's separate moves back home to Tennessee brought them together again, this time for life. In each other, they found the kernel of the community that they had known as teenagers in the church, and that they would gather around themselves in years to come. Their erotic attraction to each other was unmistakable: Jean found George as appealing as ever, and George later remembered that "Jean had all the qualities I really liked. She played the piano, and she was full of fun and laughter and things like that. I was a little somber, serious type, and we hit it off well."[100] But Jean's understanding of their connection, and of what marriage to George would mean to her, went deeper, at least in retrospect. Later, comparing her two marriages, she focused on the shared commitment to nonviolence that grounded her more mature partnership. "When I married George," she recalled, "my goals were much clearer. I knew what I wanted then. I knew I wanted to work in the church. I knew I wanted to work with children. I knew that those were compatible, and I knew that we would never, ever argue about pacifism. We were convinced pacifists, both of us, and we had been so traumatized by that war that it was something we would never, ever argue about. We never did."[101] George's memory was similar, although characteristically more reserved. He noted that when he and Jean met again in 1947, "There were a lot of good memories there, from our previous experiences, and she was very open to me. She didn't care whether I had been a CO or not. In fact, she felt very sympathetic toward that."[102]

---

98. Ibid., 14.
99. Ibid., 14–15.
100. George Edwards interview with K'Meyer, 30.
101. Jean Edwards interview with K'Meyer, 28.
102. George Edwards interview with K'Meyer, 29.

The faith they shared in nonviolence and in each other saw George and Jean through her initial conflict with her parents over their engagement. As Jean remembered the dispute, the Maneys had two objections to the match: on a practical level, they were afraid George's background as a CO would keep him from getting a job, and on a theological and political level, they were opposed to pacifism. The Maney family's closeness made her parents' opposition all the more traumatic for Jean; at "the time that I really opposed [my father]," it was a "really awful experience."[103] Jean was "really torn," but although her parents saw her decision as "very, very sudden," she possessed a confidence that was rooted in having known George "for so many years." She also had the support of other elders in their community: the "teachers, and advisors, and youth workers and people like that who had known him through the years" thought the proposed match was "just marvelous." "It was a terrible decision to make," Jean remembered, but "I finally said I was going."[104] Recalling their decision, George later reflected, "My goodness. By the time we got married, I was twenty-seven . . . She was a year younger than I was, so we were both old enough to know what we wanted to do."[105] True to the Maney family tradition, the conflict evaporated when Jean would not be deterred. The families of the bride and groom were among the few guests at the simple wedding at Westminster Presbyterian Church on December 30, 1947. Jean's pastor, W. E. Phifer, Jr., and George's family's minister, John Millard, officiated together, while Jean's sister Helen served as her attendant and George's brother was his best man. George and Jean left Nashville for Louisville as soon as they were married, so instead of a reception after the service, the Maneys had hosted "a buffet supper and open house" the preceding evening for the two families and "those who had come from other cities to attend the nuptials."[106] After the wedding, Jean's parents continued to be "just as gracious as anybody could possibly be," coming to respect George for his achievements in seminary.[107]

Louisville Seminary proved to be a congenial and supportive community for George and Jean in their first three years of marriage. Founded in 1901 by the merger of a Southern and a Northern Presbyterian

103. Jean Edwards interview with K'Meyer, 27.
104. Ibid., 17.
105. George Edwards interview with K'Meyer, 29.
106. "Westminster Church Scene of Nuptials," Nashville *Tennesseean*, December 30, 1947.
107. Jean Edwards interview with K'Meyer, 28.

seminary, it was the only Presbyterian school for future clergy supported by both churches.[108] Its small community of students grew quickly in George's three years there, from 56 in 1948–49 to 78 a year later and 112 in 1950–51. Among them were members of the northern church seeking a more conservative, Southern Presbyterian education, and Southerners wanting to study at a northern seminary—a combination that facilitated theological cross-fertilization and occasionally provoked conflict.[109] Louisville itself was a curious mix of North and South, a place where racial equality was the law and entrenched racism the reality of daily life. The local branch of the National Association for the Advancement of Colored People (NAACP), founded in 1914, had won early victories, stopping the showing of D. W. Griffith's *Birth of a Nation* after two screenings in 1918, and successfully lobbying for the passage of the first state anti-lynching law in 1920. The group's campaigns to desegregate Louisville's educational system and its parks were more protracted, the latter lasting from 1924 to 1955. Neither Louisville nor Kentucky legally mandated segregated parks, but a judge had ruled in 1924 that segregation was established practice and thus could be enforced. In 1947 the NAACP filed suit against segregated public accommodations, and in 1956 began using nonviolent direct action to push for integration.[110] That was the year city schools were formally desegregated, but to little effect: a system allowing students to transfer to a school other than the one to which they had been assigned kept *de facto* segregation intact.[111] NAACP pressure had already led to a limited victory in 1949: the amendment of Kentucky's Day Law, the foundation of educational segregation, to allow the integration of colleges and universities. Louisville Seminary then admitted its first African-American student to receive a degree, Snowden Isaiah McKinnon, whose time at the seminary overlapped with George's and whose residence on campus with his white colleagues violated the amended law.[112]

For George and Jean, Louisville Seminary provided Christian community, theological space, and financial support. George had a Patterson

108. Nutt, *Many Lamps, One Light*, ix.

109. Ibid., 121.

110. Wright, *Life Behind a Veil*, 274–75. On racial segregation in Louisville from the 1920s on, see Wright, *A History of Blacks in Kentucky*, vol. 2, and Fosl, *Subversive Southerner*. On the post-Second World War freedom struggle in Louisville, see K'Meyer, *Civil Rights in the Gateway to the South*.

111. Carmichael and James, *Louisville Story*.

112. Nutt, *Many Lamps, One Light*, 156.

Scholarship in biblical theology and a job teaching introductory Greek, Jean worked as a faculty secretary, and they knew that at least one professor, Julian Price Love, was sympathetic to conscientious objectors.[113] George later remembered those years as "a very joyous time," both "because of my wife, which was an abundant joy" and also because "I was able to renew my older religious freedom" in an environment that allowed for the expression of differing theological convictions.[114] Finding himself accepted as a conscientious objector, "I felt like there was a future here for me. I could work with these people and learn from them."[115] He also taught by example, through small gestures that made an impression on his white classmates. One of them, George Gunn, remembered years later "one of the defining moments in my justice education": George, responsible for leading the chapel service one Friday, invited the seminary custodian to read the Scripture in the service. William Warfield, an African-American man, was "the best-known minority member" of what seminary president Frank H. Caldwell called "the Seminary Family"; he had never before been asked to participate in its life that way, but graciously accepted George's invitation. Gunn remembered "this affirmation of the inclusiveness of the community of faith" as an example of George's "personal conviction."[116]

Encouraged and emboldened by the freedom he found in seminary, George continued his witness for peace within the larger church. In 1949, along with Olof Anderson, the Louisville pastor who had visited him during the war, and seventeen others, George founded the Southern Presbyterian Peace Fellowship, a denominational group affiliated with the national Fellowship of Reconciliation. The group described themselves as "a demonstration group within our denomination determined to practice at home what we think Christians around the world should practice: refuse to participate in civil or international war in order that unadulterated Christian good will may more adequately determine our behavior toward others."[117] The group also refused "to sanction military prepara-

113. On Love's support for the Louisville chapter of the pacifist Fellowship of Reconciliation during the Second World War, see Lee, "'Admit Guilt—And Tell the Truth.'"

114. George and Jean Edwards interview with K'Meyer, March 12, 1996, Tape 1, 34.

115. George Edwards interview with K'Meyer, 33.

116. George Gunn in Harrod, "George and Jean Edwards: Living Peace."

117. Nutt, *Toward Peacemaking*, 51. By 1961, George Edwards had also joined the national Fellowship of Reconciliation, with Jean following by 1962; Jean Edwards

tions," and vowed both to "work to abolish war and to foster goodwill among nations, races and classes" and to "build a social order which will suffer no individual or group to be exploited for the profit or pleasure of another." George, a member of the founding executive committee of the Fellowship, wrote a fellow charter member in 1949 that he believed that the group had unspoken support beyond its small numbers, that "at least a dozen students" agreed with SPPF's aims, and that he had been treated with "sympathy and approval" at seminary, where his conscientious objection was common knowledge.[118] Given the renewed persecution of suspected American leftists in a year of communist victory in China and the detonation of an atomic bomb by the Soviet Union, it is not surprising that the SPPF stayed small. Even in the aftermath of the Vietnam War, in 1976, its membership peaked at about ninety.[119]

While George and Jean's concern for international affairs was ongoing, their life in seminary was grounded in the local church. They delayed having children, focusing on nurturing the young people of the churches they both served across the Ohio River in southern Indiana. George was student pastor to more than one small church, while Jean served as director of Christian education—or, as she later called it, "glorified youth worker"—at a church in Speed, Indiana, which provided housing along with her salary. George's extroverted wife later recounted the reaction to their move to Speed: "Everybody said I had finally found a place that really suited me. By that name."[120] She and George together invested a lot of their time and energy in developing the youth choir at her church, consciously influencing their small-town young charges, as she recalled: "We changed their musical tastes; I don't know if we should be proud of that or not. They were singing old gospel type of stuff when we went there, but when we left they were singing marvelous hymns. They were all first cousins, and they had a blend you couldn't find anywhere."[121]

Jean continued her own theological education informally, within the boundaries of women's roles of the time, in a seminary that did not

---

e-mail to Rhonda Mawhood Lee, November 19, 2005.

118. Nutt, *Toward Peacemaking*, 53. George Edwards is listed as a member of the executive committee in *The Presbyterian Outlook*, October 21, 1949, 2.

119. Nutt, *Toward Peacemaking*, 116.

120. George and Jean Edwards interview with K'Meyer, March 12, 1996, Tape 1, 37–38.

121. Ibid., Tape 2, 4. Reference to the choir at Jean's church is in George and Jean Edwards interview with K'Meyer, March 12, 1996, Tape 1, 38.

admit women until 1957 and a church that did not ordain them as clergy until 1964.[122] After a year in Louisville, she joined the seminary staff to do "old-time secretarial work," typing and mimeographing documents for faculty members. The job "fascinated" her, deepening the biblical and theological knowledge she had gained in her graduate work.[123] Her husband's gifts for academic and pastoral ministry, and her faith in his abilities, were affirmed in the prizes he won at the seminary, for the "best paper" by a first-year student "in the content of the English Bible" and at graduation for preaching, service to rural churches, New Testament studies, and for having "made the greatest progress in his field work during [his] seminary career."[124]

Given his theological principles and outspoken nature, it was fortunate that George's heart wasn't set on retaining the sympathy and respect he enjoyed in seminary. In early 1951, as graduation drew near and Jean became pregnant with their first child, George knew, in his wife's words, that "he either had to find a church or he had to accept a scholarship." Since George's Patterson Scholarship included a small grant for postgraduate study, he was considering doing a doctorate in New Testament at Duke University, but he also had an interview with a small Presbyterian church in Trenton, Tennessee, about a hundred miles east of Memphis.[125] Before making a decision about graduate school, he decided to interview with the church. His sermon at morning worship having been well received, George met the church elders for an interview, which also went well. Then came George's opportunity to ask questions of his own. He began by noting that the town's main industry was a shoe factory, and that the church included several members of its management and administrative staff. Then he followed up by saying, "But I didn't see very many working-class people" and asking, "Do they come to church here?" "Not really," came the reply. George continued, "Well, I think that's something we would have to overcome" (later he recalled, "That one passed by them"). He kept pressing: "There was another little pause and then I said, 'I know . . . you have a large black population here.' I said, 'I would feel that if we made an agreement and we came down here to do this work

---

122. The Northern Presbyterian Church began ordaining women in 1956.

123. George and Jean Edwards interview with K'Meyer, March 12, 1996, Tape 1, 38.

124. "Fellowships and Awards, 1948–49," *The Register* 39:1 (March 1950) 42; "Fellowships and Awards, 1950–51," *The Register* 41:1 (March 1952) 44.

125. George and Jean Edwards interview with K'Meyer, March 12, 1996, Tape 2, 6.

"We Really Needed to Start a New Way of Thinking"

for you . . .'" He did not finish the sentence, at which point "there was just this prolonged silence." Finally, "One of the younger men, a deacon, got up, and he said, 'Well, Mr. Edwards, I guess we won't be going to look at the manse.'"[126]

Even though George knew that there were "not many black Presbyterians anyway," in his ecclesiology any church not open to racial integration would serve as a reminder of sin's power over human beings, rather than as a sign of Jesus Christ's defeat of the evils of this world. To others, George's commitment seemed foolish; the elder who walked him and Jean to their car after his interview in Trenton remarked, "You know, discretion is the better part of valor." At that point, the path to graduate school became clear. George and Jean laughed together forty-five years later as they remembered that, in Jean's words, George "thought he would do [a doctorate] sometime or another, but it seemed that he should do it more quickly since . . ." and George finished the thought, "Trenton, Tennessee made my decision on that."[127]

George and Jean would combine prophetic witness and providing for their family's practical needs, academic life and church service, for decades to come. Over the years, they sought the freest spaces they could find in which to live the life to which they had been called together, in all its dimensions. After Louisville Seminary, the next such space they found was Duke University in the North Carolina Piedmont. Duke and the surrounding town, Durham, were enmeshed in the same system of white supremacy that George and Jean had known since childhood. During the Edwardses' years there, they mounted small challenges to that system, while focusing their combined energies on education, church leadership, and child-rearing. In later years, George would deem inadequate their first efforts at faithful witness, and he and Jean would commit themselves more fully to testifying in word and deed against the blasphemy of racism.

The family's time in North Carolina was both fruitful and exhausting. Between the end of 1951 and the beginning of 1955, Jean bore three children; George was ordained soon after their arrival and completed his doctoral studies within four years; and together they served several churches while George also taught introductory New Testament Greek at the Divinity School.[128] From August 1951 until May 1954, the fam-

---

126. George and Jean Edwards interview with K'Meyer, March 12, 1996, Tape 1, 41 and Tape 2, 2.

127. Ibid., Tape 2, 2.

128. Ibid., Tape 2, 9.

ily lived in Pittsboro, about thirty miles outside Durham. There, George pastored the seventy-member Pittsboro Presbyterian Church and three small rural churches twelve to twenty miles out of town, holding services in Pittsboro every Sunday, and at each of the three others one Sunday a month.[129] Pittsboro Presbyterian Church seems to have been willing to engage with George's theological commitments in ways that the church in Trenton, Tennessee, had not. In October 1951, in the midst of the Korean War, a national Presbyterian magazine, *Outlook*, printed a letter from George denouncing the only "imperialism in the world which is more vicious than the Russian one, and that is our own." He warned that while the United States might prevail over Communism in the immediate future, "The judgment of God . . . namely, that those who take the sword shall perish by the sword—is sure to come to us in due time. If we do not get it from Russia, it will surely be China or India or Africa, as soon as they are sufficiently developed to follow the same folly of world power and militant nationalism that has destroyed every other world power and is now choking the life out of this country we love." Paraphrasing the Apostle Paul, George asked and answered what was, for him, the central theological question for Christians: "Who shall deliver us from the body of this death? Who is there to break for us this vicious repetition of the rise and fall of military dominions? Surely Christ alone can—if Christians will only let him."[130] If George's critique of militarism disturbed anyone at his church, no record of that concern has survived.

Nor did Pittsboro Presbyterian take offense at George's concerns about racial divisions among Christians. In April 1953, the church conducted a "Negro Work Campaign," about which no details have survived except that it was financed in the amount of $141 (equivalent to about one-fifth of George's annual salary of $720). That month the session also approved the minister's request to conduct a one-week "Negro Bible School" in the summer "if it could be arranged."[131] Historical sources are silent on whether or not that vacation Bible school ever took place, but at least George knew that, within segregation's limits, the church supported his outreach efforts. Over time, they rewarded him financially for his work, more than doubling his salary, car allowance, and

---

129. Ibid., 6; George Riley Edwards curriculum vitae, n.d. (after 1985), "George R. Edwards" file, LPTS.

130. George R. Edwards letter, *The Presbyterian Outlook*, October 1, 1951.

131. Minutes of Session, April 19, 1953, PPC.

annuity contribution in 1954 although the church's membership had not increased in George's two years there.[132]

George and Jean both retained fond memories of their years in Pittsboro, but over time, the strain of work, travel, and studying became too much for George. Jean focused on caring for their children: George Riley Jr. (known as Riley), born in October 1951, Virginia (Ginger), born in November 1952, and John (called Johnny), born in January 1955. Years later, Jean laughed remembering that after their two older children appeared thirteen months apart, "I became rather busy."[133] The church expected her to take an active role, as the annual report of the Women of the Church group for 1951 noted tellingly that "in July Rev. and Mrs. George R. Edwards came to us as our minister."[134] Jean limited her involvement, however: identified as "an inspiration and great help" to the congregation's female members, she did not serve as an officer of the Women of the Church until 1954.[135] By the spring of that year, it was clear that the family needed to make some changes. Working to complete a doctorate in less than four years while providing for his wife and children demanded all of George's energy and Jean's full support. As he later remembered, "I really felt exhausted all the time, because that was simply more than I think any person could do." Having decided to resign from the Pittsboro-area churches and move to Durham, George experienced "a terrible emotional crisis . . . I broke down and started crying and I couldn't stop." At that time, "things seemed unsolvable. I couldn't fight more battles than I was fighting, but I felt like I needed to fight more battles." His wife's equanimity got the family through George's breakdown: "Jean kept her head cool, and she never got completely overwhelmed, although we had three little children and you're trying to juggle a lot of other balls out there. It's just hell to pay."[136] George and Jean left Pittsboro Presbyterian on good terms; after receiving George's resignation, effective the first Sunday in June 1954, the session voted to pay his full salary for June and July.[137] The family moved

---

132. Minutes of Session, November 1, 1953, PPC. George's salary increased to $1500, his car allowance to $360 from $180, and his annuity fund to $112.50 from $54.00. The church also provided a manse.

133. George and Jean Edwards interview with K'Meyer, March 12, 1996, Tape 2, 7.

134. "History of the Women of the Pittsboro Presbyterian Church, 1951–52," PPC.

135. "History of the Women of the Pittsboro Presbyterian Church, 1952–1953," and "Officers of the Women of the Church," 1951–52 and 1952–53, PPC.

136. George and Jean Edwards interview with K'Meyer, April 23, 1996, 10.

137. Minutes of Session, May 2 and July 11, 1954, PPC.

to Durham, where George became the pastor of Blacknall Presbyterian Church, within walking distance of Duke, in October 1954.[138]

The move to Durham allowed George to focus more energy on finishing his dissertation, "The Qumran Sect and the New Testament Church," which merged new developments in biblical studies with his interest in the political dimensions of Christianity. The scrolls the Qumran community had produced, known as the Dead Sea Scrolls, came to light between 1947 and 1960, significant for biblical scholarship because they included copies of biblical books that predated by several centuries those that had previously been available. George followed his analysis of the textual evidence about the life of the Qumran community with a conclusion assessing the twentieth-century church's movement away from its roots as followers of Jesus of Nazareth. He contrasted the Qumran sect, which had lived in a communal isolation he called "hyper-nationalism," awaiting the arrival of the Messiah, with the church, born of the belief that the Messiah has come. The church, as the body of Jesus Christ and the bearer of his message, was called, George argued, not to live "in holy isolation from the secular world," but rather (obliquely referencing Galatians 3:28) to live within it, offering "a message of salvation which makes one of Gentile and Jew."[139] George introduced a careful critique into his argument, noting that the contemporary church had "often failed to retain the depth of its Christological foundations." Whereas a truly Christian church would rise above divisions of race and nation, "nationalism has made great inroads in Christian practice, even where the theoretical understanding of the 'body of Christ' has not been lacking." The church needed to return to "the fertile depths of New Testament ecclesiology" if it was to "transcend the divisions of race and culture" that (he did not state openly) led to racial oppression and war.[140]

In his time in North Carolina, George was challenged by his own convictions about the church's obligations to be true to the New Testament vision of oneness in Christ. Although he didn't say so directly when speaking of the breakdown he experienced in 1954, it is likely that some of the battles George thought he should be fighting at that time were against racism and segregation. Fights over the future of Jim Crow were entering a new, active phase during his years at Duke, a period of

---

138. Minutes of congregational meeting, October 10, 1954, BPC.
139. Edwards, "Qumran Sect and the New Testament Church," 275–76.
140. Ibid., 276–77.

"We Really Needed to Start a New Way of Thinking"

growth for the NAACP and allied groups, and also for militant white supremacists.[141] At least some of George's colleagues wanted to see their institution open its doors wider. Students at Duke Divinity School had petitioned their administration to desegregate in 1948, the first such effort to come from within the university, but Duke remained closed to African-American graduate students until 1961, and to undergraduates until 1963.[142] Despite his concern for interracial fellowship, George later remembered with "regret" that he had refused when asked to travel farther south "to reinforce the black movement."[143] He couldn't remember when the call had come, but it may have been in early 1956, when national pacifist organizations like the FOR and the WRL were seeking volunteers to go to Montgomery to support the bus boycott there.[144] Looking back forty years later, George remembered receiving the appeal to travel south while he was still pastoring the Chatham County churches and working on his dissertation. Given the fact that he graduated in the spring of 1955, however, it is more likely that George associated the stress of his time in Pittsboro with the family's entire five years in North Carolina. He remembered citing "professional reasons"—his workload—as a reason why he couldn't join the movement, but he was also "apprehensive about the children and Jean, and I used that in my own conscience to say no, I couldn't go."[145] George's appointment to a seminary faculty position in a couple of years would allow him and Jean to devote more of their energy to public witness, but dividing that energy between working for international peace and for racial justice at home would always be a challenge.

The second half of the Edwardses' sojourn in North Carolina passed more quietly than the first. George served Blacknall Presbyterian Church on a part-time basis until graduation in June 1955, and then full time for another year.[146] Much larger than Pittsboro Presbyterian, with 255 members, Blacknall could support its own full-time pastor.[147] Its members were disappointed when George resigned "with regret" in the summer

---

141. On organizing by the NAACP, other liberation groups, and the Ku Klux Klan in North Carolina in this time period, see Greene, *Our Separate Ways*, 42–44.

142. Kotelanski, "Prolonged and Patient Efforts," 13–14, 136–37, 140.

143. George and Jean Edwards interview with K'Meyer, April 23, 1996, 10.

144. D'Emilio, *Lost Prophet*, 239–40.

145. George and Jean Edwards interview with K'Meyer, April 23, 1996, 10.

146. Minutes of Session, June 17, 1956, BPC.

147. "Session's annual statistical report—Presbyterian Church in the United States, for the year ending December 31, 1954," BPC.

of 1956 to return to Louisville Seminary, this time as a professor of New Testament.[148] So disappointed, in fact, that the moderator of the congregational meeting held to appoint George's successor stated that "he had understood that it was the feeling in the church that we might not want another minister who might decide he wanted to go into teaching."[149] As difficult as it was for Blacknall Presbyterian to lose George, the move to Louisville was a gift for him and Jean. The seminary position he held for thirty years offered their family financial and geographic stability, and allowed both spouses to grow into their vocations as ministers, parents, and prophets. Over the following decades, they would work together to build a community that, in witnessing against war and working for peace, would fulfill the promise they had made to each other on the night in Nashville when they got engaged.

---

148. Minutes of congregational meeting, June 3, 1956, BPC.

149. Ibid., August 26, 1956, BPC.

2

"At Least We Make a Witness"

Anti-Communism and the Vietnam War

ON GRADUATION DAY 1967, George Edwards stood in the pulpit of Louisville Seminary's chapel. Chosen by the graduating class to preach that day, George had not yet begun to speak when fourteen Presbyterian laymen in the congregation rose to protest his being given the pulpit at a church-supported institution. From his pew, Deacon Ben Johnson of Louisville's Second Presbyterian Church laid two charges against George: his theology and biblical interpretation were "not consistent with the confessional standards" of the church, and "his positions on public matters and his public conduct in giving expression to them have been in contradiction with his offices as gospel minister and professor" at Louisville Seminary.[1] Another protestor, George and Jean's neighbor and an elder at Strathmoor Presbyterian Church, Chester B. Hall, had already circulated a memo asking his fellow church members to "review your own will and your own schedule of giving. Decide for yourself whether in good conscience you can continue to support financially any institution which offers itself as a place of refuge for psychos, Marxists, Communists,

---

1. "Protestor Interrupts Commencement," *The Presbyterian Outlook*, June 12, 1967.

and anti-'Christians'"—meaning Louisville Seminary.² As Hall, Johnson, and their associates registered their protest, the institution they decried literally stood with the man they targeted. First, President Albert C. Winn rose and moved to George's side so that the preacher no longer faced the protestors alone; then the graduating class and finally the whole congregation stood and turned in the same direction. After Winn told them, "You have been heard!" Hall and Johnson's group left.³

Although the protestors did not hear the sermon George had prepared in advance, their actions vividly illustrated his argument. Preaching on Mark 5:17, "And they began to beg Jesus to depart from their neighborhood," George warned the graduates that they could not afford to wait for human permission to preach God's message. "The church, the ministry, and the institutions of the church, including this seminary, stand today under the tests of freedom," he noted. "The shrill cries of the racists, the nationalists, the birchers, and the anticommunists are raised at every corner where the Christian faith seeks its unhampered application." Seen in the proper perspective, these objections were good news: "The stridency of their complaints is sign and proof that the apostolic freedom of the modern ministry is coming to new expression. Where we are exempted from the defamations and attacks of these reactions, it is evidence that the church lies under suburban captivity and purchases its peace at the price of justice and human rights."⁴ In other words, worshippers of the Son of God who followed in his disruptive, nonviolent footsteps should not expect approval—even from the church.

The incident at the 1967 graduation service illustrated the place George and Jean Edwards had come to occupy in Louisville by the middle of that struggle-filled decade. George stood in a pulpit, chosen by his students to speak a prophetic word that might be disturbing, comforting, or both, depending on the listener. Jean sat in the congregation, offering her support. A vocal minority attacked George on political and theological grounds, while the seminary community—not always in agreement with George's views on peace, war, and liberation—affirmed him as their brother in faith. These complex and challenging relationships were the

---

2. "Louisville Seminary Worship Disrupted by Protestors," *Presbyterian Survey*, July 1967.

3. Ibid.

4. Edwards, "Boundaries," 6, "George Edwards" file, LPTS. The phrase "suburban captivity" comes from a widely read appeal for churches to remain in urban areas: Winter, *The Suburban Captivity of the Churches*.

stuff of George and Jean's lives after they returned to Louisville, as they sought to answer, through their daily actions, a series of interrelated questions. How would they arrange their family life so that both spouses could fulfill the vocations to which they had been called? Which calls for social witness and liberation would they answer and extend to others? In the absence of a significant peace testimony within their church, how could they develop a network to spread the gospel message of nonviolence?

Until the end of the Vietnam era, the Edwardses' answers to these questions were shaped largely by their children's needs. While both George and Jean nurtured Riley, Ginger, and Johnny, their division of labor was fairly traditional: Jean was the homemaker, living out her call to work with children within her own family, while George was the primary breadwinner and the public face of his and Jean's commitment to peace. A scholar with a gracious demeanor, but whose personality tended toward the argumentative and melancholy, George struggled in the oppressive political atmosphere of the 1950s and early 1960s to build up a citywide network of witnesses for peace. After the Vietnam War had ended and the children left home, Jean would add her organizing skills and extroverted, persuasive personality to the cause, but in the challenging '60s, allies could be hard to find.

Controversy, in contrast, found them as soon as they moved back to Kentucky from Durham in the fall of 1956. At first, life moved according to a familiar rhythm. They made their home in Pewee Valley, a rural community twenty-five miles outside Louisville, where George pastored the Presbyterian church while teaching New Testament and Greek part time at Louisville Seminary. The next autumn, they moved to Louisville for George to serve a "probationary" year as full-time instructor of biblical Greek and New Testament before joining the faculty as a tenured professor, succeeding his former teacher, W. D. Chamberlain.[5] Their life in Pewee Valley was full, as Jean told family and friends in the spring of 1957, in the letter she had been too busy to write since before Christmas. "Ginger and Riley and I are having a great time keeping the grass mowed—two acres of it," she remarked, while "I have finished making curtains for all of the windows as well as more cherub choir surplices, so that we are beginning to feel on top of things." With the end of the semester approaching, "We hope George's schedule will slow down too,"

---

5. Minutes of the faculty, December 2, 1955 (resolving to offer George a lectureship), and March 3, 1958 (resolving to elect him professor), LPTS. Chamberlain died just weeks before he was to retire; Minutes of the faculty, May 23, 1958, LPTS.

as "He has had to do all of his studying and grading of papers at night after coming in from the church meetings." Their "many responsibilities at the church" seemed "worthwhile," leading them on "to more and greater undertakings, and the snow ball has become quite gigantic at this point."[6]

Among those undertakings, not mentioned directly, was George's work with Kentucky's most visible dissidents: Anne and Carl Braden, journalists with leftist views, to whom a Pewee Valley parishioner, LaRue Spiker, had introduced the Edwardses. The Bradens had become household names in 1954, a couple of months before the U. S. Supreme Court ruled racially segregated schools unconstitutional. In an attempt to advance residential desegregation in Louisville, the Bradens had bought a house in a white neighborhood and, as had been prearranged, immediately sold it to an African-American couple, Charlotte and Andrew Wade. That scheme exposed the depths of white Louisvillians' support for the status quo, and demonstrated the extent to which white Americans—conservative and liberal alike—equated criticism of government policy, or advocacy for racial integration, with Communism. After the Wades moved into their new home, dynamite planted under their daughter's bedroom exploded and destroyed the building; the family later left the neighborhood. A grand jury hearing on the bombing turned into a quest to denounce the Bradens and their associates as Communists and a smear campaign to suggest that they, or other opponents of segregation, had planted the dynamite as an act of provocation or a publicity stunt. As a result, both Bradens and several of their friends—all white—were indicted on charges of sedition against the state of Kentucky. Of the Braden group of associates, only Carl was tried: he served eight months in prison before the U.S. Supreme Court voided his conviction in 1956.[7] Writing about the incident a few years later, Anne Braden remembered the contrast between the massive and violent white opposition to the two families' act, and her perception until then that "Louisville's race relations, such as they were, had always been quiet," without "open clashes." White Louisvillians, she believed, self-consciously presented their border city as different from the Lower South, in a manner that struck her as "complacent, self-satisfied, locked in a fancied security."[8] White Louisvillians,

---

6. Jean Edwards letter to "Dear Friends and Loved Ones," May 4, 1957, Jean Edwards papers.

7. Fosl, *Subversive Southerner*, chs. 6 and 7.

8. Braden, *Wall Between*, 4–5.

including most clergy, identified the Bradens, not racial segregation, as the problem and, almost to a person, ostracized them for decades.

George and Jean Edwards were among the few exceptions. The pacifist convictions they shared with LaRue Spiker brought them and the Bradens together: Spiker was a member of what Anne Braden's biographer, historian Catherine Fosl, calls the "tiny" Louisville chapter of WILPF. Spiker's association with Pewee Valley Presbyterian Church did not last long: finding herself unemployable in Kentucky, she soon left the state.[9] Her brief acquaintance with George and Jean, however, and the dearth of white support for racial justice and civil liberties in Louisville, led Carl Braden to visit George at home in Pewee Valley. When Carl asked him to become a member of the local chapter of the NAACP, George answered that he "already had all the meetings I could say grace over, but I didn't mind joining the NAACP if it meant anything to him."[10] When George and Jean's white acquaintances learned that George was associating with the Bradens and their friends, they warned him away, a couple of parishioners offering "written materials to bring me up to date" on Carl's recent trial. Reflecting that "they thought it was just ignorance on my part that I would be even willing to talk to somebody like that," George acknowledged his ignorance but framed it in a positive light: "I had nothing against Carl. I didn't know anything about him."[11] George and Carl got to know each other over the years, working together politically until Braden's death in 1975, but they never became intimate friends. Although they shared some political goals, their activities were rooted in fundamentally different ways of seeing the world. George's political work was the fruit of his commitment to Christian nonviolence while, as he later remembered, "Carl was not heavy on that type of emphasis," having "much more conviction about the class warfare notion" than George did.[12]

Although George and Jean were never rooted in leftist thought as Carl Braden was, neither of them had any patience for the

---

9. Fosl, *Subversive Southerner*, 150, 162, 199.

10. George and Jean Edwards interview with K'Meyer, March 12, 1996, Tape 2, 14–15.

11. Ibid., 15.

12. Ibid., 32. Anne Braden's biographer, Catherine Fosl, has noted that Anne, a practicing Episcopalian, pursued social justice "with a zeal that looked secular but felt spiritual to her." *Subversive Southerner*, 102. Braden wrote about her motivations in the Wade case for an independent Episcopal publication: "Church Leader in Kentucky Indicted for Sedition: Tells Story of What Happens When Christian Principles Are Put to Work," *The Witness*, February 17, 1955.

anti-Communism that stifled American political—and theological—debate for decades. That became further evident in 1958, when George was invited to speak at Indiana University's Jeffersonville campus, just across the Ohio River from Louisville. He accepted, not knowing that the invitation had originally been extended to his senior colleague, Julian Price Love. Told that any campus speaker must take a loyalty oath to the United States, Love had refused, calling the requirement "childish and insulting."[13] Shortly after George accepted Indiana's invitation to speak, he caught sight of Love's photo in the *Louisville Courier-Journal*, under a headline trumpeting his refusal to sign the oath. "Finding myself in the unsavory position of being blindsided in my communications with the I.U. branch," George later remembered, "I called up the school dean to inform him it was impossible for me to do the work refused by Dr. Love." When George's refusal became public, the seminary president, Frank H. Caldwell, telephoned to entreat him not to speak to the press about the incident, "expressing strong disapproval that Dr. Love had created for the Seminary such an embarrassing situation." At that time, George's relationship with the seminary president "was at best strained," and the remonstrance, rather than "bridling" George's activism, had the opposite effect.[14] Concerns about George's, or Love's, patriotism may have been the presenting issue when, in 1961, the Louisville Seminary faculty sent a letter to their school's board affirming their "unqualified confidence in the Christian integrity" of each professor. The letter mentioned no names as the professors stated that no one among them "is teaching or preaching communism, nor is any of us promoting communist objectives." "On the contrary," they protested, "we are all devoutly concerned with eliminating the social swamps in which communism breeds."[15]

As a tenured seminary professor, George enjoyed more freedom of conscience than did pastors of congregations, whose jobs could be on the line in theological disagreements with their lay leadership. As a Calvinist who took seriously the seventeenth-century Westminster Confession of Faith, a foundational document for Presbyterian churches, George both affirmed the sovereignty of God as revealed in Scripture, and insisted on the believer's duty to heed her conscience as guided by the Holy Spirit. When he found himself at odds with his church and his colleagues over

---

13. Nutt, *Many Lamps, One Light*, 158.

14. George R. Edwards letter to Rick Nutt, 27 February 1993, 5–6, "George Edwards" file, LPTS.

15. Minutes of the faculty, November 21, 1961, LPTS.

issues of faith, he cited the Confession's statement that "God alone is Lord of the conscience, and hath left it free from the doctrines and commandments of men which are in anything contrary to his Word, or beside it in matters of faith or worship."[16] George knew that, although John Calvin had insisted on the divine authority of rulers, the founding figure of Presbyterian Christianity had also stated that obedience to God must ultimately be placed above obedience to civil authorities when the two conflicted.[17]

These affirmations, coupled with George and Jean's insistence that the way of Christ was the way of nonviolence, made them an unusual blend of radicalism and tradition. Even as they were out of step with most of their brothers and sisters in the church, their faith and their conventional home life distinguished them from some secular people, like Carl Braden, who shared many of their political commitments. Their oldest son, Riley, remembered his parents' stability and observance of many social standards as an asset to his father's political work. "Being married and living a responsible family life," working as a professor, always appearing in public in a coat and tie, demonstrating a "scrupulous attention to detail" and a "command of the facts," with "humor and [a] resonant voice," in his son's view, "George simply commanded respect."[18] Although George's views often incited virulent opposition, his commitment to the Presbyterian Church made it difficult to question his faith.

In addition to offering George freedom of conscience, his job at Louisville Seminary gave his family a new financial security. Although its faculty was poorly paid by the standards of Presbyterian seminaries, his starting salary in the range of $7,500 plus housing allowance freed him from cobbling together a living from preaching and teaching, and allowed Jean to stay home, or work part time, while their children were young.[19] Jean "loved" her work at home "very much," and when she was ready to work outside the home again, she remembered, "I always kept my job limited so that I could also take care of my family." The paid work Jean chose broadened her horizons and those of her children: when the family moved back to Louisville, her first job was teaching at the preschool of a synagogue in their neighborhood. "I was concerned," Jean

16. *Book of Confessions*, 195.
17. Calvin, *Institutes of Christian Religion*, bk. IV, ch. 20.
18. Riley Edwards-Raudonat e-mail to Rhonda Mawhood Lee, February 7, 2011.
19. Nutt, *Many Lamps, One Light*, 125.

remembered, "about relating to the community in more than just how I would through my church," and the preschool job allowed her "to sort of get acquainted with the Jewish community a little bit." At the time, Johnny was ready to enter preschool, so he accompanied his mother, learning "that Jewish children were part of our life too." Riley and Ginger were already attending their local public school, whose student body "reflected this neighborhood, which is 50 percent Jewish, and we were very glad of that, that they would have this opportunity in their school."[20]

Both George and Jean were devoted to their children, all of whom share memories of, in eldest son Riley's words, "being part of a happy family" that, like Jean's family of origin, "used to laugh a lot, especially at mealtimes."[21] Reflecting as an adult on her upbringing, Ginger believed that George and Jean "overexerted themselves" trying to be "ideal parents."[22] For Jean, at home with three children less than four years apart in age, parenting involved structures and schedules her adult children described as "strict." According to Riley, "She knew whether we'd done our homework and practiced our musical instruments. If we had difficulty with an assignment, she would ask questions and offer hints, but leave it to us to get the job done." George, in contrast, "was more relaxed. If we asked him for help with our homework, he was likely to tell us the answers. You can imagine," he concluded, "whom we preferred to ask."[23] George was indulgent in other ways: with the "sweets and chocolate" that Ginger remembered as "his downfall," which he hid in his desk but "never seemed to notice when we helped ourselves," and with pocket money, so that the children "asked him for change when we had the feeling Jean would be too strict." Like Jean, George was a teacher at home, passing on his carpentry and home repair skills to all three children in what Ginger called "his inexhaustible patient way," and washing the dishes for what he called "therapy" while the children dried.[24] Perhaps not surprisingly, given George and Jean's vocational directions, the one thing their youngest son Johnny said his parents did not offer him was "a good skill set for

---

20. George and Jean Edwards interview with K'Meyer, April 23, 1996, 3.

21. Edwards-Raudonat e-mail to Rhonda Mawhood Lee, February 7, 2011.

22. Virginia Edwards-Menz e-mail to Rhonda Mawhood Lee, February 20, 2011. In his seventies, George described himself and Jean as "almost inordinately attached to our children"; George and Jean Edwards interview with K'Meyer, April 23, 1996, 17.

23. Edwards-Raudonat e-mail to Lee, February 7, 2011.

24. Edwards-Menz e-mail to Lee.

navigating a capitalist world."²⁵ As a musician who later went into corporate work, Johnny had to learn the basics of moneymaking on his own.

As in any human community, life in the Edwards home was not idyllic. Both Riley and Ginger remembered their parents arguing frequently. Their disputes were never about what Ginger called "the big issues": peace, church work, parenting, or finances.²⁶ Instead, these two strong-willed and temperamentally different people clashed over everyday matters, such as Jean's tendency to be late for outings, which Riley remembered as "a constant source of tension." While the two pacifists did not explicitly teach their children strategies for peacemaking at home, they did develop habits that worked for them. Small conflicts would often be aired at the dinner table, where the family gathered daily and, in Riley's words, "whatever was up in the air was vocalized."²⁷ Alternatively, they would be pushed aside in the strategy of deflection that Jean had learned in her parents' home: as Ginger recalled, when "little hassles" such as what to include in the week's shopping list "went on and on," "Jean usually ended it by saying, 'OK, let's go!'" Their daughter also remembered that "Jean refused to be discouraged by George's pondering over unsolved political issues or theological questions."²⁸ Both parents agreed on the need to raise their children to abhor war: as Jean later remembered, her and George's "total agreement" about pacifism was always "just a given" in their household.²⁹ They used all available means to form their children in that faith: as a young boy, Riley accompanied his father to see the film *On the Beach*, set in a world devastated by nuclear war. In that scenario, as George later wrote, there was "not a soul to be seen, not even a Rachel weeping for her children and refusing to be comforted because they are not (Jeremiah 31:15), because she is not." When he and Riley walked out of the cinema, "our firstborn son looked up at me and said: 'Daddy, are we going to die like that?'"³⁰ The hope that neither they nor any other

---

25. John Douglas (Johnny) Edwards interview.
26. Edwards-Menz e-mail to Lee.
27. Edwards-Raudonat e-mail to Lee, February 7, 2011.
28. Edwards-Menz e-mail to Lee.
29. George and Jean Edwards interview with K'Meyer, April 23, 1996, 1/–18.
30. George R. Edwards, "The Abolition of War in the Twenty-First Century," September 19, 1996, Jean Edwards papers. George remembered taking Riley to see the film in 1963, the year in which it was set, but as it was released in late 1959, it is more likely that they saw it then.

children would perish that way was one motivation for George and Jean's work for peace.

In the midst of their awareness of the world's dangers, a sense of humor sustained both spouses, George frequently serving as the target of Jean's jokes and good-naturedly repeating them. Invited to preach at the seminary's opening worship service when he was promoted to professor of New Testament in 1959, George began by noting that he had only been employed full time at the seminary for one year, while several senior colleagues had served as instructors much longer before being promoted. When George wondered at home whether he should be flattered by this discrepancy, his wife replied, "You don't get the point. In their case it was unnecessary to hurry because their permanence and competence were quite evident. In your case, frankly, the powers that be are afraid you will peter out before the service is held, so they had to hurry things up a bit." George closed the story by insisting that Jean's suspicion should "be assigned to the realm of rumor."[31]

Balancing their combined vocations to teaching, scholarship, and parenthood without making an idol of any of those commitments was a challenging task. To accomplish it, George and Jean had to remain grounded in their primary and overarching call: as Christian disciples. Seen from that perspective, their various calls could not be separated, although time, energy, and money had to be judiciously allocated among them. Discerning that allocation was an ongoing challenge for every Christian, as George reminded the seminary community in his inaugural address in 1959. Taking the Gospel and Epistles of John, Jesus' "beloved disciple," as his reference points, George exhorted the congregation to lead integrated lives that focused as much on the divine call to love one's neighbor as on each person's individual relationship with God. For George, love of neighbor should motivate Christians not only to engage in their own costly acts of self-sacrifice, but also to pressure civil authorities to change laws and policies that denied human dignity and the inherent worth of certain persons. Recalling John's probing question to his contemporaries, "But if anyone has the world's goods and sees his brother in need, yet closes his heart against him, how does God's love abide in him?" George wondered, "May we revise this a bit to read: 'But if any

31. "The Beloved Disciple: An Address by Dr. George R. Edwards on the Occasion of His Installation as Professor of New Testament at the Formal Opening Service of the 107th School Year at Louisville Presbyterian Theological Seminary, 22 September 1959," 1, "George Edwards" file, LPTS.

nation has this world's goods and sees its fellow nation in need, yet closes its heart against it, how does God's love abide in it?'"[32]

George knew that not everyone in the congregation would agree with his biblical exegesis, but he insisted that Christians could not separate study and faithful action. Just as John had been "more than a historian of Christian beginnings," doing "a very dangerous thing" by "[letting] Christ speak to the environment in which John found himself," the seminary community must combine study of the Christian tradition with social action to make a vibrant witness to the world. Doing so, George warned, would require laboring as the first apostles had, "with gigantic exertions against the powers of unbelief, using every ounce of insight and intellectual power" at their disposal. Drawing on his own experience, George noted that "we often find that the hours are long and our mental and physical energies seem time and again to have reached their limit." But he reassured his listeners that this "exertion" and "the stimulating exchange of student-faculty relationships" would bring rewards, before closing with a final caution: "The beloved disciple was fast on his feet. In fact he outpaced Peter when the two of them raced to the tomb to see the risen Lord. The study of the New Testament is not a rat race as some say, but it is like a track meet, and the devil *will* catch the hindermost."[33]

Although George's evocation of the devil was humorous, playing on the reputation he had already earned as a strict teacher, neither he nor Jean ever underestimated the power of sin. They saw it manifested in the white supremacy that permeated every aspect of American life, in military budgets that relied on the threat of mutually assured destruction as the foundation for national security, and in the trust Christians placed in these systems. The conviction that their activism could not be separated from teaching, scholarship, family and church life as forms of witness to God's reconciling power, gave their political work an evangelistic zeal. George's scholarship and witness overlapped: while he published a few articles in scholarly journals and books, most of his writing took the form of sermons, public addresses, and pamphlets, some of which were distributed by the national Fellowship of Reconciliation.[34] After more than

---

32. Ibid., 8.

33. Ibid., 9–10.

34. Among George's pamphlets available from the Fellowship of Reconciliation was "Christianity and War: Two Positions," contrasting "the Christian militarist position" with "some responses from the pacifist side," 1965, Jean Edwards papers.

a decade as a seminary professor, George remarked to an interviewer, "I don't write books—I write pamphlets."[35]

Although George eventually wrote two books, the first, *Jesus and the Politics of Violence*, was published in 1972, when he was fifty-two years old, and the second, *Gay/Lesbian Liberation: A Biblical Perspective*, appeared a dozen years later as he was about to retire from teaching. As George noted in his seventies, "I was fifty-five before I ever read a paper at the Society of Biblical Literature."[36] He taught his students not to confuse biblical scholarship with Scripture itself. William Shackleford, who studied at Louisville Seminary in the late 1960s, remembered George coming to class one day "with a stack of books" by renowned scholars. Although Shackleford didn't remember the topic under discussion, he recalled that George "proceeded through the stack one book at a time," using each author's thesis in turn "to refute the thesis of the previous author." When he reached the end of the stack, George "tossed the last book on the table with a loud thud, and declared, 'That's scholarship, people, that's scholarship!'"[37] Despite that humorous skepticism, George's relatively scanty publication list led him to feel "intimidated" at professional meetings in the presence of scholars who wrote for "serious journals," as though he "wasn't cut from that cloth." "But," he summarized in retrospect, "I published enough," and "I did a lot of other things besides that."[38]

Those "other things" were focused as much on persuading his fellow Christians to make a public witness for peace as on showing the U.S. government that not everyone supported the Cold War. George's arguments for nonviolence were rooted in two articles of faith: that the innocent Jesus had willingly accepted crucifixion, and that God had raised him from the dead. Reacting against what he often called the "fundamentalism" of the church of his youth, George joined many of his contemporaries in questioning the physical nature of Jesus' resurrection. Generations of Louisville Seminary students would remember, after graduation, George's oft-repeated statement that the resurrection was not a "photographable event": if cameras had existed in the first century, they could not have captured an image of the risen Jesus. Rather, for George it was "a visible event only to the eye of faith," a reality that had first been perceived in

---

35. Notes from internal seminary publication interview with George R. Edwards, 1970, "George Edwards" file, LPTS.

36. George and Jean Edwards interview with K'Meyer, May 9, 1996, 51.

37. William Shackleford in Harrod, "George and Jean Edwards: Living Peace."

38. George and Jean Edwards interview with K'Meyer, May 9, 1996, 51.

encounters with "the Christ of the Church's Table fellowship."[39] The fact that the resurrection could be seen only through the lens of faith did not make it less real. When George argued that no one could behold Jesus Christ's risen body without their world, and their place in it, being irrevocably changed, he was not only describing his own experience, but challenging himself and others to live boldly the new life that the risen Christ offered. For the believer, as George paraphrased Paul's proclamation in Romans 6, "[Christ's] dying and rising are my dying and rising." This death and rebirth were nothing to fear, being suffused and nourished by the power of the resurrection, as "the renewing, liberating, and empowering Presence of Jesus, made known to us in breaking bread, comes to us from 'the other side' as God's gift."[40] That gift was nothing less than "to possess true life, to be freed from death, to enter into God's kind of life."[41] God's kind of life offered joy—and required sacrifice. Christians could not, George insisted, separate christology and ethics. Citing Peter's proclamation of Jesus as the Messiah, and Jesus' response that his disciples must take up their cross and follow him, George proclaimed, "There is, in fact, no 'you are the Christ' without 'take up your cross.'"[42]

For George, taking up his cross often meant making a solitary witness. On the University of Louisville campus in October 1962, distributing pamphlets calling for a negotiated end to the Cuban missile crisis, George was soon surrounded by a few dozen students who, in the words of a reporter, "began to question his views." Escorted by campus police to the office of a vice principal who feared a riot might start, George agreed to leave the premises.[43] He continued his advocacy of international dialogue, working to gather a network of Christians and Jews who would join him in speaking out for peace. Rather than forming a local chapter of the pacifist FOR, he called the group the "Louisville Peace Council," opening it to just war advocates who wanted to work for nuclear arms control, believing that a nuclear war would be inherently unjust.[44] Progress was

39. George R. Edwards, "Resurrection and the Empty Tomb" (undated, unpublished lecture), 2, 4, Jean Edwards papers.

40. Ibid., 6.

41. Ibid., 7.

42. Edwards, "Christology and Ethics," 94. The passage under study is Mark 8:27—9:1.

43. "Professor's Handouts for Pacifists Halted," *Presbyterian Journal*, November 21, 1962, 4.

44. The two best-known organizations focusing on nuclear arms control were

slow. As George reported to a colleague in the summer of 1963, after several months of trying to "draw together people of various perspectives on peace," "to date we have 'drawn together' about twelve people, the rest of the religious community seeming to want our fellowship about like they want leprosy." "But," he concluded, "we will keep trying."[45] At the same time, George kept an eye on developments in Southeast Asia, preaching against American military involvement there in the autumn of 1963, before many Americans were even aware of their country's presence in Vietnam. Guy Wilcox, a new member of the student body, recalled wondering during that sermon, "Who is this guy? What's with Viet Nam?"[46] George's denunciation of U.S. support for South Vietnam placed him in the small group of American clergy who were taking a stand on the issue at that time. They included Reinhold Niebuhr, who, true to his just war convictions, had joined Harry Emerson Fosdick and ten other clergy in signing a public statement against American alignment with "a regime universally regarded as unjust, undemocratic, and unstable."[47]

George had few companions in speaking out about the Vietnam War that fall, but a new phase of the African-American freedom struggle was underway, and George and Jean Edwards were among its supporters. The self-congratulatory attitude that Anne Braden had so detested in the 1950s had been evident in the city's decision to desegregate its schools in 1956, after several years of pressure from the NAACP, WILPF, and other organizations. The city's plan included allowing students to transfer to a school other than the one to which they had been assigned. Without the transfer option, city school superintendent Omer Carmichael argued, "you'd make integration compulsory," while the Supreme Court's decision in *Brown* had, he believed, simply forbidden *forced* segregation.[48] The transfer option kept de facto segregation intact for another two decades.

SANE, founded in 1957, and Women Strike for Peace, founded in 1961. Their work is discussed in Katz, *Ban the Bomb*, and Swerdlow, *Women Strike for Peace*.

45. George R. Edwards letter to Paul Peachey, July 2, 1963, CPM.

46. Guy Wilcox in Harrod, "George and Jean Edwards: Living Peace." George mentions having "recently worked over Vietnam in chapel" in a letter to Paul Peachey, October 28, 1963, "Correspondence with Dr. George Edwards, Louisville Seminary" file, CPM.

47. The statement appeared in *The New York Times* on September 15, 1963; Hall, *Because of Their Faith*, 8.

48. K'Meyer, *Civil Rights in the Gateway to the South*, 51. The superintendent of schools' reflections on city desegregation illustrate Anne Braden's point: Carmichael and James, *The Louisville Story*.

A campaign of nonviolent direct action next targeted segregation in public facilities and commercial establishments, from the late 1950s through the passage of Louisville's open accommodations law in May 1963. Even as that law was lauded by Louisville boosters as "first in the South," it was contested by proponents of the status quo, and wasn't enforced until the Kentucky Court of Appeals upheld it in 1965, after the passage of the federal Civil Rights Act of 1964.[49]

The city's foot-dragging, and most white Louisvillians' opposition to change, reflected the national white consensus against acknowledging the citizenship rights of African-Americans. In the summer of 1963, a year before Lyndon B. Johnson signed the federal Civil Rights Act, a Gallup poll found that half of Americans and three-quarters of white Southerners thought the federal government was already "pushing too fast" on these issues.[50] George and Jean, and George's seminary colleagues, were in the minority. While Louisville's open accommodations law was still being contested, the faculty of Louisville Seminary threw its support behind the campaign to compel the state of Kentucky to pass its own act forbidding discrimination in public accommodations and employment. They proclaimed March 5, 1964 "a holiday from classes" so that faculty and students could join the march on the state capital, Frankfort, in support of the civil rights bill before the legislature.[51] An estimated crowd of ten thousand participated in that march; although George and Jean were on sabbatical in Germany at the time, Jean wrote George's mother that "Buddy is in his glory over the latest news."[52] A number of Louisville Seminary supporters felt differently: Tyler Long, a Presbyterian layman in Shelbyville, Kentucky, was among those who wrote President Frank Caldwell before the march to ask that he "disassociate your office, the faculty, student body and the name of the institution from this dangerous and un-American 'March on Frankfort.'"[53] The faculty minutes a month after the march noted that Caldwell "described some of the reactions he had received as a result of the Seminary's participation in the recent March on Frankfort" and "told how he had dealt with them." In response, the faculty went "on record as warmly expressing its appreciation to the

---

49. K'Meyer, *Civil Rights in the Gateway to the South*, chs. 2 and 3, especially 105–8.
50. Stevens, "Public Opinion and Public Policy," 123, 125.
51. Minutes of the faculty, February 19, 1964, LPTS.
52. Jean Edwards letter to Analee Flaniken, March 8, 1964, Jean Edwards papers.
53. Tyler Long letter to Frank H. Caldwell, February 24, 1964, "Correspondence" file, Frank H. Caldwell Papers, LPTS.

President for his effective administration in the additional burdens which our recent involvement in civil rights brought to his office."[54] Tyler Long and other opponents of integration had many vocal companions, and the state of Kentucky did not gain its own civil rights bill until 1966.[55]

While George and Jean were involved in the struggle for civil rights throughout the 1960s, they channeled their most consistent efforts for integration into building an interracial church. Around 1959, they accepted an invitation to help organize a new congregation affiliated with the Northern Presbyterian Church in Newburg, a predominantly African-American inner suburb of Louisville. Peace Presbyterian Church, pastored by Irvin S. Moxley, a black graduate of Louisville Seminary, was intended to be something like the church George and Jean had envisioned building in Trenton, Tennessee, almost a decade earlier: a Presbyterian church whose membership would reflect the neighborhood around it. In practice, the Edwardses were virtually the only white members of Peace Church. Jean and George so valued the opportunity to worship and fellowship across racial lines, and saw it as such an advantage for their children, that they drove six miles to Newburg instead of continuing to walk six blocks to the neighborhood church they had been attending, Strathmoor Presbyterian. When asked years later about their white neighbors' reaction to their family joining Peace Church, Jean Edwards laughingly remembered, "By that time, they realized we were just different, that's all."[56] Not everyone applauded those differences: within a few years, at least one member of Strathmoor, church elder Chester B. Hall, would be one of the most vocal opponents of George's anti-war work.

The Edwards family's time at Peace Church was formative for all of them. Following the custom they had established early in their marriage, Jean served as church pianist and George as a leader in the choir where, their daughter Ginger remembered, "he practically taught me to sing the alto voice."[57] Riley later believed that growing up in the racial minority at church prepared him well for the years he served as a minister in the Presbyterian Church of Ghana.[58] His parents were challenged to confront their internalized racism: as Jean commented years later, "I think white

54. Minutes of the faculty, April 1, 1964, LPTS.
55. K'Meyer, *Civil Rights in the Gateway to the South*, 107–8.
56. George and Jean Edwards interview with K'Meyer, March 12, 1996, Tape 2, 22–23.
57. Edwards-Menz e-mail to Lee.
58. Edwards-Raudonat e-mail to Lee, February 7, 2011.

people, almost without realizing it, have a basic fear of black people," acknowledging that "it took me a while, also, to overcome that, when we first went to that church."[59] The family would stay with Peace Church until the mid-1970s, when internal church dynamics led them to move to a downtown congregation, Central Presbyterian.

In early 1964, George, Jean, and the children left Louisville and its struggles to spend several months in Göttingen, West Germany. For George, his first sabbatical leave was an opportunity to study in the homeland of some of the New Testament scholars who most influenced his work. They included Rudolf Bultmann—whose quest to "demythologize" Christian faith George admired, and whose existentialist theology resonated with George's frequent sense of isolation and his emphasis on individual conscience—and Ernst Käsemann, a leader in the quest for the historical Jesus. The wartime experience of both men illustrated the complicity in the Holocaust of even those Christians who opposed Nazism, as well as the challenge of taking a principled stand under a totalitarian regime. Both had joined the Confessing Church movement, which resisted Nazi attempts to control religious life in Germany but said little about the persecution of Jews.[60] As George later wrote of Bultmann, in response to a question from his younger son Johnny, "[Bultmann] was not an advocate of Hitlerism. But his opposition to it was hardly vigorous enough to get him into serious trouble."[61] Käsemann was briefly imprisoned for his political activities, but served in the Third Reich's army after being drafted in 1942, when Bultmann was above the age of conscription. Käsemann had lacked the options that were available to George during the war: Nazi Germany neither exempted clergy from military service nor recognized the right of conscientious objection, and the penalty for refusal was death.[62] While in Germany, George had the opportunity to meet Bultmann, discuss the upcoming U.S. presidential election with him, and chide him gently for his view that the church should not take a stand on political issues such as the use of nuclear weapons. When

---

59. George and Jean Edwards interview with K'Meyer, April 23, 1996, 18.

60. For more about the Confessing Church and the churches generally in the Nazi era, see Gerlach, *And the Witnesses Were Silent*, and Ericksen and Heschel, *Betrayal*.

61. George Riley Edwards letter to "John and Family," April 27, 1997, Jean Edwards papers.

62. Wette, *Wehrmacht*, 157. The Third Reich executed about three hundred conscientious objectors, most of them Jehovah's Witnesses; ibid., 157–58. Käsemann offers a brief autobiography in *On Being a Disciple of the Crucified Nazarene*.

Bultmann "expressed in good humor his hope that 'America wouldn't elect Goldwater president,'" George asked "how he felt competent to express such an opinion." In response, Bultmann was silent.[63]

In Göttingen, the Edwardses lived in an apartment in the home of legal scholar Gerhard Leibholz and his wife, Sabine, the twin sister of Dietrich Bonhoeffer, the theologian executed for his part in a conspiracy to assassinate Hitler. Before leaving for Germany, George and Jean had read Bonhoeffer's *Letters and Papers from Prison*, recently translated into English, and Jean had included one of Bonhoeffer's poems in her Christmas letter of 1963, in light of "the tragedy that has befallen our nation in the death of President Kennedy." "In this poem," she noted, "man is challenged to participate in the sufferings of God at the hands of a godless world," quoting Bonhoeffer's verse, "God goeth to every man when sore bestead, / Feedeth body and spirit with His bread, / For Christians, heathens alike he hangeth dead: / And both alike forgiving."[64] Meeting Sabine Leibholz in Göttingen made a lasting impression on Ginger, although "the significance of this meeting," as she later recalled, only "became clear to me many years later," after she had moved to Germany and become active in its peace movement herself.[65] The family's stay in Germany was also significant for her brothers: Johnny remembered it as a "big highlight" of his childhood, and it affected Riley's decision as a young man to study theology at Tübingen.[66]

The Edwardses' sojourn in Germany brought home the significance of the Cold War in new ways. Jean wrote to her mother in the spring of 1964 that the family had driven fifteen miles east of Tübingen to see the border between East and West Germany. "It made us very sad," she remarked. "There was a little town on either side, each with its little cluster of houses and the church steeple high above all. Before the war the people in these towns must have been neighbors and even relatives. Now they cannot have any contact." Standing at the border, separated from East

---

63. George R. Edwards, *Jesus and the Politics of Violence*, 154 n.6. In "Theology for Freedom and Responsibility," Bultmann had declared in 1958 that "the church's task is to proclaim the word of God, not to pronounce political judgments." This statement was apparently his response to the attempt by German Protestants like Karl Barth to drive their church to condemn nuclear weapons.

64. Jean Edwards letter to family and friends, Christmas 1963, Jean Edwards papers.

65. Edwards-Raudonat e-mail to Lee, February 7, 2011; Edwards-Menz e-mail to Lee.

66. Johnny Edwards interview; Edwards-Raudonat e-mail to Lee, February 7, 2011.

"At Least We Make a Witness"

Germany by a fence, a watchtower with two guards, and "a no-man's area which is mined," the Edwardses realized "we could see people standing at the fence on the other side also." The family reached across the border in the only way they could: "We sang 'My Bonnie' to them, and they waved and whistled a tune back."[67] Another encounter discouraged George while reinforcing his convictions about nonviolence. He talked about it upon his return to Kentucky, illustrating the human tendency to expand the definition of "defensive" uses of force by recalling his conversation with "an intelligent and cultured German woman and her daughter . . . a third-year theological student," who had "stoutly maintained that the campaign of Hitler against Russia from 1940 [sic] to '44 was strictly defensive."[68]

At the end of their time in Germany, Jean and George received a hint that their struggle against war was about to enter a new phase. As they were waiting in Bremerhaven in August 1964 to board the ship that would carry them back to the United States, Jean later recalled, "I happened to hear a news broadcast stating that an 'incident' had occurred in Vietnam which had placed us at the brink of war." "Little did I dream," she remarked, "of what the next ten years would bring."[69] Although the number of American military "advisers" in South Vietnam had been increasing since 1960, the Gulf of Tonkin incident was a turning point for both the United States and the Edwards family. In the incident's aftermath, a congressional resolution authorized the administration of President Lyndon B. Johnson to wage war as they saw fit in Vietnam.[70] As the war escalated, George recommitted himself to organizing, lamenting to a colleague in the spring of 1965 that "the Louisville Peace Council is about dead. While I was out of the country they had no meetings at all." Pacifists and just war opponents of the war argued rather than working together, he sighed: "There were old gripes about the FOR and the non-FOR viewpoints not being compatible." Although pacifists and non-pacifists had legitimate disagreements, George saw the probable cause of their inactivity elsewhere: "This, I think, is only a front for the lethargy which

---

67. Jean Edwards letter to Virginia Maney, May 3, 1964, Jean Edwards papers.

68. George R. Edwards, "Some Moods from Modern Europe," September 8, 1964, 5, Jean Edwards papers. In fact, the German campaign began in 1941.

69. Jean Edwards e-mail to Susan Kute, March 21, 2008, Jean Edwards papers.

70. An accessible general history of the Vietnam War is Herring, *America's Longest War*. The movement against the war is detailed in DeBenedetti with Chatfield, *An American Ordeal*.

all of us feel about more meetings and organizations."[71] That "lethargy" was in evidence in January 1965, when only Olof Anderson and Louisville Seminary student Al Schneider joined George in a demonstration outside Louisville's City Hall against the "civil defense" exercise taking place that day. In a letter to the mayor a few days earlier, the three had argued that the civil defense exercise was unethical for two reasons. The first was practical: it would falsely "perpetuate the illusion of safety in the event of nuclear war"; the second was ideological: the exercise would "condition the public to accept the inevitability of nuclear warfare as the final arbiter of international tensions."[72] Although the demonstration was tiny, George found the television and radio coverage "amazingly good and sympathetic."[73]

George would soon become a familiar presence in the media, as he and Schneider took the lead in organizing their city's opposition to the war. By early 1966, around the time Louisville's most famous draft resister, boxer Muhammad Ali, declared, "I ain't got no quarrel with them Vietcong," the two Presbyterians were a familiar sight in downtown Louisville, standing weekly in an hour-long silent vigil with about thirty fellow opponents of the war, including Jean.[74] A larger demonstration gathered about fifty people on Friday, March 25, 1966 in front of the city's federal building, home of the area's Selective Service offices, as part of a weekend of rallies across the country. The next day, an estimated seventy-five thousand protestors marched against the war in New York City. George told a reporter that he had called most of the participants and prepared the signs for the Louisville demonstration, but, conscious of his position at the seminary, he noted that (in the reporter's paraphrase), "The participants in yesterday's demonstration did not represent specific organizations but picketed as individuals."[75]

71. George R. Edwards letter to Paul Peachey, April 5, 1965, CPM.

72. Olof Anderson Jr., George R. Edwards, and Alan R. Schneider letter to Louisville Mayor William O. Cowger, January 7, 1965, enclosed with George R. Edwards letter to Paul Peachey, January 18, 1965, CPM. For the history of the movement against civil defense, see Garrison, *Bracing for Armageddon*.

73. George R. Edwards letter to Paul Peachey, January 18, 1965, CPM.

74. Quoted in Remnick, *King of the World*, 287. The description of the vigils comes from Jean Edwards holiday letter, addressed to "Dear Friends," December 29, 1966, Jean Edwards papers.

75. "Pickets Protest Viet Nam War," *Courier-Journal*, Saturday, March 26, 1966. George made it a habit to begin public presentations with the disclaimer that "I speak for myself and not as a representative of any organization or institution," as when he

Despite his attempts to draw boundary lines between his peace witness and the beliefs shared by the larger seminary community, George's political commitments brought attention to his employer. A month after the March 25 demonstration, he was the subject of a regular *Louisville Times* feature, "People You Should Know," which described him as "one of those troublemakers who believe the Bible means what it says." In the interview he outlined his view that the early church had been pacifist until the Roman emperor Constantine legalized the religion, believing that the power of the Christian God had helped him win a key battle for control of the empire. The legalization of Christianity, George asserted, had resulted in "a wedding between the power of the Cross and the power of the sword." Since that time, George maintained, Christians have "been confused by the conjunction of those two forms of power."[76] Taking into account not only the nuclear arms race but also the calls of "hawks" to use nuclear weapons against North Vietnam, George argued, "For Christians to go all the way with the nuclear deterrent is to me a rather total antithesis to the position of the New Testament itself." If enough people realized that, radical social change might result; but if they didn't, there was still value in bearing witness: "Some people don't like to take part in demonstrations. They think it's demeaning, I guess. But demonstrations at least say that there's some people around who feel this way. Only when the Negroes went into the streets and made demands did the power structure react to them." As far as protests against the war were concerned, "Fifty in front of the Federal Building didn't shake the structure, but seventy-five thousand in New York City March 26 did."[77] One reader, W. R. Cole Jr., went to some trouble to express his disagreement with George's beliefs, clipping the article and sending it to George with the comment, "American heroes, and the parents of American heroes (living or dead), will be particularly disgusted with this tripe."[78]

---

gave the address "The War in Vietnam Is Militarily, Politically, and Morally Wrong" to the Temple Brith Sholom Men's Association (Louisville), September 21, 1966, Jean Edwards papers.

76. "Dr. Edwards Says He Can't Reconcile War with Christianity," *Louisville Times*, April 23, 1966. Scholars have begun to rethink Constantine's complex legacy, questioning whether he was the hypocrite that many—particularly pacifists like John Howard Yoder as well as George Edwards—have long understood him to be. See Leithart, *Defending Constantine*, favorably reviewed by pacifist Christian ethicist Stanley Hauerwas in *The Christian Century*, October 19, 2010.

77. "Dr. Edwards Says He Can't Reconcile War with Christianity."

78. Note provided to Rhonda Mawhood Lee by George R. Edwards.

The Vietnam era was the time when Jean joined George on the picket line. Writing to friends and family at the end of 1966, Jean described her decision to become involved in her own right in the movement to end the war. Her letter opened with an explanation for her recent silence: "Frankly, we have been so depressed by the war for these past two Christmases that it seemed out of the question to wish anyone a Merry Christmas while such slaughter is going on." Jean followed that brief lament with cheerful news of her children's exuberance and the dividends paid by the musical practice she had supervised for years: "Our house has 'rocked' during the holidays, with all three children playing the piano, plus Riley on the guitar and Johnny on the drums . . . The Beatles, The Monkees, and The Lovin' Spoonful dictate most of the policies around here." She also wrote playfully of a change that had occurred in her life that year, with the two older children in high school and Johnny in middle school. She had returned to work, "and of all places at the [Southern] BAPTIST SEMINARY," a few blocks from the Presbyterian Seminary. "My job is to handle the subscriptions and bookkeeping records of the quarterly publication sent out by the faculty of that institution. *The Review and Expositor* is the title of their publication. Fortunately, for the Baptists, none of my ideas get into print in this journal."[79]

Mixing dry humor with earnest seriousness, Jean devoted most of the letter to her and George's witness against the war. Noting that "George has been doing everything possible to try to bring about peace in the world; but, so far his efforts seem to have met with little success," she sketched their weekly silent vigils downtown "on one of the busiest corners in downtown Louisville." In her pragmatic yet hopeful way, she drew comfort from the fact that "we hear that a number of these vigils are being carried on through the nation." Although they might not change government policy, Jean echoed George's conviction that "at least we make a witness that there are those opposed." As she reflected on her decision to participate in the vigils, perhaps hoping to influence some of her patriotic correspondents, Jean asked rhetorically, "How can patriotic citizens tell, before it is too late, whether their beloved country is in the hands of leaders gone mad with power? As we look back over the pages of history, we see instances where Christian people have waited until it was too late." It was "this realization," Jean stated, that made it "clear to me that I must be counted among those who protest our government's policies in Vietnam."

---

79. Jean Edwards holiday letter, December 29, 1966, Jean Edwards papers.

She closed her meditation on a hopeful note: "Surely the wind will soon blow from a different direction."[80]

Political and theological winds did swirl around George in 1967, a tumultuous year in Louisville as the struggle for full citizenship and freedom rights entered a new phase: the campaign for open housing. Beginning in Chicago in 1966, the move to dismantle barriers to African-American residential mobility had become a nationwide priority for civil rights organizations such as the Southern Christian Leadership Conference (SCLC). Louisville, one of the most residentially segregated cities in the country, became a focus of efforts later that year.[81] The goal was to persuade or force the local government to pass an ordinance prohibiting racial discrimination in the sale or rental of housing. A diverse coalition of local organizations, religious and secular, many of them mostly black and some predominantly white, supported the ordinance.[82] Although Louisville Seminary, as an institution, was not on that list, some of its faculty and students stood in favor of open housing, with Harold (Hal) Warheim, who had joined the seminary in 1962 as a professor of "Christianity and Society," emerging as a leader in the movement.[83] When the board of aldermen voted down the ordinance in April 1967, Warheim and George participated in almost daily protest marches and sit-ins for the next month in the face of broad and bitter white opposition, and in violation of injunctions limiting citizens' freedom of assembly and expression.[84] By the end of the month, the colleagues were counted among the more than five hundred people arrested on such charges as "banding together to commit a felony" and "criminal syndicalism." That fall, the U.S. District Court dismissed almost all the charges against protestors because they were so vague as to be unconstitutional.[85] Seminary colleagues affirmed Warheim's and George's actions, voting at the beginning of May to "reaffirm" their collective support for an open housing ordinance and to "commend to both students and faculty the use of whatever

---

80. Jean Edwards holiday letter, December 29, 1966, Jean Edwards papers.

81. K'Meyer, *Civil Rights in the Gateway to the South*, 118, 131. On the initial open housing movement in Chicago, see Garrow, *Chicago 1966*.

82. K'Meyer, *Civil Rights in the Gateway to the South*, 121.

83. Ibid., 133; Nutt, *Many Lamps, One Light*, 127, 164.

84. K'Meyer, *Civil Rights in the Gateway to the South*, 129, 132–33.

85. Ibid., 133.

means of expressing their concern in this matter which they find in harmony with Christian conscience."[86]

An incident later that month became Jean's most vivid memory from the push for open housing: Martin Luther King Jr.'s visit to support the movement (which included his brother, the Reverend A. D. King, pastor of Louisville's Zion Baptist Church). During a march, a white heckler threw a rock at Martin Luther King; it missed, but the leader pocketed the missile. That night, King held up the rock and proclaimed the words Jean remembered decades later: "Upon this rock we are going to build an open city."[87] The city moved in that direction in December, when Louisville passed an open housing ordinance; the state of Kentucky followed a few months later. The victory was short-lived, however: research showed that by the mid-1970s residential segregation by race had increased in Louisville.[88]

George's support for open housing ensured that he would remain a controversial figure in Presbyterian circles, but it was his renewed relationship with Carl and Anne Braden that made him notorious in 1967. That was the year George joined the board of the Southern Conference Educational Fund (SCEF, pronounced "skef"). SCEF, an active force for African-American citizenship rights since its founding in 1938 as the Southern Conference for Human Welfare, was suspect to many because it had never purged itself of known or suspected Communists. In 1966, the Bradens became SCEF's directors, moving its headquarters to Louisville and joining George in revitalizing the Louisville Peace Council, linking the American use of force in Vietnam to the violent maintenance of white racial domination at home.[89] When the Bradens invited George to join SCEF's board, he agreed; he remained a member, serving one year as treasurer, until he resigned in 1970 to take a sabbatical year in Toronto.[90] Soon afterward, the Bradens were again indicted for sedition because of

86. Minutes of the faculty, May 1, 1967, LPTS.

87. Jean Edwards conversation with Rhonda Mawhood Lee, January 14, 2011. The details of the rock-throwing incident, and King's response, are in K'Meyer, *Civil Rights in the Gateway to the South*, 137.

88. K'Meyer, *Civil Rights in the Gateway to the South*, 141–42.

89. Klibaner, *Conscience of a Troubled South*, 225–26. The Bradens' involvement in the Louisville anti-war movement, and the place of the Louisville Peace Council within it, is detailed in Ernst and Baldwin, "The Not So Silent Minority."

90. *Southern Patriot*, June 1969 and May 1970. The Bradens left SCEF by 1974; it lasted a couple of years longer, in historian Catherine Fosl's words "all but immobilized" by internal "dissension," *Subversive Southerner*, 320–21.

SCEF's organizing work in the Appalachian region of Pikeville, Kentucky. They were released after a panel of federal judges ruled Kentucky's sedition law unconstitutional, finally wiping it off the books.[91]

While George never faced criminal charges because of his association with SCEF, his presence on its board led to a chorus of calls from his fellow Presbyterians for Louisville Seminary to dismiss him. Although the PCUS had recently adopted a report titled "The Theological Basis for Christian Social Action," many of its members continued to identify their faith with the established political order.[92] Albert Curry Winn, a colleague and friend generally supportive of George's activism who had become president of the seminary in 1965, received letters about George's work with SCEF that ranged from concerned to biting. To the most caustic, he made only brief responses. When Sarah Haley Howe of Louisville wrote that "the Rev. Dr. Edwards and his fellow-travelers" made it easy for her to feel "unmitigated contempt for a clergyman" and asked Winn how to go about making a complaint to church authorities, the president simply referred her to the Book of Discipline and her pastor or clerk of session.[93] Winn may have known Sarah Howe's husband, Laurence Lee Howe, a professor of history at the University of Louisville, as a member of the right-wing John Birch Society—George's *bête noire*—and defender of white fraternities' right to discriminate on the basis of race when choosing their membership.[94] More measured complaints facilitated greater dialogue. One pastor in eastern Tennessee, noting that he was glad Americans were free to "support or criticize those who are in places of leadership," added that a seminary professor "must consider his

91. Fosl, *Subversive Southerner*, 306–9. The incident is examined in Kiffmeyer, "From Self-Help to Sedition."

92. The report, adopted in 1966, is discussed in Nutt, *Toward Peacemaking*, 35.

93. Sarah Haley (Mrs. Laurence) Howe letter to Albert C. Winn, June 10, 1967, and Albert C. Winn letter to Mrs. Laurence Howe, June 13, 1967, "Right Wing" file, Albert C. Winn Papers, LPTS. Together with the Central Committee for Conscientious Objectors, George helped one of Winn's sons register as a CO; George R. Edwards letter to Rick Nutt, 9, "George Edwards" file, LPTS. In retirement, Winn proposed that "the abolition of war" replace "just war" as a Christian commitment, in *Ain't Gonna Study War No More*.

94. Laurence Lee Howe's membership in the John Birch Society is asserted in the University of Louisville Archives' "Libguide" to his papers. Howe defended fraternities' right to racial discrimination in a letter to *Time*, July 2, 1965. On the John Birch Society, see Schoenwald, "We Are an Action Group." Rick Nutt has found that the Society had "influence" in some Louisville Presbyterian churches, "particularly" Strathmoor; Nutt, *Many Lamps, One Light*, 168.

position as well as his opinions." He cut to what was, for many American Christians, the political heart of the matter: "Personally, I would hesitate to take a position that would bring any comfort to the Communists."[95] In his reply, Winn reported that "several members of the Board and I have had a long conversation with Dr. Edwards" about his involvement with SCEF, a "matter" that "has been widely publicized by extreme right wing groups here in the city and elsewhere." "Of course," Winn added in George's defense, "there is no question in our minds concerning the loyalty of Dr. Edwards as a citizen or his integrity as a man of Christian conscience. The question is his wisdom in making this particular association." In this "very delicate matter," "the principles of academic freedom and liberty of conscience must constantly be kept in mind."[96]

The meeting of representatives of the board with their troublesome faculty member was, as George remembered it years later, "at best a standoff." The committee, led by board president Henry P. Mobley, tried to impress upon George that "the bulk of the institution's public image problem would vanish into thin air if I would sever all association with Carl Braden." George refused to do so, for two reasons: "my association with the Bradens was not extensive, and I felt that solidarity with those opposing the Vietnam War was morally appropriate, as was cooperative effort against racial discrimination." Mobley, George recalled, "did not seem surprised at my refusal to make any promises to the committee."[97] He added, however, that his relationship with many board members was "cordial" and that their exchanges never involved "discourteous language," although even years later, "our perspectives on some social and political questions remain unreconciled."[98]

Strained though his relationship with the seminary's board could be, George enjoyed the admiration of its students. The sermon he delivered at the graduating seniors' invitation in 1967, the year he joined SCEF's board, offered the trenchant exegesis and lively exhortation students had come to expect from George. Substituting the word *boundaries* for *neighborhood* in Mark 5:17, "And they began to beg Jesus to depart from their neighborhood," George offered a message that obliquely referred to

95. Dewey R. Greenhoe (First Presbyterian Church, Sweetwater, Tennessee) letter to Albert C. Winn, February 2, 1967, "Right Wing" file, Albert C. Winn Papers, LPTS.

96. Albert C. Winn letter to Dewey R. Greenhoe, February 7, 1967, "Right Wing" file, Albert C. Winn Papers, LPTS.

97. George R. Edwards letter to Rick Nutt, 7–8, "George Edwards" file, LPTS.

98. George R. Edwards letter to Rick Nutt, 12, "George Edwards" file, LPTS.

the battle many white Louisvillians were waging against open housing, to keep the racial boundaries of their neighborhoods in place. George summed up the aftermath of Jesus' exorcism of the demons known as Legion by casting them into a herd of swine: "The way things come out, the pigs are lost. People get upset. 'Our pigs are dead,' they complain. So they entreat the Healer to leave their boundaries. They want things to remain under their control." "After all," George continued, "whose boundaries are these? They have laid the limits and defined the proceedings, and those proceedings do not include the healing" of the demoniac, who "has his place: in the tombs." "So," he concluded, "they entreat Jesus to depart from their boundaries."[99]

The church, by contrast, was called to serve on various boundaries. One was the boundary between "self and society." Without referring to his own periodic emotional crises, George reminded the congregation that "every one of us needs to come under the healing ministry of Jesus." The story of Legion should be a constant warning "against the disregard of those subterranean forces which unsettle the soul and threaten to break down our self control."[100] Openness to healing, however, could not stop at the boundary of the self; "ministry to the troubled souls of men, including our own," was "adjacent to a territory beyond the self: the res publica, the common weal."[101] The common welfare was the subject of the new Confession of 1967, adopted by the (Northern) United Presbyterian Church to supplement the centuries-old Westminster Confession of Faith, in what many in the Southern church saw as an unwarranted innovation.[102] George noted approvingly that the new confession "has laid out with clarity the horizons of our social responsibility when it speaks of the problems of war, racial injustice, and poverty." Denying the distinction that churches often drew between the personal "spiritual" realm and the social "political" world, George asserted, "The creative aspects of our vocation consist precisely in its location at the boundary between self and society and its refusal to be bound by one or the other."[103] Years later, Terry Davis, a student who had stood vigil with Jean and George against the war and been arrested with George at a march for open housing, singled

---

99. George R. Edwards, "Boundaries," 2.
100. Ibid., 3.
101. Ibid., 4.
102. *Book of Confessions*, 321–30.
103. George R. Edwards, "Boundaries," 4.

out "Boundaries" as George's "most memorable and influential sermon," inspiring "all of us who were willing to take the risk of, like Jesus, being asked to shut up and get out."[104]

After the graduation service was disrupted, George elaborated on the connection between Jesus' earthly ministry and social change in a magazine interview. Explicitly denying both that he was a Communist and that SCEF was a "communist front organization," George noted, "There are sixteen ministers and some most dedicated laymen on that board," and stated that the one board meeting he had attended by the spring of 1967 had "opened with prayer." George turned his accusers' questions about his Christian faith back on them, stating, "I feel that every Christian must be involved and related to the issues of our time." Believing that "the Bradens have been persecuted unjustly," George charged, "For Christians to remain aloof and watch people endure character assassination is the grossest form of cowardice." When asked directly if he was a pacifist, George explained that he was "a Christian pacifist" because of his "understanding of the New Testament: namely, that the cross of Christ is the power of God to salvation for all who believe." "That cross," which he called "the ultimate in human destructiveness," through the crucifixion became "the symbol of Jesus' refusal to take the instruments of men to accomplish the purposes of God." "I therefore," George concluded, "am on New Testament grounds opposed to the principle of war itself.[105]

In the wake of the chapel protest, Ben Johnson's fellow members of Second Presbyterian's session unanimously instructed him to apologize, not to George, but to the president of the seminary.[106] Strathmoor Presbyterian continued its campaign, informing President Winn of their plan to present certain "Questions and Comments" to the seminary board at its first meeting after graduation. Seven questions were addressed to George, the only professor mentioned by name, asking his opinion of SCEF and its leadership, and inquiring, "With reference to the open-housing controversy, the Court issued an injunction prohibiting night marches; you were arrested for participating in such a march. Do you advocate civil disobedience?" Some members of Strathmoor believed "that the attitude of Dr. Edwards and some of his faculty colleagues no longer mirrors the simple, all-inclusive admonition of Christ: 'Love Thy Neighbor.'" Having

104. Terry Davis in Harrod, "George and Jean Edwards: Living Peace."

105. "Louisville Seminary Worship Disrupted by Protestors." George's statement about "the cross of Christ" alludes to Romans 1:16.

106. W. R. Clarke letter, *Presbyterian Survey*, September 1967.

"lost compassion for those who cannot agree on the causes such faculty members support or the actions they take," these professors had become "non-Christian, possibly even heretic, certainly dangerous."[107] One member of Strathmoor Presbyterian, Chester B. Hall, had particular difficulty loving his neighbor George Edwards. During this period, Riley Edwards remembers George receiving an envelope containing a coin and a suggestion from Hall presumably inspired by some opponents of the Vietnam War having immolated themselves as an act of protest: "Edwards, here's a quarter. Go get yourself a gallon of gas and burn yourself alive. See you in hell." Riley Edwards recalled that his family "laughed a lot about that letter. Looking back, though, I wonder why it didn't frighten us. The content was, after all, pure hate." Riley gave the writer some credit, however, noting, "at least Chess Hall was willing to sign his name. Others wrote anonymously."[108] The controversy dogged the seminary: that fall, the number of Southern Presbyterian students enrolled dropped sharply, donations lagged, and some local congregations stopped accepting student interns.[109]

George admitted the truth in his fellow Presbyterians' view that he did not always behave lovingly toward all his neighbors. In one interview, George described himself as still having the "fundamentalist spirit" of his youth, shorthand for being, in his words, "belligerent as all get-out." "Theoretically," he believed that other Christians could interpret the Bible differently than he did, and take a position in favor of just war. Seeing the Vietnam War as unjustifiable, however, he felt "sick and tired of sermons that pussyfoot around" the conflict; he realized that he was "intolerant about that."[110] George also had little patience for Christians who dismissed out of hand the legitimacy of civil disobedience. In a pamphlet written for the Fellowship of Reconciliation in 1965, George had argued that Romans 13, which counseled obedience to governing authorities and was often invoked by Christian opponents of civil disobedience, "must

---

107. D. B. Hancock (clerk of session) letter to Albert C. Winn, June 2, 1967, "Right Wing" file, Albert C. Winn Papers, LPTS.

108. Edwards-Raudonat e-mail to Lee, February 7, 2011.

109. Nutt, *Many Lamps, One Light*, 170. Around 1967, students at the Baptist and Presbyterian seminaries formed a cooperative group called Seminary Students Concerned about the War and the Draft, which participated in the local anti-war movement. Nutt, *Many Lamps, One Light*, 167.

110. Notes from internal seminary publication interview with George R. Edwards, 1970, "George Edwards" file, LPTS.

be weighed against" Revelation 13, in which "Rome is pictured as 'the beast.'" Citing the most notorious recent example of a corrupt government, George asked, "Should we obey God or men when the two are in conflict? Were German Christians right to support Hitler?"[111] In 1968, in the wake of the struggle for open housing, and as the movement against the war grew, George pointed to biblical translator William Tyndale, American revolutionaries, those who struggled for India's independence from Great Britain, and resisters against Nazism as lawbreakers whom American Christians routinely celebrated. Noting that civil disobedience was not "a privilege to be enjoyed" but rather "a duty to be fulfilled in obedience to a higher morality" than that embodied in "public laws," George warned that "persons who lack a considerable degree of self-discipline" should consider carefully any venture into disobedience. He foresaw its continued use, however, against racial oppression, "legalized forms of international violence" supported by military practices like conscription, and "legalized economic exploitation" like "unjust forms of taxation" and "using public funds to feed the military-industrial complex rather than to develop a viable economy based on peace."[112]

Perhaps George's riskiest act of disobedience during the Vietnam era was assisting deserters from Fort Knox, the Army base thirty-five miles south of Louisville. "People would call me," he remembered, and would ask, "Can you go out to Fort Knox and get people in your car?" He would drive to the post exchange and pick up the men, keeping conversation to a minimum: "Don't ask them their names, don't tell 'em your name. Take them to the airport, they have their tickets." George had sympathy for men who entered the Army and then decided, as he put it, "We don't believe in this, we're not gonna do this," so, he concluded, "we helped them out."[113] Anne Braden, who later described George as "the most militant pacifist you ever saw," remarked, "George was so funny. I don't know why he didn't get put in jail. It's against the law to help people desert the army

---

111. George R. Edwards, "Christianity and War: Two Positions," 1965, Jean Edwards papers.

112. George R. Edwards, "Civil Disobedience," February 1968, Jean Edwards papers.

113. George and Jean Edwards interview with K'Meyer, March 12, 1996, Tape 1, 23. Although the Vietnam War saw very few battlefield desertions among Americans, as there was no easy escape route for a man seeking to leave combat, the war saw new highs in rates of desertion by men who were still in the United States, or in transit in Asia. The rates rose steeply as the war continued: fifteen per thousand troops in 1966, fifty per thousand in 1969, and seventy per thousand in 1972. Baskir and Strauss, *Chance and Circumstance*, 112-13, 121-22.

and George was doing it all over the place."[114] Measured against George's statement that he only infrequently helped deserters, Braden's memory may be exaggerated.

George spent far more time on draft counseling, working with men who might be COs, referred to him through what he called the "Quaker grapevine," and organizing seminars to educate clergy, parents, and other concerned elders about the Selective Service law.[115] At least one LPTS student, Bryce McGowan, gave up his seminary deferment "through [George's] influence," registering as a conscientious objector but then being rejected for service after his physical exam.[116] Most of McGowan's colleagues were unwilling to take that step: in 1967 Louisville Seminary students voted against a resolution proposed by the school's Social Action Committee recommending that the student draft deferment be abolished. Their elders on the faculty disagreed, going on record as recommending to the government that "no special Selective Service classification be given to seminarians or clergy"—essentially challenging their students with the example George had set during the Second World War.[117]

The Edwards children found themselves in an unusual position during the Vietnam era: unlike many of their peers, who clashed with their elders over the war, they joined their parents in protest. Given what George and Jean had taught him about conscientious objection, Johnny would tell his high school friends, "You don't *have* to join the military."[118] For Riley, "As far as politics were concerned, there wasn't any gap between me and my parents." As a result, he was out of step "with the mood of those years," when parents "were supposed to be uncool."[119] Ginger had a different experience. As a child, she had known that her father had been a conscientious objector, but had had difficulty understanding what that meant; the Vietnam War was the time when she became acutely aware of her parents' peace witness. Although Ginger opposed the war, she "was not the kind to

114. Anne Braden, interviewed in 1999, quoted in Ernst and Baldwin, "The Not So Silent Minority," 111.

115. George and Jean Edwards interview with K'Meyer, March 26, 1996, Tape 1, 11. A flyer for a "Louisville Seminar on Draft Counseling," led by Joe Letson of the American Friends Service Committee, and listing George Edwards as a contact, is held in the "George Edwards" file, LPTS.

116. Bryce McGowan remembrance in Harrod, "George and Jean Edwards: Living Peace."

117. Minutes of the faculty, December 4, 1967, LPTS.

118. Johnny Edwards interview.

119. Edwards-Raudonat e-mail to Lee, February 7, 2011.

get on the barricades," but in her radical family she did not find the space she needed to say so. Whether it was intended or not, she felt "a kind of pressure that was somehow applied" leading her to participate in some demonstrations, being arrested once, and once having "to endure tear gas." Ginger became a peace activist in her own right as an adult, eventually working with the Armaments Information Office in Germany, but she chose quieter tactics, finding that she had inherited "Jean's organizing talents" more than "George's eloquence on peace issues."[120]

Riley was the most involved of the three Edwards children in the movement against the Vietnam War, driving to Washington, DC, with George and three University of Louisville students for the March on the Pentagon in October 1967. That march, the culmination of a week of protests to "Stop the Draft" brought a diverse group of perhaps fifty thousand protestors to the capital. Riley, only sixteen at the time, later reflected that none of his classmates had participated in the protest, "let alone with their fathers."[121] Earlier that year, his father had spoken publicly of his concern for his sons, noting that, although his firstborn's "frame is not quite full enough, nor his coordination smooth enough," he would soon reach the age to be called up to fight.[122] He decried Christians' equation of God and country in words his elder son would remember decades later: "Onward Christian soldiers, marching as to war—with the cross of Jesus *hid behind the door*."[123] Riley continued his activism throughout the war, joining his father in September 1968 at a protest outside a fund-raiser for Hubert H. Humphrey, who had defeated the war opponents' candidate, Eugene McCarthy, to win the Democratic Party's nomination for president. Described by a journalist as a "lanky, long-haired guitarist with [a] fierce look in his eye," Riley stood outside Freedom Hall in downtown Louisville singing the anti-war anthem "Waist Deep in the Big Muddy" ("We're waist deep in the Big Muddy, and the big fool says to press on").[124]

---

120. Edwards-Menz e-mail to Lee.

121. Edwards-Raudonat e-mail to Lee, February 7, 2011.

122. George R. Edwards, "The Preferred Age," March 1967, 1, Jean Edwards papers.

123. "The Preferred Age," 2; Riley Edwards-Raudonat e-mail to Rhonda Mawhood Lee, February 9, 2011.

124. "Peace-Freedom Songs Exceeded by Cheering," *The Louisville Times*, September 1968, A3. George Edwards is not mentioned by name, but the adjacent story, "Police Numerous and Troubles Few at Humphrey Rally," is accompanied by a photo of a group of protestors that includes him.

Born in 1951, Riley was the only one of the Edwards children to be vulnerable to the draft; his younger brother just escaped conscription when the draft was abolished in 1973. Registering as a conscientious objector when he turned eighteen, Riley used a student deferment while registered at Antioch College, but when he dropped out after two years, that action triggered a hearing before his local draft board. His confrontation with the board taught him a lesson about living nonviolently on a day-to-day basis. While still in college, Riley had gotten creative with the status update that college students were required to send their local boards, listing his major as "Genocide" and, in the space designated for his professional ambition, writing, "Preparing for a seat on my local draft board." By the time he arrived at his hearing, he had forgotten that caustic jest, but the draft board had those updates before them. As Riley later remembered, "We got into a discussion on the power of love to overcome hate. The board asked me if I loved my draft board. I replied that I did. They went on to read me my statements and to ask me if I considered this to be a loving attitude. 'No,' I had to admit. 'That was improper. I wrote those things without considering the feelings of those who would read them.'" He "never expected to be granted CO status after such a derailment," but he was.[125] Unlike his father, Riley never performed alternative service as a conscientious objector. When he was called for service around 1971, knowing that he had a high lottery number and the call-up was probably an error, he hired a lawyer who successfully contested the draft notice. Reflecting on his actions decades later, Riley sometimes "felt that I should have gone ahead and done alternative service. That would have been a stronger show of commitment." He had, however, already been doing "CO-type work" for about a year as a janitor's assistant at the alternative Green Valley School, accredited as a CO service site, in Orange City, Florida, and shrank from the prospect of two more years of the same. Three years' service "seemed to me in those years to be interminably long. On the other hand," he reflected, "my father's length of service was three years!"[126]

Throughout the 1960s, Louisville's anti-war movement remained small, but George did have a few companions among the city's clergy. Rabbi Martin Perley resigned from Temple Brith Sholom in early 1968 after twenty-two years as its leader, to become director of the Louisville-Jefferson County Human Relations Commission. In his farewell address,

125. Riley Edwards-Raudonat e-mail to Rhonda Mawhood Lee, February 9, 2011.
126. Edwards-Raudonat e-mail to Lee, February 9, 2011.

Perley noted that his congregation had supported his work for civil rights but that many could not accept his vocal opposition to the Vietnam War. He sardonically remarked that his preaching had clearly failed to make a compelling case for peace, "for the most vocal critics of my social action activities have been people who have rarely missed a Friday evening service." Reminding his congregants that Leviticus 19:16 commanded the faithful not to "stand idly by the blood of thy neighbor," Perley asked, "What is this, if not a call to social action?"[127] A Catholic colleague, Father Bill Zahner, saw about two hundred members of his downtown cathedral congregation walk out over the course of one morning's services as he preached against the war in the fall of 1970. Quoting Pope Paul VI's 1965 plea to the General Assembly of the United Nations, "If you wish to be brothers, let the weapons fall from your hands," Zahner proclaimed that "schizophrenia" had metamorphosed into "normalcy" for "us American Christians" after years of war. "Like a philanthropist who wrings his money from exploited people with his right hand, and gives it to good causes with his left," he admonished his flock, "we make war with one hand and with the other we make Eucharist."[128] Like many in Perley's temple, and like George's Presbyterian opponents, those who walked out of the cathedral resisted religious leaders' appeals for them to acknowledge the conflict between the call of their faith and the demands of patriotism, and to ground their identity and actions in the former.

By 1970, when George was due another sabbatical year, he and Jean were ready for a break from Louisville, moving their family north to Toronto. Although Riley was already enrolled at Antioch College and Ginger was to begin studies at Friends World College early in the new year, the Edwards household did not shrink. George's mother, Analee, by then widowed for the second time, joined them for the year. In a letter to friends written soon after their arrival, Jean described a July scene in their front yard, after "Ginger decided that she must try out the push mower." While she mowed, "Johnny edged the walk and Analee directed and swept and sang 'On this solid rock I stand,' as she leaned on the broom. If the neighbors haven't realized already that we are slightly touched," Jean concluded, "I am sure they did after last night." Analee

---

127. Martin M. Perley, "Why I Am Resigning—After 22 Years as Your Rabbi," March 29, 1968, Perley papers.

128. Fr. Bill Zahner untitled sermon preached at the Cathedral of the Assumption, October 4, 1970, in author's possession. The incident is described in Crews, "Hallowed Ground."

rented a piano to add to the electric organ she had brought with her, "so that," Jean noted, "we can have duets." The family enjoyed the differences they found in their temporary home: Johnny, at fifteen, reveled in the lack of a dress code at his high school, while seventeen-year-old Ginger "likes it up here because she sees so many freaks. All the guys have long hair."[129] That year, the Edwardses joined the counterculture in a new way, becoming vegetarians in order to live more simply and avoid participating in the wastefulness of grain-fed meat production.[130]

In Toronto, Jean and George were present at the creation of what became known as the "Louisville Ghetto": a building about three blocks from their rented house in which the few families from their home city who had fled the draft all had apartments.[131] Spending Christmas away from Riley for the first time since his birth, George and Jean found that despite his absence, their house was "overflowing with kids the whole time." Three "exile" couples from Louisville had "latched on" to them: "Our fireplace is really enticing, and our easy chairs are a welcome change from their scantily furnished apartments." "During the holidays," Jean remarked, "we tried to fill the void that they felt from being separated from their parents . . . Six months ago we were all strangers, and now we are like a family."[132] When summer jobs and studies took all three Edwards children away from home for the first time in the summer of 1971, Jean and George found that "our 'adopted' draft dodger children in Toronto kept us from getting lonesome."[133] One unattached man, Joe Sigur, moved into the Edwards home after arriving in Toronto from Louisville in October. Sigur had lost his basketball scholarship to the University of Louisville when he disobeyed the coach's order to cut his hair.[134] No longer eligible for a student deferment, and finding the draft board un-

129. Jean Edwards letter to "Dear Friends in America," July 24, 1970, and a draft of the same letter, Jean Edwards papers.

130. Jean Edwards conversation with Rhonda Mawhood Lee, January 14, 2011.

131. Partial draft of Jean Edwards New Year letter, 1971, Jean Edwards papers. The "Louisville Ghetto" is mentioned in Ernst, "Vietnam War," 912. An estimated thirty thousand draft resisters and deserters moved to Canada during the war years, and ten thousand more moved to other countries, mainly Sweden; Baskir and Strauss, *Chance and Circumstance*, 180.

132. Partial draft of Jean Edwards New Year letter, 1971, Jean Edwards papers.

133. Jean Edwards letter to "Dear Earth Friends" (a humorous reference to it being "blast-off time for us" from Toronto), August 5, 1971, Jean Edwards papers.

134. Bill Peterson, "When Principles Collide: U of L Student Puts Long Hair Over Basketball Letter," *Louisville Courier-Journal*, February 19, 1970.

impressed with his "meager plea" that he was a CO, Sigur flew to Toronto on the day he was due to be inducted into the army.[135] "Not know[ing] a single soul" as Jean said, but "eventually" being "directed" to her and George, he ended up being "an integral part of our family," living with them for nine months, contributing to household expenses and taking piano lessons from Analee.[136]

The sabbatical year in Toronto allowed George to finish writing his first book, *Jesus and the Politics of Violence*. In it, he took on the then-fashionable thesis of biblical scholar S. G. F. Brandon that Jesus' followers were Zealots and that Jesus himself was sympathetic to the aims and tactics of those armed fighters against Roman imperial rule. George's study of the Gospels of Matthew and Mark painstakingly reconstructed the biblical argument for a Jesus who renounced violence by his willingness to die on the cross. Mark, the earliest canonical gospel, had "[preached] Christ by means of a 'visual' representation' of the Jesus tradition"—in other words, by painting a word picture of Jesus' historical life that culminated in him hanging on a cross. Mark reinforced Paul, who stated in his first letter to the Corinthians that "we proclaim Christ crucified, a stumbling block to Jews and foolishness to Gentiles, but to those who are called, both Jews and Greeks, Christ the power of God and the wisdom of God." If Christians were to preach—and imitate—Christ crucified, George argued that "nonviolence as a positive expression of love" must be "the salient feature of Christian moral understanding."[137]

George likewise applied the pacifist lesson of the New Testament to violence in the service of liberation. Sympathetic to African-American freedom struggles, George opened the book with a reference to the shooting of Jackson State University students in 1970 by Mississippi state troopers, acknowledging that the call to nonviolence could be seen as "a convenient tool for keeping deprived people submissive to their masters." George pointed to the hypocrisy of the "Christian majority," which, "though not endorsing pacifism itself, seems determined to apply the criterion of nonviolence to all the liberation movements" of nonwhite

---

135. Joseph Sigur e-mail to Rhonda Mawhood Lee, February 11, 2011.

136. Partial draft of Jean Edwards New Year letter, 1971, Jean Edwards papers. After President Jimmy Carter pardoned draft evaders on his first day in office, Sigur, "broke" and with "winter coming on," returned home "with ambivalent feelings." Sigur e-mails to Rhonda Mawhood Lee, February 3, 2011.

137. Edwards, *Jesus and the Politics of Violence*, 108–9.

"At Least We Make a Witness"

people.¹³⁸ Nonetheless, George warned against seeing the successful use of violence, by nations or by oppressed people, as a sign of God's favor. Noting that the liberation of the Hebrews from Egypt had not been good news for the Canaanites, and that Native peoples rejected a divinely approved "Manifest Destiny" for the United States, George asked: if a black revolution were mounted and failed, "What moral or theological wisdom could be pronounced on this disaster? Would it confirm that God is on the side of the white supremacists?"¹³⁹ Arguing against tyrannicide, George used the example of Dietrich Bonhoeffer, whose "courage" he did not question, as a reminder of "how premeditated styles of behavior may melt away in the heat of existential involvement."¹⁴⁰ Perhaps speaking as much to himself as to his readers, he noted that faithfulness could not be measured by political accomplishments. Rather, "Those who take the *theologia crucis* seriously as the basis of discipleship are certainly misinformed to found their position on the hopes of pragmatic success."¹⁴¹

When George and Jean returned to Louisville in 1971, the local peace movement was in transition. The Louisville Peace Council had disbanded, but in the Edwardses' absence, a Louisville chapter of the national group Clergy and Laymen Concerned About Vietnam (CALCAV; CALCK in Kentucky and Southern Indiana) had formed. The pastor of Peace Presbyterian Church, Irvin S. Moxley, was a founding member, and George's colleague Z. Burton Cooper, who had joined the Louisville Seminary faculty a year earlier, was a charter member of the steering committee.¹⁴² After the Edwardses' return to Louisville, George became cochair along with a local activist, Pat Bricking.¹⁴³ In the election year

138. Ibid., 2, 129.

139. Ibid., 10–11. The comparison between Canaanites and Native Americans was developed by Warrior, "Canaanites, Cowboys, and Indians."

140. Edwards, *Jesus and the Politics of Violence*, 14–15.

141. Ibid., 109. George did not, however, tolerate criticism that he believed to be unfair. When the pastor of Second Presbyterian Church, William Glenn Dorris, attacked pacifism in general and George's book in particular from the pulpit in November 1972, George insisted on the right of rebuttal. Second Presbyterian Church finally mailed that rebuttal to the congregation in February 1973, as they had mailed copies of the original sermon. Sermon, "A Critique of Pacifism," and correspondence between George Edwards and Glenn Dorris, in author's possession.

142. Minutes of the "Interim Steering Committee for Kentuckyana Clergy and Laymen Concerned," Sunday June 6, 1971, "Planning Committee, 1971–73" file, Box 1, CALCK. For a history of the national group, founded in 1966 by Jews, Protestants, and Catholics, see Hall, *Because of Their Faith*.

143. "Agreement form for political broadcasts," WAKY Radio, Louisville, October

79

1972, CALCK became involved in CALCAV's campaign to "Unsell the War" by publicizing the ongoing American bombing in Southeast Asia, to "[make] Nixon's 'invisible' automated war visible to public scrutiny and sentiment."[144] The campaign placed ads in a diverse array of publications, including *Business Week*, *Rolling Stone*, and, thanks to the generosity of Hugh Hefner, *Playboy*.[145] In the spring and fall of 1972, CALCK paid for radio and television announcements reaching, among others, morning viewers of *The Today Show*.[146]

In the wake of Richard Nixon's reelection that year, followed by the "Christmas bombing" of North Vietnam, a new organization sprang up, channeling the energy of the majority of the American public that, since 1971, were opposed to the war.[147] Two women, Suzy Post of the Kentucky Civil Liberties Union and Blanche Cooper (wife of Burton), organized a new local group as part of a national campaign to pressure President Nixon to sign the peace accord his administration had partially negotiated in October. They called their group "People for Peace," organizing a two-mile "Walk for Conscience" on inauguration day, January 20, 1973. People for Peace was intended to unite as many Louisville citizens as possible, of whatever political stripe, around their common desire for an end to the war. The group's newspaper advertisement read, "We are deeply distressed! . . . Many of us have never marched before, but we who march today and we who support the marchers do so to protest the senseless bombing of civilian populations and the continuation of this endless war . . . However we voted in November, we did not vote for more war."[148]

The ad was financed by the single dollar paid by each of its hundreds of signatories, who included George and Jean. Jean later remembered the march as an inclusive event, "just People for Peace": "You don't have to belong to any certain group, or have any certain theology."[149] Twenty-five hundred people attended the march, and a further hundred or so Kentuckians joined the thousands of demonstrators who filled the streets of

---

30, 1972, "Unsell editorials," Box 1, CALCK.

144. CALCAV, "An Occasional Memo," March 20, 1972, The Virtual Vietnam Archive.

145. *Ibid*. Hefner donated a full advertising page, worth $39,000.

146. "Agreement form for political broadcasts," CALCK; CALCAV, "An Occasional Memo," March 20, 1972.

147. Herring, *America's Longest War*, 212.

148. *Courier-Journal*, January 19, 1973.

149. George and Jean Edwards interview with K'Meyer, March 26, 1996, Tape 1, 35.

Washington that day. Their numbers included, as Jean remembered, "a lot of the clergy," most of whom, as she well knew, "wouldn't do anything like that before." Few shared George and Jean's conviction about the immorality of all war, but the crowd could agree on one thing, summarized by Blanche Cooper: "All we know is that we cannot go back to the ordinary ways of doing things until this war is completely ended."[150] The end came a week later, when the Paris peace agreement was finally signed. If Jean and George took any satisfaction in the growth of the anti-war movement, or harbored any bitterness about their years of solitary protest, they did not let it show. Years later, George and Jean described the end of the war against which they had preached, taught, organized, counseled, and demonstrated for ten years simply as "a great victory for the peace movement."[151] George's contribution to that victory was recognized in 1974 when he received the United (or Northern) Presbyterian Peace Fellowship's Peaceseeker Award, praising him as "a professor of peace to hundreds of students, a witty and eloquent advocate of the rights of conscience, a scholar of non-violence for the whole church of Christ, and a well-traveled bridge between two sister denominations."[152] Although it would be years before Jean's peace witness would be publicly recognized, that day was approaching.

When, following the Vietnam War, the Edwardses founded the Louisville Fellowship of Reconciliation (LFOR), Jean came into her own as a public witness for peace and George gained the activist ally he had long needed, now that his wife's daily work of raising their children had come to an end. As a group that mobilized opposition, not just to one war, but to all armed conflict, the LFOR would grow to play a crucial theological and political role in Louisville, bringing activists together for mutual support and challenge, and acting as a clearinghouse for information about peace initiatives. After the Fellowship's founding, its story and George and Jean's were inseparable: their historical memory and passionate commitment drove the LFOR's work, while it led them into a new era of their shared vocations as spouses and as witnesses for peace.

150. George and Jean Edwards interview with K'Meyer, March 26, 1996, 36; "Louisville Marchers Protest Continuation of Vietnam War," and "Kentuckians Join War Protest," *Courier-Journal*, January 21, 1973.

151. George and Jean Edwards interview with K'Meyer, March 26, 1996, Tape 1, 36.

152. United Presbyterian Peace Fellowship Peaceseeker Award, June 24, 1974, Jean Edwards papers.

3

"When People Become Peacemakers, This Is Their Vocation"

The Founding of the Louisville Fellowship of Reconciliation

1975 MARKED A TURNING point for the Edwards family. The United States completed its withdrawal from Vietnam as the North and South united to form a single republic, and the youngest of George and Jean's children, Johnny, left his teen years behind. That summer, Jean wrote about a new challenge of parenting, as Johnny's band used his family's basement to practice in "scorching hot" weather that left everyone "panting." The six young men's choice of refreshment was beer, which they brought in until "the basement smelled like a brewery and looked like the recycling center for tin cans." "Afterwards, of course," Jean noted, "they were driving their cars, which didn't seem too safe." Her response was characteristically indirect and generous, yet clear: "Now I fill the refrigerator with lemonade, orange juice, iced tea, milk, Cokes, Seven-Up, Dr. Pepper and Pepsi. I encourage them to drink all they want! So far, no beer has appeared since I started this new approach (mainly because they are all so hard up for money!)."[1]

---

1. Jean Edwards unaddressed letter, June 23, 1975, Jean Edwards papers.

"When People Become Peacemakers, This Is Their Vocation"

While the fact that her children were grown up presented Jean with new trials like the mountain of beer cans in her basement, it also meant that she had more freedom than ever to join George in witnessing publicly for peace. The challenge in the post-Vietnam era was to find the energy to build a new movement. In 1975, Jean later remembered, "everyone was so tired." There was no organized peace group in Louisville: "it seemed," Jean reflected, that the people who had been active in the later years of the Vietnam War "had all gone back into the woodwork."[2] At first, when George and a few friends started talking about reanimating the peace movement, Jean was apprehensive about the personal cost that might be attached. Fifteen years later, recalling that period, she made an error that probably reflected earlier concerns. "I was not saying very much" about founding a new peace group, Jean remembered, because she "knew" that "George would be the one they would look to for leadership, and I felt that it was going to be more than we could handle with three little children."[3] At the time she was recalling, their children were no longer "little": Riley and Ginger were beginning graduate study and Johnny was starting his musical career. It seems likely, then, that Jean's memory of 1975 was colored by the decades in which she and George had striven to combine their peace witness with their other vocations. Jean finally decided that companions would make the work possible: "I thought about it and I said if there would turn up another couple that was completely dedicated to doing it . . . then that would be all right." Another couple, Disciples of Christ minister A. C. Cuppy and his wife V. G., did "turn up," and the Louisville Fellowship of Reconciliation (LFOR) was born on Armistice Day 1975.[4]

After that time, the story of George and Jean's life together was inseparable from the struggles and adventures of the LFOR. The couple devoted themselves to building the alliance that George had long desired but that required the gifts of both to become reality. George continued to enunciate the scriptural and theological grounds for peacemaking, while Jean's extroverted personality, persuasiveness, and administrative skills brought new members into the Fellowship and connected it to

2. George Morrison, "Question and Answer Interview with Jean Edwards," *FORSooth*, April 1990, LFOR.

3. "Question and Answer interview with Jean Edwards." Jean made the same comment in her and George's interview with Rhonda Mawhood Lee. On both occasions, Jean was aware that she was being asked about 1975.

4. "Question and Answer interview with Jean Edwards."

other organizations with similar concerns. Over the course of a few years, the LFOR grew into a political and spiritual force in Louisville, uniting diverse people around their common commitment to nonviolence and serving as a primary or secondary faith community for those who, like George and Jean, were a pacifist minority in their churches. In the Fellowship's first ten years, its members took up the warning calls that George had long sounded—about the wastefulness of military spending and the heresy of trusting weapons to achieve international stability—and issued new cautions about the dangers of nuclear power. Despite the LFOR's achievements in forming a tightly knit community and becoming known as a consistent, clear voice for peace, it faced one significant internal challenge: reaching beyond its core of white, Christian members to become an interracial and interfaith alliance.

The LFOR's growth and the bridges it built depended largely on Jean Edwards. Jean's initiation into political organizing had come a couple of years earlier when she was elected treasurer of People for Amnesty, the successor to People for Peace.[5] After People for Peace's mass rally in January 1973, the group's leadership had pondered their next move, noting that "the resumed bombing of North Vietnam brought a lot of people into the realm of peace activity, many for the first time. If we could reach these people, convince them that their support is needed, and give them a handle by which to take hold of an issue, we could broaden the base of the peace community in this city."[6] The issue they chose was amnesty: lobbying the federal government to grant immunity from prosecution for draft evaders like those George and Jean had known in Toronto. The parents of one inhabitant of Toronto's "Louisville Ghetto," Sandy Sutton, sought George and Jean's help in speaking to a federal prosecutor about their son's case.

Their meeting at Louisville's federal building was an emotional breaking point for George. Angry that the U.S. government was admitting South Vietnamese allies fleeing unification, while still threatening to prosecute those whom George called "our boys up there who stood for the truth while the government was lying," George broke down in the prosecutor's office. As he later remembered, "This is an indictment of my weak personality, but I got hysterical. I was so emotionally overcome in

---

5. "Notes from the March 24th [1973] Meeting," "Amnesty" file, 1970s Peace Movement Literature, Box 1, CALCK.

6. "Honeywell Campaign Report/Peace for Peace," February 24, 1973, "Planning committee, 1971–73" file, Box 1, CALCK.

my effort . . . I got speechless. I was crying, and I had to get Jean to take it over." The prosecutor was patient with them: as George reminded Jean more than twenty years later, "Dear, he listened to us." The attorney took Sutton's parents, the Edwardses, and a few other supporters to a conference room, where "we really told him our story, and he sat there and listened to it, and I never recall him saying an angry word to any of us."[7] Sandy Sutton and his wife, Geny, never did return to the United States to live: they bought a farm north of Toronto and settled into life there, having decided, in Sandy's words, that "this is our home now."[8] After President Jimmy Carter signed an amnesty for draft evaders as one of the first acts of his presidency, the Suttons and others like them were free once more to visit their native land.

As important as amnesty was to the peace movement, another issue brought George and Jean Edwards together with the people who would form the core of the LFOR. It had little to do with military affairs, but everything to do with violence: the merger of Louisville's city and county school systems in the autumn of 1975. Despite the nominal integration of the city schools in 1956, in the early 1970s Louisville's system was more segregated by race than that of any Southern city of comparable size. Since 1971, the local NAACP and the Kentucky Civil Liberties Union had sought to have the predominantly white county schools merged with the city system and desegregation implemented through busing. In December 1973, the two organizations obtained a court order for merger. When a court-mandated desegregation plan was implemented in the fall of 1975, not quite 20 percent—half African-American and half white—of the system's 130,000 students were bused the first year.[9] The plan met with organized white resistance reminiscent of the opposition to open housing. More than 50 percent of county students boycotted classes on the first day of school. On the second day, white protestors vandalized parked buses and schools and attacked buses carrying students; in response, nine hundred National Guardsmen were called up to reinforce the city and county police forces and to serve as armed guards on school

---

7. George and Jean Edwards interview with K'Meyer, March 26, 1996, 39–40.

8. Quoted in "The War and Kentucky," *Courier-Journal*, January 24, 1973.

9. Obituary for U.S. District Court Judge James F. Gordon, *Courier-Journal*, February 11, 1990; Kleber, "Busing, Public School," in Kleber, *Encyclopedia of Louisville*, 148–49. Louisville's experience with busing is discussed in Clotfelter, *After Brown*, and Orfield and Eaton, *Dismantling Desegregation*.

buses.[10] White opposition to busing was channeled through such groups as Christians United, Union Labor Against Busing, and the Ku Klux Klan; over a month of street demonstrations culminated in a rally of five thousand opponents of busing, sponsored by Union Labor Against Busing on October 19.[11]

In the face of this resistance, Jean and George and other white Louisvillians who supported busing joined the black parents and community members who had been organizing for over a year to prepare for desegregation. George and Jean worked with some old friends and made some new ones through Progress in Education (PIE), an interracial group that counted Anne Braden among its organizers and the Edwardses among its first members. Founded in September 1975 in the throes of anti-busing violence, PIE coordinated its efforts with predominantly African-American organizations already in existence: the West End and Mid-City Citizens for Desegregation, and United Black Protective Parents. The latter group included George's former student Louis Coleman, one of the first African-Americans to graduate from Louisville Seminary, and Bob Cunningham, who in the 1990s would become a Fellowship of Reconciliation activist.[12] Anne Braden had recently entered a new phase of her personal and political life: by 1974, she and Carl had left the directorship of SCEF, which soon disintegrated, and Carl had died of a heart attack in February 1975. Having decided "that I would never spend another minute of my life building something all-white or predominantly white. That is just not what's going to change things in this country," Braden devoted her energies to the Kentucky Alliance Against

---

10. "The Guard—900 Sent to County Get Orders to Act with Caution, Tact," *Courier-Journal*, September 7, 1975; "Jefferson County School Buses to Carry Armed Guards," *Courier-Journal*, September 8, 1975.

11. "Labor Union Busing Foes Hold Rally," *Courier-Journal*, October 20, 1975. United Labor recruited 1,729 Louisvillians to travel to Washington, DC, for an anti-busing march on the Capitol on October 25 that brought together opponents of busing from several cities, including Louisville and Boston. "1,729 Leave Tonight for March in Washington," *Courier-Journal*, October 24, 1975. Louisville members of Electrical Workers Local 761 participated in the anti-busing rallies against the orders of their international headquarters, emphasizing that they were involved as individuals, not as union representatives. "Anti-busing Leader Urges Boycotts," *Courier-Journal*, September 1, 1975.

12. Folder, "West End School Committee (1974)," Box 4, PIE.

Racist and Political Expression (known as the Kentucky Alliance).[13] In the fall of 1975, she focused on PIE.

The ninety "concerned citizens" who gathered for PIE's founding meeting in September 1975 at First Unitarian Church downtown included future members of the LFOR like Judith and John Cumbler.[14] The Cumblers, veterans of the anti-war and civil rights movements, had just moved to town for John to teach history at the University of Louisville. A conscientious objector to the Vietnam War who had been raised in the Society of Friends, John later remembered the timing of their move as "incredibly lucky" because "it immediately immersed us in the struggle for racial justice." After their experiences in anti-war protests in Madison, Wisconsin, and working for civil rights in Mississippi, the fact that "in Louisville there were riots everywhere" made them "feel at home."[15] The community the Cumblers found in PIE included George and Jean Edwards: Jean served as a telephone tree captain, and George worked with his fellow faculty members at the Louisville Presbyterian Theological Seminary to gather support in Louisville faith communities for busing.[16] A local interfaith organization, LAIOS, formed a "task force on school desegregation" and sponsored a conference titled "School Desegregation: Chaos, Order or Justice" at Louisville Seminary three weeks after school opened in 1975.[17] Around the same time, nine seminary professors, including George, signed a pro-busing letter to the *Courier-Journal*. Its themes would have been familiar to anyone who had followed George's political work over the years. Reminding readers that "those of us who take our perspective from a biblical faith may find both insight and solace in our heritage," it warned that solace did not take the form of a comfortable life. "There is nothing in the Bible that suggests that the life of faith is a life free from pain. Quite the contrary... for these times, court-ordered busing is a painful but needed attempt to move beyond racial separation in our school system." What

---

13. Fosl, *Subversive Southerner*, 321. When PIE dissolved after a couple of years, public schools remained an area of concern for the Kentucky Alliance.

14. The estimate of the number of "concerned citizens" who formed PIE is from a PIE brochure, "Progress in Education (PIE)—a report and an invitation to join Progress in Education—A pro-desegregation voice in Louisville, Kentucky," folder, "PIE General Correspondence, 1976–77," Box 1, "PIE Organizational Records," PIE.

15. John Cumbler interview.

16. Folder, "PIE Telephone Tree Lists," Box 1, "PIE Organizational Records," PIE.

17. Folder, "The Louisville Area Interchurch Organization for Service (LAIOS): Interfaith Task Force on School Desegregation (1975–76)," Box 4, "Records of Various Pro-Busing Groups and Other Organizations," PIE.

appeared to be "irresolvable community conflicts" could, the signatories affirmed, "be resolved, in time, by a community which opens itself to the power of reconciliation."[18]

That power had been invoked the day before schools opened at a prayer service at Central Presbyterian Church downtown. There, over a hundred black and white members of eight Louisville churches shared communion and sang hymns ranging from African-American spirituals to a song composed during the freedom struggle of the 1960s, "We Are One in the Spirit." Rudolph Smith, George and Jean Edwards' pastor at Peace Presbyterian Church, offered a prayer for courage, which he defined as "when a black child walks into a lion's den" and "putting trust in the Louisville police when their history leaves a lot to be desired, and their fraternal order has taken a stand against busing."[19] Pro-busing activists needed all the strength they could muster: Louisville's public schools would remain under court order, testing and revising various desegregation plans, through 2000. In 2007, the school system was the object of a successful appeal by white parents to the U.S. Supreme Court to remove racial diversity as a criterion for public school student assignments.[20]

Joining the pro-busing movement was a way for George and Jean to live out their longheld commitment to racial justice and reconciliation, but the fall of 1975 saw them preparing to leave Peace Church, the interracial church they had cofounded in 1959. Their departure was further evidence of the challenges all Christians face in living out the belief that the risen Christ has overcome the world's racial and cultural divisions. Grounded in black theology, the theological counterpart to black power, Rudolph Smith had arrived in the early 1970s to serve as the church's pastor. Working with Smith challenged George's liberal views on race: while he found that Smith's preaching against racism "stereotyp[ed] white people" and was "chauvinistic," he was reluctant to air those disagreements. When black members of the church who may have agreed with Smith's critique of whites objected to his teaching (as George remembered it) that "Jesus was a black man," George attempted to justify Smith's view. He

18. "From Nine on Seminary Faculty," *Courier-Journal*, October 4, 1975. A few days before, forty-two black and white ministers from nine denominations had issued a statement urging citizens of Louisville to "'build on the positive elements' of busing for desegregation," *Courier-Journal*, October 1, 1975.

19. "School Prayer . . . It Was Offered in Hopes of a Peaceful Start Today," (ellipsis in the original), *Courier-Journal*, September 4, 1975.

20. "Across U.S., a New Look at School Integration Efforts," *The New York Times*, June 29, 2007.

remembered telling his African-American friends, "Oh look, he's talking about black pride. You shouldn't walk out. You should try to understand what he's trying to do; he's trying to build confidence among these people"—namely, the lower-middle-class blacks who constituted most of the congregation. But, he recalled, his black friends "walked out anyway." One "good friend" had no qualms about frankly rejecting George's interpretive assistance: when George "grabbed hold of him and told him my story" about why he shouldn't leave the church, the man responded, "Oh, go to hell, George. You don't understand what's going on here."[21]

Twenty years later, George acknowledged that he could have learned from his friend's directness and that avoiding the issue had made building community across racial lines more difficult. Paralyzed by a legacy of institutionalized and internalized racism, George "tried to avoid conflicts" with Smith, later realizing that "that's a Southern guilt thing, I guess." That guilt kept George from discussing theological and liturgical disagreements with the pastor, including the fact that Smith read from a "book of black wisdom" (whose title George could not remember) as well as from the Bible during worship. George acknowledged that "I would've been more honest ... if I'd just told him off, because, ultimately, I did not approve, either, of the way he talked." George "finally got tired of listening to it," noting that "I was never into that [black power] part of the race thing." "But," he added, "I realize I am here talking like a middle-class white man. I realize that."[22] Never attempting to engage Smith in dialogue, losing faith in the reconciling power of Christ in that challenging situation, George and Jean simply left Peace Church.

George and Jean's neighborhood church, Strathmoor Presbyterian, was no more welcoming a place for them in the mid-1970s than it had been in the 1960s, so they moved to Central Presbyterian Church downtown.[23] They already had connections to Central. Their son Riley had joined it in late 1975; George's colleague Ulrich Mauser was an elder there; and Olof Anderson, the charter member of the Southern Presbyterian Peace Fellowship who had visited George in New York

21. George and Jean Edwards interview with K'Meyer, March 12, 1996, Tape 2, 26–27.

22. Ibid., 28–29, 33.

23. Riley Edwards' transfer is recorded in the session minutes of November 10, 1975, and Jean's in the session minutes of April 12, 1976, CPC. George was present at the congregational meeting held on January 30, 1977; Minutes of Congregational Meetings, CPC.

City during the Second World War, had previously been Central's assistant pastor.[24] Shortly after the Edwardses moved to Central, George wrote his mother that, given the friendliness of the members and the fact that there were "seminary people" in the congregation, "We feel at home there."[25] In the mid-1970s Central was in decline, suffering from the white flight to the suburbs that began the previous decade. The church lost members every year from 1965 until 1981, when speculation abounded that the struggling church would close.[26] Instead, Central rallied and grew steadily, attracting some African-American members but remaining overwhelmingly white. Decades later, reflecting on the webs of racism in which all Americans were caught, George remarked with apparent frustration, "Only those who have little or no experience in trying to overcome racism in our society seem to have a clear understanding of how to eradicate racial injustice."[27] He did not mention his earlier hopes for churches becoming models in this area, but those may have diminished over the years.

The complexity of the struggle against racism dogged the LFOR from its founding: although it always cooperated with the Kentucky Alliance on civil rights issues, and many African-American activists knew the Edwardses as reliable allies, the Fellowship's steering committee had no black member until the early 1990s. There were a number of possible reasons. African-Americans, who were dealing with the crisis triggered by white opposition to busing in Louisville and the immediate dangers that violence posed to their children, were not likely to shift their attention to a new pacifist group founded that same autumn. Only a minority of Americans were pacifists to begin with, and African-Americans were overrepresented in the military, a source of reliable jobs for members of an underemployed minority that faced greater discrimination in the private than in the public sector.[28] Finally, white pacifists were often slow to

24. Session minutes, December 15, 1969, and October 5, 1975, CPC.

25. George R. Edwards letter to Analee Flaniken, April 17, 1976, Jean Edwards papers.

26. "A Case Study of Central Presbyterian Church," n.d. (circa 1987), "History of C.P.C. (Harry Gans files)" file, Central Presbyterian Church Historical Documents, CPC.

27. George R. Edwards to Paul R. Dekar, March 26, 2004, in author's possession.

28. The proportion of African-Americans (both men and women) in all branches of the military rose after the introduction of the all-volunteer service in 1973. After 1990, the proportion of African-Americans in all branches of the military held firm at about 20 percent until the early twenty-first century, when it dropped slightly before

"When People Become Peacemakers, This Is Their Vocation"

acknowledge the structural violence of racism, focusing their energy on international conflict to the exclusion of domestic concerns.[29] There were practical troubles, too: the group usually held its meetings in locations to which its existing members had easy access, like the Presbyterian and Southern Baptist seminaries and the Friends meetinghouse, but which were located in predominantly white parts of town, not always easily accessible by public transportation.

The struggle to be racially inclusive was ongoing for the LFOR, but the Fellowship did draw one solid line in its quest for members: they should renounce violence as a means of settling human disputes. In the 1960s, George Edwards had decided that the peace witness in Louisville would be stronger if the Louisville Peace Council united pacifists and believers in the just war doctrine into one—never large—group. In 1975, building on this experience, he considered forming a Louisville branch of the Committee for a Sane Nuclear Policy (SANE), rather than the pacifist FOR.[30] SANE, founded in 1957, stood in what historian Milton S. Katz calls the "liberal nuclear-pacifist" wing of the peace movement, focusing on pressuring the U.S. government for nuclear disarmament without addressing larger issues of war and peace.[31] In the end, however, the activists who came together to form a new peace movement for Louisville held the line on opposing all war.

On Armistice Day, November 11, 1975, George and Jean Edwards established the Louisville Fellowship of Reconciliation with a half dozen friends, including PIE veterans A. C. and V. G. Cuppy and Sister of Loretto Sarah Concannon, Dominican Sister Mary Brigid Gregory, and Catholic theologian J. Milburn Thompson.[32] Following both its members'

---

rising again. Black Americans constituted about 13 percent of the general population throughout the period. Segal and Segal, "America's Military Population," 19–20.

29. This had been a concern of African-American peace activists for decades. See Blackwell, *No Peace without Freedom*, and Lee, "'Admit Guilt—And Tell the Truth.'"

30. Jean Edwards e-mail to Rhonda Mawhood Lee, November 7, 2006.

31. Katz, *Ban the Bomb*. SANE merged with the Nuclear Freeze Campaign in 1987 and was renamed Peace Action in 1993.

32. At the time, none of the members knew that a chapter of the FOR had existed in Louisville during the Second World War. They would only discover that fact in 1989, when Elizabeth Hartsfield, LFOR's first secretary and by then a retired Disciples of Christ minister, sent the records of the first LFOR chapter to George and Jean when the new group hosted the national Fellowship's annual meeting. Letter from Elizabeth Hartsfield to LFOR, February 26, 1989, and Jean Edwards, "A Rare Gift," undated essay from 1989 or early 1990, LFOR.

inclinations and the national association's policy, the group was intended to be ecumenical, interfaith, and politically diverse. The founding by-laws announced the LFOR's intention to bring together "men and women who recognize the essential unity of all humanity and wish to explore the power of love and truth for resolving human conflict," seeking out "those of whatever faith who wish to confront human differences with nonviolent, compassionate and reconciling love, and to resolve cultural conflicts by the united efforts of people of many faiths." Faith was defined as including not only Protestants, Catholics, and Jews, but also those of a "Humanist" orientation: the groups' members came together as individuals who shared a commitment to peace, whatever its source, instead of founding a community grounded in a shared faith. The membership parameters closed with a statement that would have resonated with those who remembered George and the Bradens' struggles with anti-Communism and internal church conflicts: "No creedal or political standards shall be required of any officer."[33] Although the LFOR's founding members did not know it, they were joining a declining organization: the national Fellowship of Reconciliation's membership had already peaked at twenty-three thousand in 1972.[34]

Jean and George quickly announced their new endeavor to their scattered family and friends. Jean's Christmas letter in 1975 was photocopied onto FOR stationery, headlined by the slogan attributed to its former leader A.J. Muste, "There is no way to peace. Peace is the way." Jean opened with her customary reference to international affairs: "Peace in Vietnam has caused us to regain our holiday spirit, even to the extent of writing a Christmas letter! We hasten to mail it before Angola accelerates and brings on ten more years of depression." She made light of the health problems George was experiencing, noting that although he was "plagued with indigestion, back ache, tooth ache, and his ever present 'publish or perish' syndrome," he was expected "to recover from

---

33. By-laws of the Louisville Fellowship of Reconciliation, approved March 25, 1976, steering committee minutes, LFOR. The national FOR had amended its statement of purpose in 1930 to include not only disciples of Jesus but those who had "received their inspiration from other religious leaders" and some who had "reached their faith in love and nonviolence in still other ways." In 1965, the statement was modified again, explicitly to include "those of whatever faith who wish to confront human differences with nonviolent, compassionate, and reconciling love." Dekar, *Creating the Beloved Community*, 37–38, 146.

34. DeBenedetti with Chatfield, *American Ordeal*, 320. Individuals who joined a local branch of the FOR were counted among the national organization's membership.

all except the latter!"[35] In fact, George's back troubles worsened over the years, sharply curving his spine and requiring him to rely increasingly on Jean's physical strength as they aged.[36] In 1975, living for the first time in their empty nest, Jean noted the changes in their family: "Our children have grown up and each has gone his/her unpredictable way."[37]

Riley and Ginger were both in West Germany. Ginger had gone first: after completing an undergraduate degree in German and history at the University of Louisville, she began studying to be a psychiatric nurse.[38] Riley had decided to study theology at Tübingen with a view to being ordained. His parents "strongly encouraged" him to heed that call, "believing that my gifts were the right ones" for that vocation.[39] Although Riley and Ginger remained emotionally close to their parents, the fact that they both moved abroad to establish themselves in fields where George and Jean had preceded them illustrates a statement Riley made when reflecting upon life with his parents. Far from having to bridge a "generation gap" with George and Jean, as many of his contemporaries had, his "struggle" as he matured was "establishing my own identity." "With both parents having such strong identities of their own," he noted as he approached the age of sixty, "it took me years to find my own place in my own right."[40] Ginger and Riley's younger brother, Johnny, followed his own vocational and geographic path, touring for years with the band he cofounded, Buster Brown, and others, before returning to Louisville from California in 2000 to live with his family a few blocks from George and Jean, to be near them as they aged.

The peace work that would come to define Jean was still relatively new to her at the end of 1975, when she informed family and friends that "George and I have involved ourselves this fall in organizing a local chapter of the Fellowship of Reconciliation."[41] "Involved" was an understatement: Jean and George served together as the first cochairs of the LFOR, from the beginning the group's office was located in their home,

---

35. Jean Edwards letter to "Friends of Yore," Christmas 1975, Jean Edwards papers.

36. In a letter to his mother the following year, George noted that a recent X-ray had shown a problem with "the bottom disc" in his spine. George R. Edwards letter to Analee Flaniken, April 17, 1976, Jean Edwards papers.

37. Jean Edwards letter to "Friends of Yore," Christmas 1975.

38. Edwards-Menz e-mail to Lee, February 20, 2011.

39. Edwards-Raudonat e-mail to Lee, February 7, 2011.

40. Ibid.

41. Jean Edwards letter to "Friends of Yore."

and their family telephone was the Fellowship's contact number.[42] Jean quickly became LFOR's lead organizer and administrator, volunteering her time to write flyers, make telephone calls, maintain the membership list, and coordinate mailings once the group started publishing a newsletter in 1977. The use of volunteer labor was a conscious decision to keep the group's expenses low and allow it to rely exclusively on its members for financial support. As Jean remembered, "We decided we were not going to be an organization that tried to hire staff because we didn't want to have to do all that fundraising."[43] The nucleus of the organization was its steering committee, described in 1978 as "about seven people who are completely dedicated and absolutely dependable." The committee's membership changed over the years, but its role as the core of the Fellowship persisted.[44] Steering committee members devoted time and energy to planning educational events and demonstrations in which the LFOR's general members could participate, and, starting in 1977, putting out the newsletter that kept the membership informed about issues related to war, violence, and peace.

The first focus for the LFOR's energy in those early years was the national campaign to stop the building of the B-1 long-range bomber. The replacement for the twenty-five-year-old B-52 had a long history. The Eisenhower administration had first envisioned it; Gerald Ford approved its funding in the summer of 1976; and the grassroots campaign against it, led by the American Friends Service Committee, confronted President Jimmy Carter when he took office in January 1977.[45] Following up on a campaign promise to make deep cuts in military spending, Carter turned his attention to the $1 billion appropriated for the B-1. When his administration announced the decision to scrap the bomber, the LFOR credited the peace movement, arguing that Carter had "needed all of the

42. Louisville Chapter, Fellowship of Reconciliation, "Application for Recognition of Exemption," Form 1023, Internal Revenue Service, January 1976, steering committee minutes, LFOR; by-laws, approved March 25, 1976, steering committee minutes, LFOR.

43. George and Jean Edwards interview with K'Meyer, April 23, 1996, 51.

44. "What makes our F.O.R. tick?" Unattributed article attached to steering committee minutes, November 16, 1978, LFOR.

45. For the history of the B-1 and the movement against it, see Kotz, *Wild Blue Yonder*. The B-1 reemerged, deemed a "strategic-weapons launcher," in the Reagan years. One hundred B-1s were eventually built by the mid-1980s, costing a total of more than $28 billion and dogged by concerns about their military usefulness. Ibid., 3–6; 221–33.

backing that he could get to fight the military-industrial complex. We helped to make it an issue and alerted our neighbors to the facts." The victory, the LFOR encouraged its membership, meant "that a tiny group of people who are organized, who are armed with truthful arguments and humane sentiments, and who are truly dedicated can win great victories."[46] The campaign had brought new members into the LFOR, including Eileen Blanton, who became a close associate and friend of the Edwardses. Blanton and Jean met when the younger woman was working as an undergraduate teaching aide in the education department of the Catholic Bellarmine College, where Jean was the departmental secretary. As Blanton later remembered, Jean approached her one day to ask, "Can I get you to sign a petition [against] the B-1 bomber?" At the time, Blanton "had no clue what the B-1 bomber was," so Jean, who "didn't ask you sign something blindly," explained the issue. Blanton's encounter with Jean, she reflected, "changed my life," leading her to commit herself more and more deeply over time to the cause of peace, work that she saw as a natural outgrowth of the Catholic faith in which she had been raised. Jean's ministry skills were clearly at work as she approached Blanton. Knowing, in Blanton's words, "how important it was for people to feel like they were making a difference, in the face of so many things that felt overwhelming," Jean gave the younger woman a focus for her desire to live out her faith in nonviolence. Ultimately, Blanton affirmed, Jean "really introduced me, as a lot of people would say, to the peace movement in town."[47]

Blanton's initial involvement in the B-1 campaign led her to participate in the LFOR's first act of civil disobedience: their occupation of the Marble Hill nuclear plant under construction in Madison, Indiana, fifty miles from Louisville. Marble Hill was part of a buildup of power plants in the Ohio River Valley in the mid-1970s, one response to the decade's energy crisis.[48] In 1976 twelve plants existed or were planned in the 160 miles between Louisville and Maysville, Kentucky, to the east, and six new plants were proposed for the sixty-mile stretch of the

46. Newsletter, July 1977, LFOR.
47. Eileen Blanton interview.
48. Jimmy Carter made the first of his speeches about the energy crisis in April 1977, calling "the energy problem" the "greatest challenge" facing the country other than "preventing war" and citing the "need to shift to plentiful coal" as one element of a comprehensive American energy policy. Most of the plants planned for the Ohio River Valley, however, predated the Carter administration. "The Energy Problem," April 18, 1977, in Horowitz, *Jimmy Carter and the Energy Crisis of the 1970s*, 36, 40.

Ohio River between Cincinnati and Madison to the southwest. Marble Hill was the only nuclear plant; the others would be coal-burning, conveniently located close to Kentucky coal fields.[49] Opposed to the use of atomic energy, whether for war or for electricity, the Fellowship joined an environmental group, the Paddlewheel Alliance, to form a network to try to prevent the nuclear plant's construction. While Fellowship and Alliance members were also concerned about the pollution caused by coal-burning plants, they accepted a strategic alliance with the coal companies and miners, who opposed the nuclear plant for economic reasons. As George Edwards later pointed out, "We had a [base] here that was larger than just people morally opposed, for whatever reasons, to nuclear power."[50] The network's actions against the plant started with a three-day bluegrass festival on a farm outside Madison on the last weekend in July 1976.[51] The fact that well-known bluegrass artists like Mac Wiseman, not given to supporting radical causes, participated in the festival supported George's observation about the widespread opposition to Marble Hill.[52]

After a public hearing in February 1977 failed to stop the project and construction began, the LFOR and the Paddlewheel Alliance stepped up their protests. A demonstration at the site on August 6, 1977—the anniversary of the U.S. bombing of Hiroshima—ended with the release of balloons with notes attached reading, "If this had been radioactive, it would have gotten you!"[53] As the group moved from festivals and demonstrations outside the plant to planning direct action against it, two Paddlewheel members, University of Louisville students Sarah Lynn Cunningham and Scott Houchen, visited the Clamshell Alliance that was fighting the proposed Seabrook nuclear power station in New Hampshire. They returned having, in Jean's words, "learned a whole lot," bringing back "a lot of marvelous ideas . . . to start training us" to occupy the Marble Hill plant.[54] The protestors divided into small "affinity groups,"

49. "New Army of Environmentalists Focuses on Ohio River Power Plants," *Courier-Journal*, July 12, 1976.

50. George and Jean Edwards interview with K'Meyer, June 18, 1996, 12. The LFOR did not receive support from the Kentucky Coal Association for its activism against Marble Hill.

51. "Festival to Raise Funds to Oppose Nuclear Plant," *Courier-Journal*, July 25, 1976.

52. Thanks to music historian Charles Hughes for this observation.

53. Newsletter, July 1977, LFOR.

54. George and Jean Edwards interview with K'Meyer, June 18, 1996, 10–11. Jean

each consisting of individuals who committed to occupying the sites and contact persons who would support them from the outside. Jean Edwards later remembered the affinity groups as "very, very important," meeting "just about every week" in order to build the trust required to engage in risky protests together.[55] The protestors followed the principles of civil disobedience that George Edwards knew so well. They announced their intention to engage in illegal activities in advance, justifying their actions in a press release two weeks ahead of the action planned for Saturday, October 7, 1978. Noting that "Indiana and Kentucky residents have testified at the Nuclear Regulatory Commission's permit hearing and have supported all legal attempts to stop the plant," but that "all these efforts have fallen on deaf ears," they declared themselves compelled "to pursue extralegal means" to try to force "a full public hearing" on nuclear power.[56]

October 7 was a day of coordinated anti-nuclear protests across the country. Forty-two people occupied the Seabrook plant in New Hampshire, and about 450 protestors against the Black Fox nuclear plant in Inola, Oklahoma, received tickets for trespassing after they marched on its construction site.[57] In the Louisville area, more than 150 protestors, including George and Jean Edwards, processed that morning behind an American flag to the Marble Hill plant, still only one-fifth built. They ranged in age from college students to people in their sixties, and included students, teachers, a Catholic nun, Baptist, Presbyterian, and Catholic clergy, and at least one engineer. Thirty-one of them climbed over the fence encircling the facility and sat down cross-legged on the grass; the majority, including George and Jean, stayed on the outside. Sheriff's deputies waited until the first dozen protestors had scaled the fence before starting to arrest them for trespassing; two more waves of occupiers followed. The trial of the thirty protestors who pleaded not guilty ended with a hung jury, a fact that "appalled" Judith Cumbler, the wife of John, one of the occupiers. According to her husband, "She said, 'You trespassed! They have pictures! They have films of you going over the fence . . . and you're

---

Edwards remembered the Seabrook power station being in Massachusetts, possibly because it is located about forty miles from Boston.

55. "Question and Answer interview with Jean Edwards."

56. Paddlewheel Alliance news release collected in "Marble Hill Occupation Handbook" (2nd ed.), September 30, 1978, 1, LFOR.

57. "31 Arrested after Scaling Fence at Marble Hill Nuclear Plant," *Courier-Journal*, October 8, 1978. The Seabrook plant was completed in 1986 and began production of energy in 1990; the Black Fox project was abandoned in 1982.

not found guilty! What did you have to do *to* be found guilty?'" "Clearly," her husband smiled, "the people in Madison, Indiana, were much more pissed at Marble Hill than they were at us."[58]

Despite popular concerns, plant construction continued after the trial, leading the Paddlewheel Alliance and its partners to stage a much larger occupation in June 1979. This time, eighty-nine activists occupied the plant, including George Edwards and the writer and farmer Wendell Berry. Over two hundred allies cheered them on, including Jean, who stayed outside the fence as George's support person.[59] George brought his own prophetic style to the event: as Jean later dryly remarked, "When [George] got up to the top of the ladder," he read from the Bible briefly and then "decided he would make a speech" before descending the ladder into the enclosure.[60] The occupiers were immediately arrested for trespassing but were never tried, thus being deprived of a public forum for their views on nuclear energy.[61] Prosecutors may have considered a trial unnecessary, as Marble Hill's future was already uncertain. The American move toward nuclear power had been compromised by the public fear that had followed the meltdown at the Three Mile Island nuclear reactor in Pennsylvania that March, and then in May, Marble Hill itself had been struck by allegations of shoddy construction. Charles Cutshall, a construction worker at the plant, filed an affidavit stating that he and other workers had been told to cover up defects like air holes in the concrete walls of the containment unit. Construction halted that summer so the plant could be inspected, and Marble Hill was finally abandoned in early 1984.[62]

The grassroots campaign against Marble Hill drew LFOR members together early in the group's history. Eileen Blanton remembered her time in an affinity group for the Marble Hill occupation as a formative experience: her "first experience of collaboration for social change on that

---

58. Cumbler interview. One occupier, a Catholic priest named Philip Field who had been a leader of the occupation, pleaded guilty, paying a fine and court costs of just under $50. "30 of 31 Nuclear Foes Enter Innocent Pleas," *Courier-Journal*, October 11, 1978.

59. "89 Are Arrested in Calm Protest at Marble Hill," *Courier-Journal*, June 4, 1979.

60. George and Jean Edwards interview with K'Meyer, June 18, 1996, 14. Eileen Blanton and John Cumbler also remembered George reading and preaching at the top of the ladder, but could not recall the text he read or what he said; Blanton and Cumbler interviews.

61. "Prosecutor's Plan Upsets Builder of Marble Hill," *Courier-Journal*, June 5, 1979.

62. Blair, "Return to Marble Hill."

level," where people with shared commitments "learned how to work and support each other in a group" and where each member was "important." As one who "chose not to go over" the fence into the plant, Blanton was all the more gratified to feel "a part of that success" in a group that recognized support persons as vital to nonviolent civil disobedience. Blanton remembered the Marble Hill occupation as "a good time . . . to build stronger relationships, and to have people to make commitments with."[63] For Blanton, the LFOR eventually served as her primary faith community, after she became estranged from the Catholic Church in which she had been brought up. Working from 1981 until 1990 as the associate director of the Peace and Justice Center of the Catholic archdiocese of Louisville, Blanton found herself in an ambivalent position. She later remembered that she "loved" her work there because of "the pride I felt in the Catholic Church *having* a Peace and Justice Center." "But," she continued, "I also remember the day that I found out that we didn't challenge ourselves internally, that the Peace and Justice Center was only there to talk about social issues, and challenge the community, but there was no question about ordination of women, or any of those things, and I just remember being so shocked and disappointed and heartbroken." She struggled with the conflict between her desire to be a force for reconciliation in the world, not wanting "to alienate people," and her seeking to "live and work in a way that always pushes me to greater integrity and whatever organization I'm a part of, to that greater integrity." "And," she reflected with twenty-five years of perspective, "it's hard to do that, you know; it is just hard." Blanton moved back and forth among different parishes, seeking a congregation where she could live out her faith, but she "never did quite find a home."[64]

In the wake of the Marble Hill action, the LFOR made a couple of changes to expand its alliances; both bore the stamp of Jean Edwards' practical nature. In 1979 the Fellowship invited people who were "not quite pacifists" to become "friends" rather than members in order to stay informed about its activities and participate in those they could support; and a few months later, the Fellowship started including a "Calendar for Peacemakers" in its newsletter, to spread the news of peace-related activities around town.[65] Groups whose meetings were listed included

63. Blanton interview.
64. Ibid.
65. Newsletter, March 1979, LFOR.

the Louisville Anti-Klan Coalition (formed in response to Ku Klux Klan leadership in the anti-busing movement), Amnesty International, and the Committee in Solidarity with the People of El Salvador (CISPES).[66] The list of events grew quickly; as David Horvath, a longtime Fellowship member, later recalled, Jean "really did beat the bushes" to put together the calendar, which was "the thing you needed to get in the mail every month" in the 1980s.[67] John Cumbler also remembered the calendar serving as both a source of information in the pre-Internet era and a marker of community that "linked together diverse groups, diverse interests." By the late 1980s, Cumbler recalled, if "you walked into any progressive family's house" in Louisville," "there were two things on the refrigerator: the Vogue [independent cinema] schedule, and the FOR calendar of events." The experienced activist reflected that, compared to some political activities, the "Calendar for Peacemakers" "didn't make an incremental difference. That made a *big* difference in this community."[68]

The LFOR avoided one significant theological and political issue because of its potential for conflict: abortion. While many pacifists saw an abhorrence of abortion as integral to their reverence for God-given life, others believed that forcing a woman to carry a pregnancy against her will was itself a violent act. Discussions about this issue in pacifist circles typically focused on the legal conflict between a woman's right to terminate a pregnancy and the fetus' right to life, rather than on the actions that communities of faith could take to support pregnant women and reduce abortion rates.[69] On both sides of the legalization-prohibition divide, feelings were strong. Juli Loesch, a Catholic feminist and peace activist and founder of the Pax Center in Erie, Pennsylvania, wrote the national FOR's *Fellowship* magazine in 1978 to invite members to attend the National Right-to-Life Convention that year and participate in mobilizing "pro-life non-violent direction action." She argued that the "right-to-life" movement, seeking the recriminalization of abortion, "contains hopeful

---

66. The calendar appeared in LFOR's newsletter as early as the summer of 1980. It was untitled at first, but by the summer of 1983 had been dubbed the "Calendar for Peacemakers."

67. David Horvath interview.

68. Cumbler interview.

69. For a recent Christian "pro-life" argument that moves beyond the language of competing rights, see Stassen and Gushee, *Kingdom Ethics*. For a discussion of "personhood" and abortion from a "pro-choice" point of view, see Simmons, "Personhood, the Bible, and the Abortion Debate."

seeds of pacifism and even feminism," as some members found that their "anti-abortion, anti-euthanasia principles" had led them to "near-pacifist views on war" as well.[70] In response, Jean Peterman, a National Organization for Women activist from Ohio, decried the tactics that protestors had used at abortion clinics, including "blocking doors, ganging up on patients and calling them murderers or accusing them of killing their babies, and barging into the operating room during procedures." Arguing that "feminists" had been working for "genuinely helpful ways to reduce the number of abortions" such as "adequate day care, educational and job opportunities for women" and contraceptives, Peterman concluded, "Of course non-violent types will disavow all the firebombings that have occurred. Is forcing a fourteen-year-old to continue a pregnancy or bleed to death from an illegal abortion really any less violent?"[71]

The LFOR was leery of joining such a dialogue of the deaf. At a meeting about a year after its founding, "The question was raised as to whether the FOR has a position on abortion," and "It was decided that we would do well to discuss this controversial issue when all groups are represented."[72] If that discussion occurred, it was not recorded in the minutes; the group seems to have decided not to address the subject, not a surprising decision given that the steering committee included members of a variety of churches, including Catholic nuns. Two decades later, when the LFOR's newsletter published a rare article defending the practice of late-term (sometimes called partial-birth) abortions, the group was swiftly rebuked by David Brown Kinloch, an active Mennonite member "outraged that an organization with a pacifist orientation would publish articles supporting abortion, let alone partial birth abortions." Adding that "acts of violence and murder are no less heinous just because it is [sic] advocated by those on the left of the political spectrum," Brown Kinloch warned, "A pacifist journal needs to stick to articles that do not advocate violence, or else it will lose its focus and audience."[73]

Around the same time, George Edwards admitted to an interviewer that the fact that he and Jean were "certainly not opposed to abortion, especially under certain critical conditions" amounted to "a certain

70. Juli Loesch letter to *Fellowship*, April–May 1978.
71. Jean Peterman letter to *Fellowship*, July–August 1978.
72. Steering committee minutes, November 8, 1976, LFOR.
73. David Brown Kinloch letter, "Abortion story improper," *FORSooth*, January 1997, responding to "Late term abortions wrongly vilified, speaker said," *FORSooth*, October 1996, LFOR.

inconsistency in ... our morality," but added that he didn't feel "compelled to accept" that "every fertilized egg is a fetus."[74] He added caustically that he was not the only Christian with inconsistent views on reverence for life, as both Catholics and Protestants had "not found this right to life to exist with reference to adults, specifically in the case of war, because of the 'just war' theory."[75] While George and Jean made small financial contributions to the Kentucky Religious Coalition for Reproductive Choice, and George served after his retirement from the seminary as a counselor for women in distress over a pregnancy, the issue was secondary to their concern about war.[76] When he signed up to be a counselor in 1995, George wrote, "Please note: My age is now seventy-five. My wife and I do considerable work as volunteers for various groups, mainly the church and Fellowship of Reconciliation, so I am not in a position to take on much more," signing his note, "Peace."[77] Lacking consensus on how abortion, war, and various forms of violence might be theologically connected, George and Jean and their fellow members of the LFOR chose not to address abortion together, leaving public and private commitments on the matter to members and their faith communities.

Despite the desire stated in its bylaws to "represent as many religious heritages and institutions of the community as possible," interfaith cooperation proved elusive for the Fellowship. It had sought a Jewish member for its steering committee as early as six months after the group's founding; Muslims would join the chapter in the 1990s as their numbers in Louisville increased, but in the 1970s and 1980s, "interfaith" work in Louisville meant Christians and Jews working together. The city had a significant Jewish community, particularly in the Reform tradition, dating from at least 1814. The first Jewish congregation, Adas (later Adath) Israel, was chartered in 1843; over time, all the major American branches of Judaism came to be represented in the city.[78] In its quest for a Jewish member for

74. George and Jean Edwards interview with K'Meyer, May 9, 1996, 4.

75. Ibid., 4–5.

76. George and Jean donated $20 to the KRCRC in July 1989, "Fundraising" folder, KRCRC; George is listed as a "clergy counselor" from 1994 through 1997, "Clergy counselors" folder, KRCRC.

77. George R. Edwards clergy counselor agreement, February 9, 1995, "Clergy counselors" file, KRCRC.

78. Ely, *Jewish Louisville*, 21; "Laws of Kentucky, passed at December Session, 1842" (approved January 12, 1843), archives of The Temple. Adath Israel was a founding member of the Reform umbrella organization, the Union of American Hebrew Congregations (now Union for Reform Judaism), established in Cincinnati in 1873.

its steering committee, the LFOR used George's acquaintance with Martin Perley, the rabbi who had resigned his pulpit in 1968 over the Vietnam War and who was now the chair of the Louisville-Jefferson County Human Relations Commission.[79] That search was unsuccessful, and the steering committee minutes contain no further notes about seeking a Jewish member. The irritant in the relationship between LFOR leaders and Jews in Louisville was U.S. support for the state of Israel. LFOR members objected to the displacement of Palestinians in 1948, the ongoing occupation of the Palestinian territories, and the United States' financial underwriting of Israel's military. George and Jean Edwards, however, never condoned the violent tactics of groups like the Palestine Liberation Organization that sought Palestinian statehood. George denied explicitly in *Jesus and the Politics of Violence* that organized violence by one group against another could ever receive "divine sanction" and described the conflict in the Middle East as "escalation toward disaster," but he was particularly critical of Israel, the United States' principal ally in the region.[80]

The LFOR's attempts to connect with Louisville's Jewish community were compromised in 1980 when the Fellowship joined with the Liturgy in Life Committee of the Presbyterian Seminary to bring Allan Solomonow to Louisville. Solomonow, an activist with the Jewish Peace Fellowship and former director of national FOR's Middle East Program, made an argument that was provocative at the time: that the Palestine Liberation Organization (PLO) should be included in Middle Eastern peace negotiations.[81] While Jean Edwards found the chapel service that Solomonow led at the Presbyterian Seminary to be "one of those rare occasions when we are taken completely out of ourselves into a realm of new insights and reconciliation," others saw his visit differently.[82] Solomonow's sojourn seems to have been arranged without discussion with local Jewish organizations; according to the *Kentucky Jewish Post and Opinion*, "[t]he Jewish community was advised of his presence only by" the newspaper itself. The *Post and Opinion* took a stance against

---

79. The steering committee minutes for May 1976 note, "In our search for a Jewish person on the steering committee, it was suggested that we talk to Martin Perley and also to the Board of Rabbis"; LFOR.

80. Edwards, *Jesus and the Politics of Violence*, 11.

81. "Transcript of a Talk in Louisville by Allan Solomonow," *Kentucky Jewish Post and Opinion*, December 12, 1980.

82. Jean Edwards, "Allan Solomonow's Visit—Reflections," Newsletter, December 1980–January 1981, LFOR.

Solomonow's position, challenging the Jewish Community Federation of Louisville to consider whether "such a speaker should be allowed to speak unanswered."[83]

One segment of the community responded by inviting George Edwards to participate in a "dialogue" about peace in the Middle East at a Friday evening service at the Conservative Congregation Adath Jeshurun in December 1980. A *Post and Opinion* story about George's visit to the synagogue noted that he was "familiar to many people here as an ardent pacific [*sic*] and civil rights activist" who "understands that he is a member of a small minority in urging that Israel should make the first move toward negotiating with the Palestine Liberation Organization." His speech, the paper noted, met with "strong opposition." Focusing on his "own personal conviction about the futility of war" and the need to find an alternative to "global suicide," George referred to peace in the Middle East as "an American problem." As the strongest U.S. ally in the region, Israel must take the "initiative for new moves that would generate hope for peace in the Middle East."[84]

George Edwards was used to his trenchant critiques of American foreign policy being poorly received, but having worked mostly in Christian circles, he may not have been adequately prepared for debate with people of another faith. He did not help his cause by stating that Americans had "very little opportunity to understand the Palestinian viewpoint" because "the Jewish vote within the United States is highly articulate, well-informed and it is carefully integrated as far as I can observe it from the outside."[85] Adath Jeshurun's rabbi, Simcha Kling, heard in George's comments overtones of Christianity's long prejudice against Judaism, responding that he saw "any intimation that there is undue Jewish power in America or on the Senate" as "a polite form of anti-Semitism." In the question-and-answer session that followed, in response to what the *Post and Opinion* reporter called "both fair and unfair challenges," George returned to his basic view that "we need dialogue between the parties."[86] Having gotten off on the wrong foot in its attempts to open a debate about the Arab-Israeli conflict, the LFOR was able to attract very few Jews to their events. The relationship between the United States, Israel, and the

83. *Kentucky Jewish Post and Opinion*, November 28, 1980.

84. "At Adath Jeshurun—'We Need Dialogue between Parties,'" *Kentucky Jewish Post and Opinion*, December 19, 1980.

85. Ibid.

86. Ibid.

Palestinian territories remained a central concern of the Fellowship, but without a Jewish presence at the table, its opportunities for true dialogue and work toward Middle Eastern reconciliation were limited.

As the 1980s opened, the LFOR focused on a new policy of the Carter administration: the reinstatement of draft registration for young men. Calling the introduction of draft registration in the summer of 1980 "an abomination," George told a journalist in June that he had already received ten inquiries by telephone about draft counseling.[87] The LFOR planned a silent vigil for the following January at the downtown post office as registration began for men born in 1962.[88] Building on members' Vietnam-era experience, the Fellowship sponsored draft counseling workshops at several churches and high schools.[89] A newsletter article publicized the fact that the new registration law made no provision for claiming conscientious objector status and that, under the law, registrants would "have only ten days to think about and claim an exemption once the draft has begun." "Therefore," the article stated, young men needed "as much objective information and assistance on this issue as possible" to "enable them to make an informed decision about something which will affect them the rest of their lives."[90] The LFOR remained vigilant against the possible reintroduction of a draft, one of its ongoing concerns.

The year that draft registration was reintroduced, George's long-standing witness for peace was recognized with the Peace Seeker Award from the Southern Presbyterian Peace Fellowship, which he had co-founded almost forty years earlier. The award praised the same qualities the northern church's Peace Fellowship had lauded a few years earlier, calling George "a tireless seeker after the things that make for peace and an elder Statesman of the Fellowship, who bridges generations of witness to educate for world responsibility and to press for the timely strategies of peacemaking."[91] A few months later, questioned by a reporter about

87. "Impending Registration a Call to Arms for Old Draft Warriors," *Louisville Times*, June 18, 1980.

88. Newsletter, December 1980–January 1981, LFOR. Under the government's rolling registration plan, nineteen- and twenty-year-olds had already been required to sign up; from then on all male citizens and permanent residents were required to register when they turned eighteen.

89. For example, in the fall of 1981, workshops were held at DeSales High School (a Catholic boys' school), Third Christian Church, and St. Matthew's Episcopal Church; steering committee minutes, September 28, 1981, LFOR.

90. Newsletter, October 1983, LFOR.

91. Southern Presbyterian Peace Fellowship Peace Seeker Award, June 1, 1980,

"the philosophical burn-out thought to be so prevalent among peace activists," George had shrugged, smiled, and replied, "I take all that with a grain of salt. When people become peacemakers, this is their vocation. This becomes part of their moral armament."[92]

That strength would be necessary for the LFOR's long-term vocation of witnessing against nuclear weapons, continuing the work that George had begun decades earlier. The centerpiece of the LFOR's witness in this area was their annual Hiroshima Day remembrance. The format varied from year to year, but the vigils or protests always incorporated liturgical elements—prayer, chant, and song—that signified the connection between witness and worship, and the Holy Spirit's active presence in both. On occasion, protests led to unforeseen complications. Jean Edwards laughed years later as she remembered the protests of 1978: together with anti-nuclear protestors around the world, LFOR members had drawn human silhouettes on sidewalks in downtown Louisville to symbolize the people vaporized in the atomic bombings of Japan. "Somehow," Jean remembered, the paint they had used "didn't wash off" as expected with the next rain. Her telephone rang off the hook with "the city and the parks commissioner and various people" calling "about these silhouettes on the streets downtown that wouldn't come off," until the LFOR's conscientious activists planned a workday to clean the sidewalks themselves. Laughing, Jean concluded, "That was terrible."[93]

A few years later, Fellowship members felt a new urgency to speak out against nuclear weapons, as their hope that President Jimmy Carter would make a significant change in the country's military policy vanished. They were horrified when, in the final year of his presidency, Carter ordered a buildup in nuclear forces, known as PD-59 after the presidential directive that set it in motion, that was intended to enable the United States to fight and win what the government termed a "limited" nuclear war.[94] The election of the more hawkish Ronald Reagan only stiffened the LFOR's resolve. In the first year of the Reagan administration, activists prepared for the annual Hiroshima remembrance by making a paper chain—a biodegradable prop, unlike the sidewalk paint—to illustrate the ideological and financial chains of war that bound human beings to de-

Jean Edwards papers.
    92. "The Peace People," *Louisville Times*, August 16, 1980.
    93. George and Jean Edwards interview with K'Meyer, June 18, 1996, 34.
    94. Freedman, "First Two Generations of Nuclear Strategists," 775.

struction. The chain was composed of thirty thousand links—in purple, the Christian liturgical color of repentance—each representing ten of the three hundred thousand people who were killed in the U.S. nuclear bombing of Hiroshima in 1945. As activists worked together for months around kitchen tables to form and join the links, each paper circle, as participant Paula Jackson later remembered, symbolized a prayer uttered silently or out loud as it was created.[95]

For those who made the chain, and for the sixty or seventy activists who stood before the Louisville federal building with it draped around them on the morning of August 6, its significance was inseparably spiritual and political.[96] As Eileen Blanton told a reporter, the purple color of the chain was "a sign of mourning—a sign of a prayerful atmosphere." George took a shift in the line "before going to work," yawning at the early hour and wearing a sign around his neck bearing a photo of a mushroom cloud and the words, "No more Hiroshimas." Riley, home for a visit, and Jean stood with him. Jean told a reporter why she believed "this [is] a time for the peaceful community to come together": "It's not just the *fear* that one [bomb] might be dropped. It's the fact that *two* have been dropped by the United States." Not all passersby agreed with the demonstrators. When a Marine sergeant entering the building asked one the purpose of the vigil, he was told, "We're here in memory of the three hundred thousand who died in Hiroshima." His reply: "Sorry we didn't get 'em all."[97] Characteristically, Jean used her time on the line as an organizing opportunity. Encountering a local Catholic priest, Jim Flynn, "standing there holding that purple chain that morning," she told him, "It's time for you to join the Fellowship of Reconciliation!" Flynn did join, eventually becoming a member of the steering committee and a key figure in the Fellowship later in the decade.[98]

The 1981 Hiroshima remembrance was a cooperative venture between the LFOR and a year-old peace group that had already surpassed it in size: the Council on Peacemaking and Religion (CPR), the local arm of the international campaign to pressure the United States and the Soviet Union to freeze the number of nuclear weapons in their arsenals. The Council's first leaders were old friends of George and Jean: Glen Stassen,

95. Paula Jackson interview.
96. The estimated number of activists comes from "Never Again Is Wish Expressed at Vigil on Hiroshima Anniversary," *Louisville Times*, August 6, 1981.
97. Ibid. The article is accompanied by a photo of George Edwards yawning widely.
98. George and Jean Edwards interview with K'Meyer, June 18, 1996, 9.

a professor of Christian ethics at the Southern Baptist Theological Seminary who had first learned from the Edwardses in the early 1960s that the United States was involved in a war in Vietnam, and Pat McCullough, who had sat on the Louisville Fellowship's steering committee since 1977.[99] Although the two organizations' membership overlapped to a great extent, the CPR appealed to a larger constituency, as membership in the group was open to anyone, pacifist or not, who agreed with the goal of a nuclear freeze. As a result, the CPR's mailing list of supporters peaked at approximately three thousand names, compared to the Fellowship's high of eleven hundred in 1996.[100] The two organizations differed in other ways. Terry Weiss, an activist with the Council from 1982 and its director from 1987 until 1994, summarized the differences in the two organizations' approaches: "We were more socially acceptable" and "less threatening," while the LFOR "to the general public, was viewed as much more radical, and they are." The former Baptist turned Episcopalian remembered with a laugh that her fellow Council activists and she "looked like people who went to the Episcopal Church . . . and who dined out on a regular basis," even though she was "stone-cold poor" when she started working with the CPR. Its leaders "wore suits" and made appeals to corporations and religious leaders to raise their budget.[101] Even though there were what Weiss remembered as "a lot of iffy years" for the CPR, it had far more resources than the LFOR—perhaps $350,000 a year by 1994—which enabled it to pay full-time staff.[102] The Fellowship of Reconciliation, in contrast, worried about meeting its monthly expenses of about $200 in the mid-1980s.[103]

In response to the CPR's growth in the early 1980s, George Edwards asked his fellow steering committee members a question he would not have been able to imagine in the 1960s: whether they thought Louisville had "a proliferation of groups and meetings" concerned with peace. After decades as a virtually lone voice for peace, George now found that he had to cooperate and negotiate with other leaders whose perspectives and tactics differed from his in ways both dramatic and innocuous. Bubbling

99. Stassen interview; McCullough's membership is attested in the steering committee minutes, October 8, 1977, LFOR.

100. Terry Weiss interview; steering committee minutes, November 25, 1996, LFOR.

101. Weiss interview.

102. Ibid. The budget figure is based on Weiss's memory of 1994, the last year she directed the Council; independent confirmation is not available.

103. Steering committee minutes, January 28, 1985, LFOR.

"When People Become Peacemakers, This Is Their Vocation"

up in him were the concerns that, in the 1960s, he had called "the old gripes" between opponents of all war and nuclear pacifists. At the end of the meeting during which George raised that issue, the steering committee emphasized "the importance of FOR's distinct contribution as a pacifist group in the community," while affirming that "we need to continue to relate to CPR."[104]

That relationship was not only strategic, it was personal: the two groups' members were friends whose priorities and tactics differed but who shared a commitment to witnessing publicly for peace. Glen Stassen, who always spoke affectionately of George and Jean, called himself "a strategist" with little patience for debates between pacifists and just war theorists in an age of nuclear proliferation. Although, like the Edwardses, Stassen saw different types of warfare and violence as interrelated, he focused on pressuring governments to make measurable reductions in their nuclear arsenals to reduce the threat of global annihilation. In the early 1980s, a new threat was on the horizon. In 1978, the Soviet Union had deployed intermediate-range nuclear missiles against Western Europe, and by 1983 the Reagan administration carried out the plan, originally formulated under President Carter, to deploy American weapons—commonly called "Euromissiles"—in West Germany, Holland, Belgium, and Italy. The missiles' proximity to Moscow concerned antinuclear activists: stored above ground, they could reach the Soviet capital in less than ten minutes. A false report of American missile activity at a tense moment could, peace advocates believed, tempt Soviet leaders to launch an attack on the vulnerable missile storage sites, precipitating a nuclear war. Under those circumstances, Stassen saw three virtues in the goal of a nuclear freeze. First, it was "clear, and easily understandable: Just stop! What more do you have to say?" Second, as the Nuclear Freeze Campaign gained strength across the country and throughout Western Europe in the early 1980s, it gave people the "belief that we could make a difference." Finally, the freeze campaign "really connected with values we have, like survival" and reverence for God-given life.[105]

Together those three factors added up to a mass movement. At its peak, the freeze campaign mobilized about a million people for a demonstration—the largest in American history—under the banner "Freeze the

104. Steering committee minutes, June 1, 1981, LFOR.
105. Stassen interview. He discusses the integration of his Baptist faith with his peacemaking commitments in Stassen, *The Journey into Peacemaking*.

Arms Race, Fund Human Needs" in New York City in June 1982.[106] The demonstrators had popular support: a poll conducted six months earlier had found that 52 percent of respondents were concerned that President Reagan "might get us into another war."[107] Further polls throughout the early 1980s consistently showed between 70 and 85 percent of the American public in favor of the freeze.[108] Several religious bodies joined the campaign, including the Presbyterian Church, the National Council of Churches, the Synagogue Council of America, and the Conference of Catholic Bishops. Despite this mobilization, the freeze campaign was unable to stop deployment of the missiles. The movement's persistence, however, and its ability to garner public support, combined with Mikhail Gorbachev's reforms and the Reagan administration's need to redeem itself from the Iran-Contra scandal of 1986, were significant factors leading to the 1987 Intermediate Nuclear Forces (INF) treaty that removed the missiles from Europe.[109]

George and Jean Edwards missed the rally in New York in 1982 because they were on their way to Edinburgh for George's final sabbatical from Louisville Seminary. George's teaching vocation had continued to be important throughout the LFOR's early years. Known as a dedicated and outspoken teacher with a good sense of humor, he was the butt of an April Fool's joke in 1980 when the seminary issued a mock press release titled "Rapture Ruptures Lecture." It announced, "Professor George Edwards of the Louisville Presbyterian Theological Seminary was stunned today. In the midst of a lecture on the self-defeatism of fundamentalists who profess a narrow interpretation of the Bible, all seven hundred members of his audience suddenly vanished without a trace. For the first time in his life, Mr. Edwards was speechless." The book George wrote during his sabbatical, *Gay/Lesbian Liberation: A Biblical Perspective*, continued his outspoken ways. His theological interest in homosexuality had been sparked by the incident at Eastern State Mental Hospital decades earlier, when he had rescued a patient named Cecil from a brutal beating by an inmate disgusted by Cecil's sexual involvement with another man. That

---

106. Meyer, *Winter of Discontent*, 184–88. On European activism against the missiles, see Wittner, *Toward Nuclear Abolition*, 226–52. For a concise overview of the anti-nuclear movement from its beginning through the twenty-first century, see Wittner, *Confronting the Bomb*.

107. Wittner, *Toward Nuclear Abolition*, 254.

108. Ibid., *Confronting the Bomb*, 157.

109. Cortright, *Peace Works*, 235–36; Wittner, *Toward Nuclear Abolition*, 395–404.

early insight into the use of violence to enforce heterosexuality eventually led George to become one of the first advocates for the full inclusion of gay and lesbian persons in the church. One of nineteen persons named in 1976 to a Northern Presbyterian task force to study homosexuality, George later remembered learning "more, technically, about [homosexuality]" through that experience than he "had ever been exposed to previously."[110]

When the task force finished its work in 1978, its majority report recommended that non-celibate gays and lesbians should not be deemed ineligible for ordination on the basis of their sexuality.[111] The church's General Assembly rejected that recommendation, however, imposing a ban that remained in place until 2011. The question of whether a life partnership between two persons of the same sex could be an integral part of the Christian life had both theological and pastoral implications. Although the church resolved in 1980 that homosexuality seemed to be "contrary to the teaching of scripture" and to "repudiate the heterosexual process which gave us life," it saw the need to "be sensitive to the difficulty of rejecting a person's sexual orientation without rejecting the person."[112] George emerged from his work on the task force on sexuality believing that such distinctions between pastoral care and theological integrity were unnecessary and that gay and lesbian persons could be fully embraced within the community, ministry, and rites of the church. His participation in the task force gave him space in which to continue the reflections on sexuality and violence that he said had motivated his "search for ethical sanity" since Cecil's beating.[113] His service on the church task force became pivotal in George's conversion to an open ally of out gays and lesbians, but he found that his first attempt to write a book offering biblical arguments for affirming gay and lesbian identities fell flat. On sabbatical in 1977 in Tübingen, where Riley was studying theology, he found that the German professors of New Testament he met "thought I

---

110. UPCUSA press release, "Appointment of nineteen persons to a task force on a study of homosexuality," September 24, 1976, "George Edwards" file, LPTS; George and Jean Edwards interview with K'Meyer, May 9, 1996, 30.

111. The report is contained in Presbyterian Church USA, *Definitive Guidance*.

112. Minutes of the 120th General Assembly (1980), Presbyterian Church in the United States, 213.

113. Edwards, *Gay/Lesbian Liberation*, 119.

was crazy" and "had no sympathy . . . whatsoever" for his interest in the issue.[114]

When George and Jean returned home in the spring of 1978, his manuscript on gay and lesbian liberation completed, they found that no American publisher would accept it. Noting, however, that "some of the evaluations were affirmative," George returned to the project in 1982, requesting a sabbatical leave to "get away from the telephone"—ringing at his and Jean's home for the LFOR—and "rewrite the entire material."[115] The sabbatical granted, George and Jean moved to Edinburgh for several months, which gave them time to enjoy their family and to focus on the new book. By then, both Riley and Ginger had married West German citizens; as George later remembered with a laugh, "You can't imagine how friendly German young people are."[116] When Johnny visited from Louisville at the same time as Ginger, her conscientious objector husband, and their baby, Jean wrote home to say that "the rock-and-roll world mingled very nicely with the vegetarian, anti-draft syndrome, and we laughed a lot." Jean and George reveled in their new role as grandparents. "Of course," Jean wrote, "we adore the baby and enjoy taking care of her. She's been on two hikes with us—one was across the mountain (covered with heather), when she slept in the harness which George was wearing; and the other was in the baby buggy which we pushed along the footpath to Leith (the next town) and picked blackberries along the way."[117] Jean and George would eventually have eight grandchildren, six in Germany and two in the United States.

While in Edinburgh, George and Jean attended an Episcopal church, a surprising development that Jean described in a letter to Spenser Simrill, a canon at Christ Church Episcopal Cathedral in Louisville and a leader in the Council on Peacemaking and Religion. Asking humorously, "Could it possibly be predestined and foreordained that we should become 'dyed in the wool' Episcopalians during our stay in Scotland?" Jean told her friend that they had "naturally" worshipped first at St. Giles Cathedral, "the pulpit of John Knox, where even the statue of John Knox is displayed." There, "The order of worship was exactly the same as the one

114. George and Jean Edwards interview with K'Meyer, May 9, 1996, 30.

115. George R. Edwards letter to Louisville Seminary President John M. Mulder, September 21, 1981, "George Edwards" file, LPTS.

116. George and Jean interview with K'Meyer, March 12, 1996, Tape 1, 25.

117. Jean Edwards letter to "Dear Steve and Katherine," September 18, 1982, Jean Edwards papers.

we had known since childhood." Even the hymns were familiar, and "The sermon left us feeling that we would like to hear more." That changed on September 19, when they accompanied Ginger, "her draft resister husband," and their new baby to church and were horrified to read in the bulletin that the church would commemorate the Battle of Britain that day. They were "amazed to see the Royal Air Force *Band* (in uniform) seated in the chancel" and "nearly fainted dead away" when RAF officers processed in, "some carrying Battle-Axes (pikes?), some wearing swords." During the service, "the national anthem was sung, and the band played a lively military tune for the recessional." Despite the militaristic liturgy, "The minister's sermon seemed to try to reconcile everybody," speaking "of peace and ending the arms race. Consequently, I felt that it would be possible to dialogue with him and wished for an opportunity to do so."[118]

That opportunity arrived almost immediately. After the service, while they were "wandering around looking at the building, waiting for the rain to stop," the minister approached them to admire the baby. Jean took advantage of this chance to ask the pastor "how he could reconcile the military incorporated into the church service, even carrying weapons down the church aisle." When the minister replied that "the church has always reflected the culture which surrounds it, and should rightly do so," Jean replied that "this used to be true in the USA more than it is now, since there seems to be a real emphasis for the church to return to its roots," adding that Jesus had come "to replace the 'eye for an eye' philosophy with a new ethic." The minister warned her "that we have to guard against being self-righteous in thinking that we have the only truth," adding "that Jesus was certainly self-righteous in his attitude toward the church of his own day!" Whatever the pastor may have meant by that last comment, Jean decided "that I shouldn't hold him too long but thanked him profusely for talking with us. Otherwise, we would have gone away feeling that we had no opportunity for dialogue." She closed her account of their conversation on a hopeful note: "He is a very likeable person and a very good preacher. Hopefully, we will have another opportunity to talk with him when Riley comes and we can invite him for tea." They stopped worshipping at St. Giles, however, seeking another church "before another Sunday came around." On the advice of Lorna MacLeod, the wife of the founder of the Iona Community, Church of Scotland minister George MacLeod—a pacifist whose beliefs were once

---

118. Jean Edwards letter to Spenser Simrill, October 3, 1982, Jean Edwards papers.

described as "half-way towards Rome, and half-way towards Moscow"—the Edwardses moved to St. John's Episcopal Church.[119]

At St. John's, they felt more at home, finding a Peace and Justice Center in the basement, noting that the church would observe the "Week of Prayer for World Peace" later that month, and learning of "a fall series of six discussions on Tuesday evenings of peace issues." The "thing that touched me the most," however, was that when the rector—improbably named Neville Chamberlain—"saw that we were having difficulty finding the right place in the prayer book he came down out of the chancel right to our pew and explained how to follow the service." Jean was impressed enough with Chamberlain's report to the congregation of his recently completed first six months with them, in which he commented on the variety of views among the congregation about nuclear disarmament, to quote it extensively to Simrill. The tensions evident in the parish, Chamberlain argued, were "the cost of being a Christian" and were "to be worked through, in love and in understanding." Without that challenging work, "there is no maturity—no resurrection." As the church continued its discussion, "it will manifest some of the hurt and cost of discipleship. If it doesn't, it will become, as in the picture of the religious community in Ezekiel's vision, a valley of dried bones."[120] Those words clearly resonated with Jean, as one who had spent her adult life within the church, holding firm to her confession of nonviolent faith while seeking opportunities for dialogue with those who believed differently.

Jean wrote to other friends about the "amazing number of peace groups working in Edinburgh" and the outspoken advocates George and she found there. They agreed with Ron Beasley, a Church of Scotland elder, who, having noted that, in Jean's words, "no government seems to be taking the Peace Movement seriously," had "reluctantly" concluded that "a carefully prepared, quiet, non-violent program of civil disobedience" had become necessary. In the same vein, Jean summarized an "interesting article" in the local newspaper about a visit to Edinburgh from Thyra Quensel of the West German Green Party. "When she spoke in Scotland," Jean wrote, Quensel "suggested that mass marches are no longer effective because they do not put 'sand in the machinery.' She stressed, 'We have to do something practical; we have to begin blockading nuclear bases.'" Quensel's conclusion resonated with Jean: "When asked if the Green

---

119. Jean Edwards letter to Simrill; the quote about George MacLeod comes from Ferguson, *George MacLeod*, 180.

120. Jean Edwards letter to Simrill.

Party consists of a bunch of hot-headed idealists or a real emerging political force, she replied simply, 'I hope we are both.'"[121] Their sabbatical leave strengthened George and Jean for the new campaigns of civil disobedience in which they would soon engage.

The distance from home and the time for reflection that Jean and George enjoyed in Edinburgh bore fruit in a completely revised manuscript of *Gay/Lesbian Liberation*. Transforming the initial draft was a joint endeavor, as both Jean and George remembered years later, repeating together, "We rewrote the whole thing."[122] The book drew upon liberation theology and George's deeply eschatological worldview to argue that advent of the kingdom of God meant freedom for gays and lesbians along with others who had long been considered outcasts. Rejecting arguments from natural law against homosexuality on the grounds that "the appeal to what is 'natural' often conceals the imposition on the community of customs that disregard the interests of some to the advantage of others," George made a case based on both the Old and New Testaments.[123] He reinterpreted the story of Sodom and Gomorrah, not as a condemnation of consensual same-sex relations, but as "an episode of gang rape" in a patriarchal, xenophobic city, in which male visitors fell prey to a "violent, aggressive abuse of power."[124] In the ancient world, George pointed out, phallic penetration was a way of violently subordinating trespassers and the conquered; he cited the example of a Greek vase celebrating a victory of Athenians over Persians in fifth century, which bore the caption, "We've buggered the Persians!"[125] He applied historical context to Paul's injunctions against homosexual relations, arguing that Paul had been primarily concerned with first-century pagan idolatry. Furthermore, just as Protestant churches were questioning some of his assumptions about women's roles in the church, twentieth-century Christians could assume the "naturalness" of gay or lesbian partnership for some.[126]

Although George's analysis used historical-critical methods of biblical scholarship, the foundation of his argument was a deep faith in God's

---

121. Jean Edwards letter to "Dear Steve and Katherine."

122. George and Jean Edwards interview with K'Meyer, May 9, 1996, 31. Jean made the initial comment that "we rewrote it," followed by George repeating, "We rewrote the whole thing, didn't we?"

123. Edwards, *Gay/Lesbian Liberation*, 66.

124. Ibid., 25.

125. Ibid., 46.

126. Ibid., 99.

grace. Early in the book, he stated his concern that liberation theology's sympathy for Marxist thought could lead some to forget that God—not human beings—would always be the agent of liberation. Analyzing Paul's letter to the Romans, he emphasized that the apostle "stubbornly refuses to dilute God's justification as gift (or grace) by allowing it to become a human or political achievement."[127] Traces of his old disagreement with Carl Braden were visible in George's contention that it was impossible "to define liberation theology in categories determined by Marxist views of economic justice" and that it was "suspect" to assume "that biblical teaching mandates a single economic ideology for human liberation"—a criticism he applied equally to Christian advocates of capitalism.[128] Citing Paul's statement that "God chose what is low and despised in the world, things that are not, to reduce to nothing things that are, so that no one might boast in the presence of God," George argued that "the perspective of Christian belief, both theological and moral, is always 'meontic,'" or "aimed not at what *is* but what, in God, has the potentiality for being." In considering Paul's perspective on sexuality, therefore, George found it necessary "to distinguish the legal from the liberative element and give precedence to the latter."[129]

George's understanding of the implications of divine grace for Christians led him to formulate an ethical framework for sexuality that would apply to all people, whatever their sexual orientation. He grounded that ethic, like his commitment to nonviolence, in the self-sacrificial love of God that was most fully seen in Jesus Christ. Christians were called to let that love, called *agape* in Greek, transform the often self-interested *eros* of lovers. "Sexual love," George noted, "is paradoxical in its ability to express self-centered, instinctive, and immediate gratification, on the one hand, and powerful self-giving on the other. The moral task of theology," therefore, was to "exemplify and teach" that sexual love should mature into "self-giving *agape*," which was "the basis for a mutuality that no longer seeks surrender and self-sacrifice from the other, pleasure and domination for the self."[130] Seeing no reason why gay Christians' relationships would be any less grounded in *agape* than heterosexual relationships, George elaborated an "ethical profile" for sexual relationships

127. Edwards, *Gay/Lesbian Liberation*, 11.

128. Ibid., 11, 12.

129. Ibid., 75. The biblical quote is from 1 Corinthians 1:28–29; *meontic* is a word derived from the Greek for "that which is not."

130. Ibid., 111.

liberated by God's saving love.¹³¹ That framework included constancy, nonviolence, and what George called "transgenital awareness," by which he meant both seeing persons as more than their sexual orientation and "[placing] sexuality in appropriate relationship to the total moral task of liberating love."¹³² Over time, lifelong monogamous relationships would transform both partners as they grew and changed together. Writing from the perspective of thirty-five years of marriage, George dismissed the false freedom that promiscuity offered gay and straight persons alike, lamenting that "too many people are denied in this way the joy of growing old together in love."¹³³

In the book's conclusion, George addressed international ethics, drawing a sharp contrast between the nonviolent social order of Christian marriage and the violence that pervaded foreign relations. "Sexual love that fulfills and enriches human relationships," he noted, "is based on mutuality, the gentle and caressing touch, responsiveness to and tenderness toward the other—what can be called 'software.' But the affairs of nations are carried out with hardware of the most lethal sort, the hallowing of martial virtues and heralding of the heroic violence prevailing over the malicious violence of each successive enemy." Returning to his theme of the links between exploitative sexuality and international violence, George remarked, "We too have buggered the Persians, and the people are tutored in the glory of it."¹³⁴ Just as married couples were called to live a life inspired by God's self-giving love, which would lead them out of a narrow erotic focus on themselves and into service in Jesus Christ's name, the church was called beyond a focus on its own members' personal relationship with Christ and into a mission of solidarity with the suffering. Drawing on Paul's letters to the Romans and the Corinthians, George argued that the body of the faithful, "constituted as church by the bodily suffering of Christ," was called to "hear the world's groaning for liberation from bondage" and "enter into it with collaborative effort," moving out of what George called "an erotic, self-centered piety into concert with the groaning heard within the whole of creation."¹³⁵

---

131. One of the sources George drew most from in his connection of *agape* and erotic love was Williams, *The Spirit and the Forms of Love*. Williams, however, did not address gay and lesbian relationships.

132. Edwards, *Gay/Lesbian Liberation*, 115, 119, 123.

133. Ibid., 115.

134. Ibid., 122.

135. Ibid., 123–24. The passages George cites in this section are Romans 8:18–21

In his advocacy for gay and lesbian Christians, George had few allies among biblical scholars. After his death, Louisville Seminary colleague Johanna Van Wijk-Bos remembered *Gay/Lesbian Liberation* as "a landmark work, one of the first to argue, on a biblical-theological basis, for full inclusion of people whose orientation and gender identity differed from the heterosexual norm."[136] In his introduction to the book, the liberationist Old Testament scholar Norman Gottwald called it "a blockbuster" which, he added, was "saying a good bit for a book that is first and foremost a work in theology, and the theology of Paul at that!"[137] Despite affirmation from those colleagues, a few years later George expressed disappointment that "to date I haven't seen a review of it even in one serious biblical or theological journal."[138] George's work bore fruit at the local level, however. When he and Jean returned home to Louisville in 1983, they played a key role in their church becoming the first Kentucky congregation to join the newly-formed More Light movement for the full inclusion of gays and lesbians within the Presbyterian Church. By joining that network in December, Central Presbyterian Church affirmed that it would "welcome into its fellowship all persons, regardless of race, color, national origin, age, sex, sexual orientation or preference, economic, cultural, or religious background." Proclaiming that "human judgment" could not "set aside" "the worth and dignity of every person as a child of God," Central affirmed that its leadership would not use any one element of "a person's total humanity" "as a basis for denying full participation and service in the body of Christ."[139] The church's outreach to gays and lesbians, numerous in its downtown neighborhood, was a factor in reversing the decline it had experienced in the previous two decades.

Over the next few years, George and Jean would enter yet another phase of their witness together, engaging in new campaigns of

---

and 1 Corinthians 12–14.

136. Van Wijk-Bos, "May the beauty of his life shine forevermore." Van Wijk-Bos, a scholar of the Old Testament, was Louisville Seminary's first female tenured professor and George's colleague for his last seven years of teaching.

137. Edwards, *Gay/Lesbian Liberation*, vii.

138. George R. Edwards letter to Virginia Edwards-Menz, August 4, 1986, Jean Edwards papers. *Gay/Lesbian Liberation* received positive reviews in at least one church and one education journal: "The Truth Can Set Us Free," *Presbyterian Survey*, June 1985, and *SIECUS Report*, May 1985, of the Sexuality Information and Education Council of the United States; both Jean Edwards papers.

139. Session minutes, December 13, 1983, CPC.

"When People Become Peacemakers, This Is Their Vocation"

civil disobedience in response to both political and personal factors: the United States' nuclear weapons stockpiling and its interventions in Central America, and the freedom they found in George's retirement from Louisville Seminary. The decade or so until the mid-1990s was the most politically active of their life together. They drew increasingly close to allies like Eileen Blanton and Jim Flynn, and continued to work with churches when those were sympathetic. More often, however, they created networks with people of any, or no religious faith who felt, as they did, a vocation to peace, and who would take the risks that witness required.

4

"Praying for Peace and Paying for War Are Inconsistent"

Radicalism in Retirement

IN APRIL 1983, A few months after their return from Edinburgh, George and Jean Edwards went public with their latest peace witness: sending 50 percent of the income taxes they owed to the World Peace Tax Fund, instead of to the Internal Revenue Service.[1] In the Louisville Fellowship of Reconciliation's newsletter that month, George outlined his and Jean's reasons for this act of civil disobedience. "Since my earliest remunerated employment," he noted, "I have paid in full the federal income tax. I do not believe that human communities can exist without laws, institutions, and services which seek to serve the common good. In recent years, however, my wife and I have increasingly realized that praying for peace and paying

---

1. George R. Edwards, "A Letter of Conscience," Newsletter, April 1983, LFOR. In later years, George and Jean estimated having begun war tax resistance around 1980, but 1983 is the first year for which there is contemporary evidence. The Escrow Account for a World Peace Tax Fund was maintained by the Conscience and Military Tax Campaign (now the Nonviolent Action Community of Cascadia, or NACC), which lobbied for legislation to allow taxpayers to direct a portion of their payment away from military purposes. Such legislation has been introduced in Congress several times since 1972. Hedeman, *War Tax Resistance*, 125.

for war are inconsistent. On this tax day, 1983, therefore, we are withholding 50 percent of our federal tax—the amount that we believe goes for the maintenance of a military system now threatening global genocide."[2]

The Edwardses had already been quietly refusing for a couple of years to give the government the proportion of their tax bill that funded past, present, and future wars. Over the next few years, as George retired from Louisville Seminary and as the Reagan administration increased military spending and sponsored new proxy wars, George and Jean would participate in various forms of civil disobedience: war tax resistance, the sanctuary movement offering safe havens to undocumented refugees, and the Pledge of Resistance against a possible U.S. invasion of Nicaragua. The size of their networks of mutual support in these ventures varied, but even when it was tiny, as was the case with war tax resistance, George and Jean had more companions in witness in the 1980s than they would ever before have dared to imagine. With their marriage serving as the core of the network of friends and fellow witnesses that grew up around the LFOR, the Edwardses found that the Reagan years—hard times for peace advocates—in Jean's words, "caused us to grow stronger." That strength was grounded in the cooperation among the LFOR's steering committee, the leaders who became "more and more integrated—working more and more together" as the 1980s unfolded.[3] The end of that era brought new challenges in the form of the Persian Gulf War and the struggle to make the national and local FOR more racially inclusive, and gave Jean and George the opportunity to continue witnessing to their longheld conviction against the death penalty. By the mid-1990s, as the Edwardses contemplated slowing the pace of their public activities, they could look back on two decades with the LFOR and give thanks for the friends who had accompanied them, while wondering what Christian peace witness would look like for the generation then coming to maturity.

When Jean and George Edwards decided that they could no longer pay for war while praying for peace, they joined a tradition with long roots—including the Radical Reformation that had birthed the historic

---

2. George R. Edwards, "A Letter of Conscience." Estimates of government spending on the military varied, in part depending on how much of the national debt was included in the estimate. In the same period, the American Friends' Committee on National Legislation calculated that 35.5 percent of tax revenues were spent on the military. Williamson Jr., "Limits on a Christian's Obedience to the State," 103.

3. "Question and Answer interview with Jean Edwards." On the LFOR in this period, see Lee, "'God Alone Is Lord of the Conscience.'"

peace churches, and the American freethinker Henry David Thoreau—but narrow appeal.[4] They had long been familiar with the risks associated with resistance. George had considered writing a book about Maurice McCrackin, a Northern Presbyterian minister and member of the radical pacifist group Peacemakers whose refusal to pay war taxes had led to his being stripped of the right to exercise his ordination in 1960.[5] Based in Cincinnati, only a hundred miles from Louisville, McCrackin knew George from their work with Anne and Carl Braden and SCEF.[6] During the Vietnam War, George had resorted to a devious trick to have McCrackin preach at a Louisville Seminary chapel service. As George later remembered, he had suggested McCrackin when a group of students asked him for the name of a preacher opposed to the war. "When the date of the appointed service came," George later remembered, seminary president Al Winn "met some of us at the chapel entrance and said he could not give permission for McCrackin to speak." When the students suggested that George preach instead, Winn acquiesced. When the moment for the sermon arrived, George stood and "said that I was not really prepared, but that a distinguished guest from Cincinnati was on hand for the occasion," then invited McCrackin to address the congregation. George's actions that day was met with silence from Winn. Although George suspected the prohibition against McCrackin preaching had come from the seminary board, as it seemed "definitely out of character" for Winn, he later remarked, "I regret the breach of trust he may have felt in my handling of the matter." In his own defense, however, he noted that McCrackin had traveled from Cincinnati in good faith, expecting the chapel pulpit to be open to him, so that "my disregard of the ban seemed less blameworthy to me than to respect it."[7]

Like George and Jean, McCrackin was a member of the national Fellowship of Reconciliation, which had encouraged war tax resistance since at least 1961, when its executive secretary A. J. Muste had refused

---

4. Thoreau wrote his essay "On Civil Disobedience" after his refusal, in 1846, to pay the Massachusetts poll tax, believing that payment of the tax would amount to supporting the United States' war against Mexico.

5. McCrackin's story is told in Bechtel and Coughlin, *Building the Beloved Community*. McCrackin was restored to good standing with his presbytery in 1987.

6. McCrackin's association with the Bradens is discussed in Bechtel and Coughlin, *Building the Beloved Community*, and in Fosl, *Subversive Southerner*, 225–26.

7. George R. Edwards letter to Rick Nutt, 27 February 1993, 12, "George Edwards" file, LPTS.

to file a tax return on the grounds that the government had no right to conscript his money. Like many, Muste believed that a government that recognized the right of citizens not to fight wars must also allow them to refuse to pay for it. That putative right, however, was not recognized in the law of the United States or any other country. From the point of view of the IRS, what pacifists called "resistance" was no different from ordinary tax evasion or fraud. In American history, there has only been one legal way to avoid paying war taxes: to keep one's income below the taxable level, voluntarily living below the poverty line. Those who owed taxes and refused to pay them for the sake of conscience could be punished by prison time, but that penalty was rarely imposed: between 1942 and 2010, only forty-nine Americans faced court action for charges related to war tax resistance.[8] A 1973 article in the national FOR's *Fellowship* magazine urging members to resist reassured them: "All IRS can do is threaten you, confiscate your bank account and wages, or, as a last resort, your property."[9] Those threats may have seemed less formidable to a lifelong bachelor like McCrackin, or an elderly widower like Muste, than to a family man like George.

For years, he and Jean had publicized the size of the military budget: since the LFOR's founding, its members had stood outside Louisville's downtown post office every Tax Day, April 15th, passing out leaflets outlining the proportion of tax revenues devoted to war. Those protests made life difficult for one member of the Louisville Seminary administration. Thomas L. Jones, vice president from 1977 to 1980, who remembered George having given him figurative "courage pills to take a stand" against the Vietnam War, later found that he did not look forward to the LFOR's Tax Day protests. "In a day when we had a liberal student body but had to raise money from a conservative constituency," the protests made extra work for him: "George's leadership meant I had to spend weeks trying to regain the angry pro-war folks!"[10]

As U.S. military spending soared from already high levels, reaching $1.6 trillion over Ronald Reagan's first five years in office (instead of the $1.2 trillion Jimmy Carter had projected for that period), Jean and

---

8. According to the War Resisters League: http://www.warresisters.org/convicted_wtr.htm.

9. Bradford Lyttle, "War Tax Resistance Expands," *Fellowship*, February 1973. Despite the title, the article made no claim that the number of American war tax resisters was increasing.

10. Tribute by Thomas L. Jones in Harrod, "George and Jean Edwards: Living Peace."

George encouraged their allies to join the tiny but committed minority of Americans protesting with their dollars.[11] When George and Jean did so, they attached a letter to their tax return explaining why their payment was half the size the Internal Revenue Service expected. Accepting that "the saying of Jesus, 'Render unto Caesar the things that are Caesar's' (Mark 12:17), does acknowledge our obligation to the state," they went on to say, "To this is added however, 'and to God the things that are God's,' which means that even the state must respect a higher authority. In 1646, our faith tradition affirmed that 'God alone is Lord of the conscience.' We therefore believe that when civil obedience violates the conscience such violation must be nonviolently resisted."[12] With their first such letter to the IRS, George and Jean moved from engaging in civil disobedience as an occasional undertaking, as in the open housing movement or the struggle against the Marble Hill nuclear reactor, to making it a constant commitment for the rest of their lives.

Each in their own way, they exhorted others to consider following the same path. Perhaps inspired by the example of the Quaker professor at Converse College who had introduced her to the idea of conscientious objection, Jean spent an evening in 1981 addressing the seniors in Bellarmine College's honors program on the topic of tax resistance. Afterward, the chair of the English department, Kathleen Lyons, who had organized the session, expressed her gratitude to Jean that the students had heard "about a subject that can take on stridency, from one as gentle as you are." "They need," Lyons concluded, "to consider the subject seriously, and they will be able to do so after your clear, gracious presentation."[13] George focused on urging older adults to resist. In an essay commissioned by the General Assembly of the Presbyterian Church (USA), which sought resources to help members discern "the responsibilities and limits of Christian citizenship in a society increasingly faced with the dangers of militarism," George pointed to the disturbing rise since 1981 in both military spending and poverty in the United States.[14] His analysis rested on the biblical passage he and Jean cited in their letter to the IRS,

---

11. Military spending figures come from LaFeber, *America, Russia, and the Cold War*, 318.

12. George R. and Jean Edwards letter to Internal Revenue Service, April 15, 1998 (outlining the argument they had made for years), Jean Edwards papers.

13. Kathleen Lyons letter to Jean Edwards, October 29, 1981, Jean Edwards papers.

14. The quote about the General Assembly comes from "Preface," in Stone and Wilbanks, *Peacemaking Struggle*, v.

but it ended with a plea that arose from his experience as a teacher, draft counselor, and father. "For too long," George charged, "the decision for Christ or Caesar has been assigned to young men and women, usually jobless and bored, or too inexperienced to measure the consequences they face when military recruiters picture for them futures bright with vocational benefits and travel to exotic places. War tax resistance places the weight of decision about the human future where it belongs: upon all of us old enough and secure enough to ask what it means to pray for peace and pay for war." He concluded, "Saying 'no' to Caesar is a tough, frightening decision, but it could be, in the grace of God, one step toward a new human future."[15]

George and Jean inspired others to take that step of refusing Caesar in order to affirm the Prince of Peace's ultimate claim on their lives. All these allies discovered how difficult it was to take an individual stand for conscience. Although the LFOR supported its small cohort of war tax resisters, it never constituted an alternative Christian community in which goods and risks could be shared and the goal of individual financial security jettisoned. George and Jean served as that community for each other, risking the wrath of the IRS together, as a mature couple whose children were grown. Another couple, LFOR steering committee member Gloria O'Neil and her husband Art, did the same, finding a creative way to continue practicing resistance after the IRS garnisheed Art's wages for nonpayment of taxes. In 1983, they donated $14,000—half their taxable income for the previous year—"to peace-related organizations," lowering their revenue to a point where they did not owe taxes.[16]

Most unmarried members of the LFOR found war tax resistance impossible to maintain for more than a few years in the absence of broader community support. Eileen Blanton agreed with George and Jean that taxation by the state was necessary as "a way of distributing wealth and taking responsibility for everything." As she worked with Jean Edwards preparing pamphlets for the Louisville Fellowship's annual Tax Day protest at the post office, however, Blanton's conscience convicted her. The pamphlets laid out "how much of our dollar is spent for building weapons and paying for the military and what I thought of as destruction." "And," she decided, "I just couldn't in conscience do that." For years, Blanton's income was low enough that she didn't owe any taxes, but by 1983 her salary had grown and she decided to practice resistance. Whereas George

15. Edwards, "Biblical and Contemporary Aspects of War Tax Resistance," 119–20.
16. Steering committee minutes, March 26, 1984, LFOR.

and Jean had notified the government of their action by means of a letter attached to their tax return, Blanton employed another strategy that was common at the time: claiming more dependents than the number to which she was legally entitled. The theory behind this practice was typically that the life and well-being of all persons depended on the willingness of citizens of democratic countries to stop paying for the weapons that could annihilate life on earth. Blanton claimed ten dependents, donating the money she withheld from the government to peace and justice organizations including the Fellowship of Reconciliation.[17] After two years the IRS caught on, auditing Blanton in 1985.[18] She forestalled legal action against her for fraud by setting up a payment plan for the unpaid taxes, interest, and penalties. Although she concluded that tax resistance had been "a great way for me to figure out what I did believe and didn't believe," Blanton remained sad that she had not been able to resolve the conflicting calls of citizenship and conscience, "to feel like a responsible citizen" and also to "voice my objection financially."[19]

Pat Geier, another Catholic member of the Fellowship's steering committee, took up where Blanton left off, starting to withhold war taxes in 1985.[20] Several factors motivated Geier. First among them was the example of George and Jean: she considered George "a spiritual father" as well as "a saint and a prophet," and "adored" Jean even as she became "furious" with her at times for her "relentlessness" in pursuing her activist objectives.[21] Both, she wrote them in 1984, "continue to be for me great sources of strength and witness to the Gospel of Jesus."[22] Geier's work with the Edwardses and the LFOR had what she later called a "conscientizing" effect, which deepened as she studied history and learned of the example of the Austrian Catholic Franz Jägerstätter, beheaded for refusing to fight for the Third Reich.[23] Reading the story of Jägerstätter, who is remembered

17. Blanton interview.
18. Steering committee Minutes, April 22, 1985, LFOR.
19. Blanton interview.
20. Steering committee minutes, April 22, 1985, LFOR.
21. Pat Geier interview, December 21, 2005.
22. Pat Geier letter to George and Jean Edwards, February 6, 1984, Jean Edwards papers.
23. Pat Geier interview, February 27, 2007. "Conscientization," or coming to consciousness, is a term used in liberation theology; it comes from Freire's *Pedagogy of the Oppressed*. The book about Jägerstätter that made such an impression on Geier was Zahn, *In Solitary Witness*.

as having often repeated the words, "I cannot turn the responsibility [for my actions] over to the Führer," Geier asked herself, "What would I have done if I had been a German Catholic?"[24] By the mid-1980s, Geier saw the United States' support for dictatorships in Central America as the central moral issue of her own time; she needed to take a stand. For Geier, God's call to reconciliation, which she tried to live through her church and through the FOR, was "a call to walk with, to be with, to suffer with, to take on the risks with, those in the world who are the most vulnerable, the most marginalized, the most unjustly treated, the most oppressed."[25] Despite that commitment, Geier gave up war tax resistance after a couple of years, having decided "pretty quickly" that "being sole support of myself," she would not be able "to continue to exist economically . . . short of joining a religious community." As a younger woman Geier had considered taking religious vows but had gone into secular social work instead. She later reflected that war tax resistance in the United States, with its individualist ethos, was an "isolating thing," because "unless you live in a [religious] community, your economics really only affect you. And that's kind of a hard thing to establish any community around."[26]

Community did gather around war tax resisters in times of crisis. When the IRS seized resister Jerry Hardt's farm in Salyersville, Kentucky, in the spring of 1984, the LFOR helped raise funds to buy the land, placing it in trust so that Hardt could continue living there without holding title. Hardt's supporters, including George and Jean Edwards and other Fellowship activists, marched together to the county courthouse to hold a worship service before the auction, at which the land trust placed the sole bid.[27] The LFOR continued to use their annual Tax Day protests to educate citizens and encourage them to take even a symbolic stand against military spending. Fellowship members handed out leaflets bearing a "pie chart" depiction of the federal budget, encouraging people to take actions that were unlikely to have severe consequences: withholding a nominal amount like $10.00, or refusing to pay the excise tax, earmarked

24. Zahn, *In Solitary Witness*, 105.
25. Geier interview, December 21, 2005.
26. Ibid., February 27, 2007.
27. Steering committee Minutes, May 28, 1984, LFOR. Besides Hardt, the IRS seized property belonging to about two dozen households for nonpayment of war taxes in the 1980s, after which the number of seizures dropped off: War Resisters League, "IRS Seizure and Court Actions against War Tax Resisters."

for military spending, on long-distance telephone service.[28] Some resisters, like Pat Geier, continued to withhold the long-distance tax, even after resuming payment of their full income tax bill, with no negative repercussions.[29] They had a small number of allies across the country: that year, the National War Tax Resistance Coordinating Committee estimated that between ten and twenty thousand citizens refused to pay "some or all of their federal income taxes" as a protest against military spending. "Thousands more" withheld the federal excise tax on long-distance telephone calls, and it was impossible to know how many deliberately kept their income below the taxable level in order not to pay for war.[30] Still others, like George's acquaintance E. Glenn Hinson, a faculty member at Southern Baptist Theological Seminary and the first editor of the *Baptist Peacemaker* magazine, sympathized with war tax resistance without following suit. As Hinson wrote the Edwardses in 1985, "I admire you both for withholding some of your tax payments because so much of it is going for military purposes. I wish I had the courage to do the same."[31] That year's protest made a clear connection between "the money going for weapons" and "the suffering which people are enduring": it began at the unemployment office with a combination rally and food drive, collecting cans of food for the Presbyterian Community Center's pantry.[32]

For George and Jean, war tax resistance undergirded the other forms of civil disobedience in which they and their LFOR allies engaged in the 1980s, publicizing and disrupting military affairs: the sanctuary movement, and the Pledge of Resistance, founded to prevent an American invasion of Nicaragua. The sanctuary movement started in the Southwestern United States in the early 1980s as churches became aware that increasing numbers of undocumented Central American refugees, most of them from Guatemala and El Salvador, were crossing the desert to flee U.S.-sponsored civil wars in their homelands. Many died along

28. The pie chart was reproduced in LFOR's April newsletter every year. The excise tax on long-distance telephone service was instituted in 1898 to help fund the Spanish-American War and has been repealed and reintroduced several times since then. It was last repealed in 2006. "U.S. to Repeal Long-Distance Phone Tax," *New York Times*, May 25, 2006.

29. Geier interview, February 27, 2007; Steering committee minutes, January 28, 1991, LFOR.

30. "War Tax Resistance Increasing," *Fellowship*, April/May 1985.

31. E. Glenn Hinson letter to George and Jean Edwards, April 19, 1985, Jean Edwards papers.

32. Steering committee minutes, March 25, 1985, LFOR.

the way. Most of those who made it to the United States were denied asylum because of the United States' support for the dictatorships that ruled their homelands, while those fleeing ideological opponents like Nicaragua were typically accepted.[33] In response, what its members called a "new underground railroad" spread throughout the country, eventually including several hundred churches and thousands of individual supporters and assisting organizations. Modeled on the Christian dissident tradition of smuggling enslaved persons out of the South before the Civil War, that railroad was "underground" because it was illegal: the right to practice one's faith by providing sanctuary was not recognized in U.S. law. Christians in the movement grounded their actions in a different authority, manifested in the biblical warrant for "cities of refuge," the historic status of churches as safe havens for fugitives, and the abolitionist movement.[34]

The sanctuary movement gave Christians an opportunity to combine what church tradition calls the corporal works of mercy, such as feeding the hungry, giving drink to the thirsty, and harboring the stranger, with the spiritual works of mercy like converting sinners, instructing the ignorant, and intercessory prayer. Sanctuary workers hoped not only to provide direct material help to those in need, but also to expose the brutality of the Central American civil wars in which the United States government had implicated its citizens, and of which many Americans remained ignorant. The leader of the movement in Louisville was Jim Flynn, the Catholic priest Jean had recruited for the LFOR as they stood side by side bound by a paper chain at the 1981 Hiroshima remembrance. Flynn, who had been ordained in 1955, a few years before the Second Vatican Council, was fond of citing a comment that he remembered hearing biblical scholar John Dominic Crossan make in the 1960s: "Sacraments are signs and symbols—not substitutes for social justice." Flynn remembered years later that Crossan's "sibilant statement" helped deepen his understanding that "my actions for justice in the streets were extensions of my spirituality at the altar and the pulpit."[35]

33. Crittenden, *Sanctuary*, 347, 358, 368–69.

34. "Cities of refuge" are mentioned in Numbers 35:11–12; Crittenden, *Sanctuary*, 62, 347. The stories of sanctuary workers in the Southwest are told in Otter and Pine, *The Sanctuary Experience*.

35. James Flynn, "50th Anniversary Reflections on My Life," unpublished address to St. Mary's Catholic Church, Park City, UT, April 10, 2005, in author's possession. On the origins and development of the theory and practice of liberation theology, see

Together with another priest, Richard F. Fowler, Flynn founded Church of the Epiphany in the eastern reaches of Jefferson County in 1971, to be a parish dedicated to both liturgical innovation and social justice. By 1981, the area around Epiphany was becoming more suburbanized, the church's distinctive commitment to social justice was wavering, and Flynn sought a new call. He went on retreat to Gethsemane Abbey in Bardstown, Kentucky, home of the monk Thomas Merton, who wrote extensively about the place of nonviolence in the Christian life before his accidental death in 1968. Flynn considered joining friends who were working in Central America, but he spoke no Spanish and wanted to serve God in the city where he had lived his whole life. Reading Merton's *Conjectures of a Guilty Bystander*, Flynn started to pray to him: "Help me decide what I'm going to do." Convinced that he was not called to return to a suburban parish, Flynn stayed in prayer "a long time," until "it all became clear to me that Central America has to be where I want to focus my concerns." A month later Flynn was called to St. William's, an urban church with a tradition of peace and justice ministries.[36]

He and his congregation were quickly challenged to work with the burgeoning sanctuary movement when a fellow American priest who had been working in El Salvador arrived in Louisville with three of his parishioners; all had fled in fear for their lives. As they told their story at St. William's, Flynn remembered, "There wasn't a dry eye in the place... I was wondering how all this was going to translate and now here it was." St. William's declared itself a sanctuary parish on the feast of Pentecost 1983. They were open about their new commitment, notifying both the Immigration and Naturalization Service (INS) and their archbishop that they intended to break the law that prohibited helping undocumented immigrants cross the U.S. border. As Flynn remembered, "We knew that we were in civil disobedience, that if [the government] wanted to they could come and arrest any of us," but they also knew that any such government action would carry its own consequences, as "we had a lot of church support." As for Archbishop Thomas Kelly, Flynn understood that he "had to retain some sort of distance, officially," but the priest believed he had received his superior's tacit permission to "do what you have to do." No other church in Louisville joined St. William's in offering sanctuary on its premises, but its sanctuary ministry received logistical and

---

Smith, *The Emergence of Liberation Theology*.

36. James Flynn interview, 17–18, 21–22.

prayer support from area churches including George and Jean's Central Presbyterian and Epiphany, the parish Jim Flynn had cofounded, where Pat Geier sat on the Social Responsibility Committee.[37] LFOR cofounders A. C. and V. G. Cuppy, who had moved to Kansas City, Kansas, in 1981, got involved in the movement there, writing Jean with the news that "their home had been declared a sanctuary in connection with the Mennonite congregation."[38] Louisville Seminary students and faculty also publicly declared their support for the movement's goal of ending U.S. military aid to El Salvador and gaining refugee status for all persons fleeing oppression in their home countries.[39]

The first refugees seeking sanctuary landed at St. William's just before Christmas 1983: their arrival was announced at an ecumenical worship service marking the third anniversary of the sexual assault and murder in El Salvador of Catholic churchwomen Ita Ford, Maura Clark, Dorothy Kazel, and Jean Donovan. That evening's liturgy included a mock trial of the four women, who were found "guilty of the Gospel" and sentenced to death, and a reminder from Patricia Ramser, a member of both St. William's and the LFOR, that Ford, Clark, Kazel, and Donovan had been "people like us, scared as we are." Jean Edwards read a roll call of martyrs, holding a clenched fist aloft as the congregation affirmed that the churchwomen and martyred Archbishop Oscar Romero of El Salvador were "Presente!" in their midst. Ramser told the congregation that the family—a toddler and, appropriately for the season, expectant parents—would be there in a few days. As Ramser cried, "We're going to have a family! We're all going to be parents!" the crowd of about one hundred cheered. Speaking to a journalist, LFOR member Sheila Pyle, an Episcopalian, summed up the reason for the worship service and the sanctuary movement: "What do we do to deal with this suffering? The Lord said: 'Love your enemies. Do good to those who hate you. Pray for those who curse you.'"[40]

Many of those prayers would have been uttered for the government officials who made and enforced immigration laws. As the sanctuary movement sought to pressure the U.S. government into changing its interventionist course in Central America, many of its leaders came under

37. "Timeline," Parish Council Minutes, April 23, 1987, and January 23, 1986, CE.

38. Steering committee minutes, 25 March, 1985, LFOR.

39. "Minutes of the Faculty," May 26, 1983, LPTS.

40. "Illegal Refugees to Find Sanctuary in Louisville," *Courier-Journal*, December 3, 1983. The photograph of Jean Edwards reading the roll call accompanies this story.

surveillance. Jim Flynn was one of them. In November 1985, while he was in El Paso studying Spanish, his room in the rectory he shared with five other men was ransacked. Leaving no sign of forced entry, the intruders sent what Flynn interpreted as a clear message. The few dollars on his desk were left untouched, while his books on liberation theology and the slides he used in presentations about Central America were thrown on the floor. A letter that he had placed deep in his files, about refugees he was planning to help across the border, was pulled out and left on his desk, in Flynn's opinion, "to let me know they knew what was going on." Flynn suspected the INS or CIA was responsible, but the burglary was never solved.[41] By early 1986 about three dozen break-ins had been committed in a dozen cities against the offices of groups opposed to U.S. government actions in Central America. None of the break-ins was ever solved, and all government agencies denied any involvement.[42] Unlike sanctuary workers in Texas and New Mexico who were convicted in the mid-1980s of illegally transporting and concealing undocumented aliens, no one in the Louisville sanctuary movement was ever indicted.[43] Jim Flynn later estimated that St. William's housed fifty to seventy-five refugees over the course of about a decade.[44] Most stayed only a short while before moving on, some to the northern United States and many to Canada, where Guatemalans and Salvadorans fleeing their country's civil wars could apply for refugee status.[45]

In the midst of his and Jean's sanctuary work, George retired from Louisville Seminary. His decision to retire as soon as he turned sixty-five, rather than continuing to teach as many academics did, was directly tied to his and Jean's civil disobedience. Not long after George and Jean began tax resistance, the seminary's business administrators informed George that the IRS would garnishee his salary if he did not sign forms to authorize withholding. George refused to sign, causing the seminary

41. Flynn interview, 21–22.
42. Crittenden, *Sanctuary*, 302.
43. The story of the trials in the Southwest is told in Crittenden, *Sanctuary*.
44. Flynn interview, 23.
45. Canada became less hospitable after the US Immigration and Reform Control Act of 1986 prescribed the deportation of any immigrants who could not prove they had entered the United States before 1982. In response to the approximately six thousand undocumented immigrants who gathered in border towns in early 1987, Canada stopped giving temporary work permits to individuals claiming refugee status, requiring them to wait on the US side of the border while their claims were reviewed. Crittenden, *Sanctuary*, 348.

comptroller, Marty Marsh, "to reply tearfully that 'she was only trying to do her job,'" and George later to reflect, "I regret putting her to this embarrassment."[46] The government followed up by auditing Jean and George in 1985. As the couple later wrote in the LFOR newsletter, the auditor who came to their home "mentioned that she [was] a loyal member of the United Methodist Church and was surprised that a minister would violate the law."[47] George and Jean briefly went over the reasons for their civil disobedience, but in the end, the auditor and the tax resisters retained their differing beliefs about the extent to which Christians must comply with secular law. Believing that his tax resistance "was a problem" for the seminary's "administrative people" and "embarrassed the institution," George retired as soon as he could draw his pension.[48] After the early 1980s, he and Jean never voluntarily paid war taxes: "from time to time," as he remembered, the IRS simply took money from their bank account.[49] Their witness was costly, as the amount withdrawn by the IRS included penalties for nonpayment in addition to the original tax liability.

Until his retirement, George had continued to be a beloved teacher known for his exacting standards and his compassion for students, and for initiating discussions others would not. Mark Baridon, who entered the seminary in the autumn of 1984, George's last year of teaching, later remembered, "He was hard! He was very hard." Although George "would never let anybody fail if they really tried," students "had to know the material very well." George taught his students, in Baridon's words, "how to think, and formulate our thoughts," so that they could speak "out of a thoughtful Christian perspective," even when they focused on questions "that George didn't particularly think were that important," such as whether or not Jesus had been married.[50] Another student, William Robertson, said of George in 1985 that "he teaches with a great deal of grace, and he is willing to slow down and take time with us."[51] Teaching with grace did not mean avoiding controversy. When Baridon took George's ethics course, he was surprised to find that his professor used a slide show from a Unitarian Universalist curriculum, "About Your Sexuality," in a

46. George R. Edwards letter to Nutt, 11.
47. Newsletter, April 1985, LFOR.
48. George and Jean Edwards interview with K'Meyer, April 23, 1996, 50.
49. George R. Edwards letter to Nutt, 11.
50. Baridon interview.
51. Clarence Matthews, "Edwards Retiring from Seminary—But Not from Peace Work," *Louisville Times*, April 27, 1985.

discussion of sexual morality. The slides depicted volunteer adult couples in a variety of intimate embraces; as Baridon later said, "You could have heard a pin drop in the room" as the pictures flashed across the screen. George's stated reason for showing the slides was pastoral, as he realized, according to Baridon, "that many of his students [preparing for ordination] had no imagination when it came to such things, and they wouldn't know what people were talking about when they came to the office!" George was direct in other ways: as Baridon remembered, "He wasn't afraid to talk back to other faculty, which was always a delight in the cafeteria." When another professor claimed, as Baridon remembered, "that God speaks through the General Assembly of the church, George started yelling, 'Don't ever tell my students that! I've seen some of the damnedest decisions come out of this General Assembly!'" More than twenty years later, Baridon chuckled, "It was hilarious."[52]

Although George was his professor, Baridon had met Jean first when she visited campus to borrow a crib the seminary kept in storage for a family visit. When Baridon, helping Jean move the crib, mentioned that he had just graduated from the University of North Carolina at Greensboro, Jean exclaimed, "We used to live in Durham! You'll have to come over for dinner!" Enjoying the Edwardses' hospitality, Baridon "just really was attracted to their style of doing things, and their justice orientation," and he began attending Central Presbyterian Church at their invitation. Other students also knew and loved Jean: on one occasion a seminarian challenged George in class, "How has Jean lived with you all these years?" Whether or not the question was asked in jest, Baridon remembered George answering it seriously: "Every day, I find something new I can appreciate about her. That's how you keep any relationship going." "You don't think of him as sappy," his former student commented, "but he almost was sappy talking about Jean . . . Something shifted in him when he would talk about her."[53]

George's retirement party reflected the playful relationship he enjoyed with his students. As a teacher given to saying, "Fasten your seatbelts" at the beginning of a particularly challenging class, George found himself in the seminary cafeteria fastened by his students into a chair with a seatbelt. Playing on George's habit of saying that the resurrection was not a "photographable event," students presented him with a photo

---

52. Baridon interview.
53. Ibid.

album they had made. One "snapshot" was of Jesus emerging from the tomb, while another depicted "Jesus and some woman in a wedding dress to show that he was married." George responded with mock regret, "Well, if I'd had this during my years of teaching ministry, think of the impact it could have had."[54] His seminary colleague, Louis B. Weeks, praised George's sense of humor, telling a reporter that "he is able to laugh at himself and institutions, while at the same time addressing issues of peace and justice." Looking back on his arrests in civil rights actions of the 1960s, George told the same journalist that he had "no regrets": he and Jean would continue to use war tax resistance and other means to witness to their conviction that "it's a sin, as far as we are concerned, to build one nuclear weapon."[55] In George and Jean's honor, friends endowed the annual "Edwards Peacemaking Lecture" at Louisville Seminary, on the theme of "the biblical concept of *shalom*, the wholeness and unity which God desires for all creation." Richard Deats, an employee of the national Fellowship of Reconciliation whom the Edwardses had known for decades, gave the first lecture on January 20, 1986, the first national observance of Martin Luther King Jr.'s birthday.[56]

In the tradition of those like King who had used civil disobedience for prophetic purposes, George and Jean continued their illegal witness after retirement, adding membership in the Pledge of Resistance to their other commitments. The Pledge began in late 1983 as a promise to engage in acts of civil disobedience in the event of an American invasion of Nicaragua. The United States had long supported the Somoza dictatorship overthrown by the socialist Sandinista revolutionary movement in 1979. When the new Nicaraguan government decided to supply small arms to revolutionaries in neighboring El Salvador during the fall of 1980, that move gave the Reagan administration the initial justification it needed to fund, train, and supply Nicaraguan counterrevolutionary forces, known as contras. The U.S. government in the Reagan years argued that the region was of vital importance to Americans' security, framing its military actions in Central America in the language of self-defense. "If we cannot defend ourselves there," Reagan declared in the spring of 1983, "we cannot expect to prevail elsewhere. Our credibility would collapse, our alliances would crumble, and the safety of our homeland would be put

---

54. Ibid.
55. Matthews, "Edwards Retiring from Seminary—But Not from Peace Work."
56. Program, "The Edwards Peacemaking Lecture," 1986, Jean Edwards papers.

in jeopardy."[57] The U.S. invasion of Grenada that October was an implicit warning to both the Sandinista government and their supporters in the United States that Nicaragua could receive the same treatment.

In response, peace workers organized the Pledge of Resistance at a meeting held eight days after the invasion of Grenada.[58] The Pledge brought together Catholics, mainline Protestants, and evangelicals like Jim Wallis, founder of *Sojourners* magazine, to pressure the U.S. government to stop aiding the contras, and to commit themselves to oppose an American invasion of Nicaragua by nonviolent means. Possible actions included traveling to Nicaragua "to stand unarmed as a loving barrier in the path of any attempted invasion, sharing the danger posed to the Nicaraguan people"; occupying congressional offices "in a nonviolent prayerful presence" until such an invasion ended; and organizing "demonstrations of public opposition to any invasion attempt."[59] By December 1984, over forty thousand people across the United States had signed the Pledge; *Sojourners* sent copies of their forms to the State Department. By June 1986 the number of signatories had doubled, and there were Pledge groups in more than three hundred cities in the United States.[60]

Louisville was one. Its Pledge group was one of the more theologically and politically inclusive movements in which the LFOR participated. Catholics were particularly likely to get involved because of the martyrdom of Archbishop Romero and the four American churchwomen serving in El Salvador, but many other people of faith joined them along with, in the words of Catholic LFOR activist David Horvath, "atheists and communists and the whole fleet."[61] The Pledge held periodic demonstrations in Louisville, bringing its activities to a head with a sit-in at the offices of U.S. Senators Mitch McConnell and Wendell Ford on June 12, 1985. That day, as Congress prepared to vote on aid to Nicaraguan contras, Pledge chapters across the country staged protests and sit-ins to pressure elected representatives not to renew their support; by the end of the day over nine hundred demonstrators had been arrested. In a reprise

57. Reagan, "Address before a Joint Session of Congress on Central America."

58. For a history of the Pledge (originally called "A Promise of Resistance"), see Smith, *Resisting Reagan*, 78–86.

59. "A Promise of Resistance," *Fellowship*, December 1983.

60. Smith, *Resisting Reagan*, 83; Vicki Kemper, "We Will Do What We Promise: Resistance Pledge Delivered to State Department," *Sojourners*, February 1985. By 1986, the Pledge movement had published a guide for members: Butigan et al., *¡Basta!*

61. Horvath interview.

of the Marble Hill occupation a decade earlier, the seventy-five people who occupied McConnell's and Ford's offices included George Edwards, supported by Jean outside. George summed up the group's intentions in four simple words, captured by a reporter: "We are not moving." Another elaborated, "We've tried all channels—marching, singing, calling, writing letters and holding vigils at the Federal Building. But we never got a positive response. Now it's time for direct action."[62] George was among the twenty-three protestors arrested and hustled out by police when they refused to leave; six more received citations for trespassing before they left on their own. Despite the activists' efforts, the aid was authorized in the amount of $27 million over nine months.[63]

The occupiers hoped to use their trial a few months later as an opportunity to witness to their beliefs and possibly influence more citizens to call for a change in government policy. The accused and their dozens of supporters created a festive mood at the courthouse on the morning of the trial: supporters set up a café on the sidewalk outside the courthouse to serve dishes like "CIA grits," improvised for the occasion.[64] The defendants had prepared briefs stating that they had been obliged to speak out as "people of faith" whose consciences had been aroused by "continuing injustices and violence in Nicaragua supported by their elected representatives." They further believed that after the trials of Nazi officials at Nuremberg, international law required private citizens to take action to prevent their government from committing crimes against humanity. The prosecution dismissed those claims, saying that the Nuremberg defense applied only to "public officials" and stating that when religious beliefs are "translated into conduct," the government is entitled to impose "reasonable" regulations on that conduct. Both sides' arguments became moot when the prosecution dropped all charges (originally trespassing but later changed, because of a legal nuance, to disorderly conduct). Assistant U.S. Attorney C. Cleveland Gambill commented, in a reporter's paraphrase,

62. "Foes of Aid to Nicaraguan Rebels Descend on Offices of Lawmakers," *Louisville Courier-Journal*, June 13, 1985.

63. "House Votes to Aid Contras," *Washington Post*, June 13, 1985. That amount constituted only a portion of the U.S. funding received by the contras. The CIA furnished the largest proportion, and a smaller amount came from the proceeds of the secret sale of arms to Iran. See Kornbluh, *Nicaragua*, and Kornbluh and Byrne, *The Iran Contral Scandal*.

64. "Federal Charges against 29 Arrested in Nicaragua Protest Are Dropped," *Louisville Courier-Journal*, November 20, 1985; George and Jean Edwards interview with K'Meyer, June 18, 1996, 28.

that the charges had been dropped "to save both sides the time and expense of trying the case," while acknowledging "that the government might have difficulty proving the identity of each of the twenty-nine people arrested in June."[65] George Edwards later offered a succinct assessment of the prosecution's dilemma. "Because there were so many of us, and we were all middle-class people, we weren't hoodlums," the prosecutors "were in an impossible political position: if they really laid it on us, they would be in more political trouble than they felt like they really wanted to fool with."[66] Dropping the charges also quashed the defendants' plan to call as a witness Reed Brody, a former assistant attorney general in New York whose evidence of thirty-seven contra attacks on civilians in Nicaragua had been substantiated by *The New York Times*.[67] As had been the case with the Marble Hill occupation a few years earlier, the lack of a trial deprived the protestors of a forum in which to air their beliefs.

In the midst of the LFOR's radical actions in the 1980s, it continued to cooperate with the Council on Peacemaking and Religion on issues where the two groups saw eye to eye. For their annual Hiroshima Day remembrance in 1984, in the aftermath of the Euromissiles' deployment, they put together a piece of street theater that connected the international threat with their home city.[68] LFOR activists had learned that trains regularly carried ten-ton cylinders of uranium hexafluoride, a radioactive material used to make nuclear weapons, through the city from Paducah in western Kentucky to plants in Tennessee and Ohio. The cylinders, nicknamed "Paducah Tigers," would sit, waiting to be transferred from one train to another, in the railroad yard across the street from Jim Flynn's St. William's Catholic Church. The yard was located in a predominantly African-American neighborhood, leading Jean later to say succinctly that if any of the deadly substance had leaked out of its containers, "they'd be the ones to get it."[69]

The Hiroshima Day remembrance began at 6:30 a.m. outside the Federal Building in downtown Louisville, with seventy-five demonstrators singing "We want an end to war right now" as the American flag was raised over the building. Activists handed out flyers reading, "In

65. "Federal Charges against 29 Arrested in Nicaragua Protest Are Dropped."

66. George and Jean Edwards interview with K'Meyer, June 18, 1996, 28.

67. "Federal Charges against 29 Arrested in Nicaragua Protest Are Dropped." Brody's findings were published as Brody, *Contra Terror in Nicaragua*.

68. George and Jean Edwards interview with K'Meyer, April 23, 1996, Tape 1, 40.

69. Ibid., June 18, 1996, 36.

"Praying for Peace and Paying for War Are Inconsistent"

every war there's a Hiroshima waiting to happen" while George Edwards proclaimed, "We commemorate this day because of the uselessness of this weapon, the crime against humanity and the very, very, very damaging precedent which was set by our own government on August the 6th, 1945." George explained the danger the Paducah Tigers posed to Louisville before the crowd turned to follow Terry Mewborn (later Weiss) of the Council on Peacemaking and Religion and her seven-year-old son, Noah, the several blocks to the railroad yard at Thirteenth and Kentucky Streets, across from St. William's Church.[70] At the yard, the demonstrators acted out their country's blindness to the dangers of nuclear weapons. A mock bomb lay on top of a coffin guarded by pallbearers and "Ronald Reagan"—Sister Ann Hardman of the Sisters of Charity of Nazareth, dressed in black and wearing a rubber Reagan mask. Several demonstrators blindfolded themselves for the march back to the federal building behind "Reagan," who commented that "he" felt "very powerful" because those following were "blindfolded and don't know what's going on."[71] As the marchers returned to the federal building, they joined fellow activists who "had been having a prayer service" at the building in their absence, swelling the crowd's numbers to over one hundred. The blindfolded demonstrators listened to excerpts from a description of the bombing of Hiroshima by Thomas Merton. At pauses in the readings, the blindfolded activists repeated in unison, "We do not see the harm." At 8:15 a.m., the time at which the bomb had been dropped on Hiroshima, they removed their blindfolds and declared together, "Today we see the harm. Today we know Hiroshima waits in every war . . . Today we pray, no more Hiroshimas."[72] As the mock bomb was dismantled and small paper cranes—a Japanese symbol of the hope for peace—attached to helium balloons floated into the air, "Reagan" tried to convince the newly enlightened protestors to put their blindfolds back on. As he proclaimed, "MX [missile] is a Peacekeeper," the crowd retorted, "You've gotta be kidding," refusing to put their blindfolds back on.[73] As had happened with their 1978 remembrance, the LFOR made some changes after the 1984 demonstration because of ecological concerns. Although, as Jean later remembered, the balloons made a "very beautiful" stream rising out of

70. "Marchers Commemorate Hiroshima Bombing," *Louisville Courier-Journal*, August 7, 1984.
71. Ibid.
72. Ibid.
73. Ibid.; George and Jean Edwards interview with K'Meyer, June 18, 1996, 38.

the coffin into the sky, "About that time, we decided we couldn't do balloons anymore because we got the word that it's destructive for the birds," who would eat the deflated props.[74]

Although George and Jean's peace witness took a more radical turn in retirement, the pattern of their life together changed very little, as they continued to live their intertwined vocations in partnership with each other. George continued to teach and provide pastoral care on an informal basis, often helping his former students with their ministries. When Mark Baridon served as a summer student chaplain at Westminster Terrace, a nursing home in Louisville, George accompanied him to serve communion to those who couldn't attend church, as Baridon was not yet licensed to do so. Baridon remembered George spending "so much time at the bedside," not serving communion "cafeteria style" but taking time to "get to know the person, talk to them, pray with them." At the time, Baridon was impressed with George's ability to "speak out in the public arena and be just as kind and peace-loving to somebody who's ill and maybe ready to die, and wants communion."[75] Both George and Jean taught Baridon about striving to live peacefully in everyday life. As he recalled, "sometimes our opponents may be aggravating," but "George and Jean had a wonderful way of defusing that, many times, and being kind to people back, whereas I'd just come from college, thinking it was OK to yell at people." George's outbursts in the seminary cafeteria notwithstanding, Baridon reflected, he and Jean "showed me a little better way, a little more productive way of handling myself." Baridon witnessed that better way during hymn-sings at the nursing home: "If [George] could pick a hymn it would always be 'Let There Be Peace on Earth,'" which he would dedicate "to somebody who had argued with him about peace stuff" as a way to defuse tension. "He'd say, 'I'd like to dedicate this to this sister over here, with whom I've had many good discussions,' and they would both laugh, and they would sing 'Let There Be Peace on Earth.'"[76]

Mark also saw George's pastoral care at work in his last two years in seminary when, as an intern at Central Presbyterian Church, part of his job was "outreach to the GLBT community" in the neighborhood. George would occasionally accompany him to meetings of a gay and lesbian student group at the University of Louisville a few blocks away, to

---

74. George and Jean Edwards interview with K'Meyer, June 18, 1996, 38.
75. Baridon interview.
76. Ibid.

make presentations on "The Bible and Sexuality." Baridon remembered those talks having great "impact" on "young, eighteen-year-old, nineteen-year-old kids that had never heard that view, that God would accept them." "George was so affirming to those people," Baridon recalled, without "belittling the views they were raised with," but telling them, "'No, really, you are accepted by God and God loves you.'"[77] George and Jean acted on their shared convictions in this area by working on the campaign for civil rights for gay and lesbian residents of Louisville. It began in 1986, as the Greater Louisville Human Rights Coalition successfully lobbied the county Human Relations Commission to endorse the idea of including sexual orientation in local civil rights ordinances. That endorsement was the beginning of a struggle by groups including the LFOR that, in 1999, produced local legislation guaranteeing equal access to employment, housing, and public accommodations for all persons regardless of sexual orientation.[78]

George and Jean's concern for the struggles many lesbians and gay men faced made their home a haven for Tony Hewitt, an African-American man with HIV who was estranged from his family and for whom they served as surrogate parents in the late 1980s. Hewitt accompanied the Edwardses in 1989 when they accepted an opportunity to spend a year working full time for the national FOR in New York as the organization planned its seventy-fifth anniversary celebration for the following year. Witnessing for peace was already a full-time job for Jean: a couple of years earlier, George had called her a "peace work professional" who worked for the LFOR without pay "about twelve hours a day, seven days a week." He noted, "If George wakes up at 2 a.m. and Jean is not in the bed, he knows she is at one of two places: at her typewriter updating the FOR mailing list, or down at the copy shop taking advantage of after midnight bargain prices."[79] In the year that Jean and George lived on the third floor of Shadowcliff, the house that serves as national FOR headquarters in Nyack, New York, both worked full time for the Fellowship as they accompanied Tony Hewitt through his final months of life. Among Jean's projects was to promote the new documentary *Weapons of the Spirit*, a

77. Baridon interview.

78. Grise-Owens et al., "Organizing for Change." The LFOR first endorsed and offered financial support to the fairness movement in 1990; steering committee minutes, March 26, 1990, LFOR.

79. George Edwards, "Some unedited paragraphs about Jean Maney Edwards," unpublished typescript, September 24, 1987, Jean Edwards papers.

French-American coproduction about the village of Le Chambon-sur-Lignon, France, whose residents, supported by the international Fellowship of Reconciliation, sheltered thousands of Jews during the Second World War as a witness to their once persecuted Huguenot faith.[80] George took care of Shadowcliff's yard and also created "a large movable display with photographs of FOR leaders (past and present)" for the anniversary celebration, while Tony produced a documentary video for the FOR and volunteered as an art teacher to children at the local community center.[81] When Tony died a few months into their time there, Jean and George were with him, and condolence wishes from Fellowship friends acknowledged the depth of their loss, one among the many younger people they had taken into their hearts and home over the years.[82]

At Shadowcliff, Jean, George, and Tony had watched with much of the world as East German citizens tore down the Berlin Wall in November 1989. The next April, the LFOR joined the chorus of calls for a "peace dividend" to be redirected from the military budget to domestic social programs. There were demonstrable needs around the country. In 1990, 18 percent of American children lived in poverty, with staggering racial disparities: just over 10 percent of white children were poor, compared to almost 40 percent of black and Native American children.[83] The number of homeless persons in shelters and on the streets in 1990 was variously estimated at a quarter of a million by the Census Bureau to over half a million by social science researchers, and about one-quarter of all Americans went without health insurance at some time between 1990 and 1992.[84] The LFOR and its allies revised their campaigns to encourage war

---

80. Jean Edwards e-mail to Rhonda Mawhood Lee, July 3, 2011. The village's story is also told in Hallie, *Lest Innocent Blood Be Shed*.

81. Memories of George's work come from Jean Edwards e-mail to Lee, July 3, 2011; information about Tony's work comes from Joanna Schoettler (national FOR staff and council) condolence letter to "Family and Friends of Tony," March 8, 1990, Jean Edwards papers.

82. A condolence card to George and Jean signed by nineteen friends from the national FOR, and a Fathers' Day card from Tony Hewitt to George, are held in the Jean Edwards papers.

83. Lichter et al., "Race and Poverty," 9. The child poverty rate for the decade would peak at 23 percent during the 1993 recession; ibid., 8.

84. "U.S. Homeless Count Is Far Below Estimates," *New York Times*, April 12, 1991; "Health Insurance Coverage: Who Had a Lapse between 1990 and 1992?" The document studies lapses in health insurance lasting at least one month between February 1990 and September 1992.

"Praying for Peace and Paying for War Are Inconsistent"

tax resistance in light of the new international situation, asking in 1990, "If the Cold War is over, why do half your taxes *still* go to the military?"[85] The LFOR's appeal used a pair of quotes chosen from two different political camps. Martin Luther King's 1967 warning that "a nation that continues year after year to spend more money on military defense than on programs of social uplift is approaching spiritual death" was paired with Reagan secretary of state Alexander Haig's reported comment about peace advocates, "Let them march all they want so long as they continue to pay their taxes."[86] Acknowledging that "choosing not to pay the full amount of taxes that the IRS says you owe is against the law," the LFOR encouraged members and friends to ease in for the sake of conscience: "Withholding a small amount (under $100.00) may only result in receiving bills from the IRS for the tax and penalties for each day the amount goes unpaid. A disarmed and peaceful world is worth this risk."[87] George and Jean, as committed resisters, were members of a small group: the War Resisters League estimated that in 1991 at least five hundred American taxpayers refused to pay some or all of their taxes, causing $105,000 to be "redirected to alternative funds and other groups."[88]

Although some Americans allowed themselves to hope for a more peaceful foreign policy in the wake of the collapse of the Soviet bloc, the Persian Gulf War soon dashed those hopes. George and Jean responded as they had so many times before. A week after the beginning of Operation Desert Storm, George once again led a rally in front of Louisville's federal building, using a microphone to engage in a call-and-response chant with the crowd ("Whadda we want?" "*Peace!*" "When do we want it?" "*Now!*") as a small counter-rally carried signs urging, "Bomb Iraq."[89] The next day, four busloads of Louisvillians, including the Edwardses, traveled to the nation's capital as part of the seventy-five thousand protestors there, who joined millions around the world in raising their voices

---

85. *FORsooth*, March 1990, LFOR.

86. Ibid., April 1991, LFOR. King's comment is from "Beyond Vietnam." Haig is alleged to have made his comment after the June 1982 demonstration in New York City by more than a million supporters of a nuclear freeze. One member of LFOR, Mennonite David Brown Kinloch, remembered that the quote attributed to Haig reinforced his commitment to war tax resistance; David Brown Kinloch interview.

87. *FORsooth*, April 1991, LFOR.

88. War Resisters League, "History of War Tax Resistance."

89. "The Peace People," *Courier-Journal*, January 26, 1991.

against the use of military force to evict Iraq from Kuwait.[90] George returned to counseling possible conscientious objectors, including young men concerned that a draft might be reinstated, and soldiers stationed at Fort Knox, six of whom were among the couple of thousand members of the regular services and reserves who applied for CO status during the war.[91] Jean offered a compassionate assessment of the soldiers' predicament: "These are people who couldn't afford an education otherwise, who enlisted to get help. They found this was the only avenue society offered them."[92]

George's argument against this latest war was almost devoid of Christian language, a new development that may reflect the fact that, in the late twentieth century, he no longer assumed that much of his audience shared his commitment to Christian faith. Instead, he emphasized war's broader moral threat. Speaking to a reporter, he recalled a recent news story about the My Lai massacre in Vietnam: "There was a soldier narrating about how, by the time the attack began on defenseless civilians, he lost all control of himself. Killing just took command of his consciousness." Rejecting the idea that My Lai was an anomaly, George insisted, "The stories of people like that are really the stories of war." Neither the soldier in combat nor the civilian at home escaped the responsibility that came with unleashing its violence: "For a soldier to defend his actions by saying 'I was just carrying out orders' is an abandonment of responsibility. So automatic support of troops comes with its own dangers." Waging an air war, as in the Gulf, could be especially morally toxic, in George's view, as he remembered talking to a friend's mother during the Second World War. When he asked the older woman why she was happy her son was a bombardier, she replied, "He doesn't have to see the people that he kills." For all those reasons, George concluded, "All war is awful, but this war in the Gulf is unnecessary, cruel and immoral."[93] Jean's comments on the war had a characteristically hopeful tone. Noting that she and George "could never, ever support war," having lived their convictions against it since World War II, she remarked that "the peace movement has changed

90. "War Protestors Changing with Time," *Winchester [Kentucky] Sun*, January 28, 1991.

91. "The Peace People"; steering committee minutes, February 25, 1991. On conscientious objection among military personnel and civilians during the Persian Gulf War, see Chambers, "Conscientious Objectors," 44–45.

92. "The Peace People."

93. Ibid.

tremendously in that time. Now we feel we have a great deal of support." She concluded, "With this conflict, there's not even a moral issue involved . . . It's a fight for oil, and young people see that."[94]

In the wake of the Persian Gulf War, the LFOR protested the use of a long-standing Louisville festival to celebrate the quick American victory. Having learned that General Norman Schwarzkopf, commander of the victorious forces, had been invited to serve as the honorary grand marshal of the annual Pegasus Parade two days before the Kentucky Derby in May 1991, many members and friends of the LFOR chose to stay away. The LFOR organized a postcard campaign for individuals to inform the city government of their decision: headlined "It's a Horse Race, Not an Arms Race," the card's text lamented the parade's shift from "a 'people's event'" to a celebration of "military might." The LFOR also sponsored a half-page newspaper advertisement on the day of the parade, noting, "While we, too, celebrate the safe return of our troops, both the presence of military tanks and aircraft in the Pegasus Parade and General Norman Schwartzkopf [sic] being the grand marshal glorifies war and distorts what has traditionally been a celebration of spring, family, and friendship." The ad reiterated the Fellowship's constant warning: "A nation which seeks first war and violence as a means to resolve conflict is a nation which will repeat such actions in the world again."[95] As always, George and Jean and their allies were in the minority. A record crowd, estimated at three hundred thousand, gathered for the parade that year. Some had waited eight hours to catch a glimpse of Schwarzkopf and greet him with signs proclaiming "Gen. Schwarzkopf for President" and "Thanks for bringing our Dad Home Safe."[96] The peace activists who had requested permission to march in the parade in a group of one hundred were not present; they had been turned down for fear, as one LFOR ally reported, that their presence would get "a violent response" from the crowd.[97]

In the early 1990s, George and Jean renewed their efforts to address a longheld concern: involving African-American allies more closely with the local and national Fellowship of Reconciliation. They started among their circle of friends. Bob Cunningham of the Kentucky Alliance Against Racist and Political Repression—the organization Anne Braden

94. Ibid.
95. Steering committee minutes, April 22, 1991, LFOR.
96. "Parade Captivates a 4-Starstruck Crowd," *Courier-Journal*, May 3, 1991.
97. Coalition for Peace in the Middle East spokeswoman Jan Taylor, quoted in ibid.

had founded in the 1970s—became involved with the Fellowship around the time of the Persian Gulf War. He first joined LFOR's steering committee as a liaison to the Alliance, which until that time had been represented on the committee by Beverly Marmion, a white activist. Cunningham had been deeply involved with Progress in Education in the mid-1970s, so when he joined the LFOR's steering committee, he already knew George and Jean and other Fellowship members who had supported school desegregation. Cunningham felt an affinity with the Edwardses, whom he described as "movement people," but before the 1990s, he had felt that "international type issues" were "white folks' issues," "not ever understanding," as he later remembered, "that slavery itself was international." In the early 1990s Cunningham came to believe that until white pacifists and black racial justice activists understood that their concerns were linked, "neither of us would do too well."[98]

Cunningham reached a turning point when he attended the annual conference of the national Fellowship of Reconciliation in Colorado in the summer of 1992. Discussions of "the war budget" opened his eyes: "I began to say, 'Wait a minute. That is money that could be used by the poor, and who's more poor than black folk?'" The key factor drawing him into the Fellowship, however, was its connection to George and Jean. Cunningham remembered that he "always saw George and Jean at any of our rallies and demonstrations around anti-racism. So I knew that was part of their agenda also." Cunningham remembered that George and Jean "attracted me in so many ways. As husband and wife, as male and female," who seemed "ideal to me" when he realized how deeply they were committed to witnessing for peace. He looked to them as models: "It kind of made me feel that, 'This is what I want to be. This is how I want my life to be.'" Remembering those "precious people," Cunningham reflected that "if they had been members of something else, I probably would have gone into another organization other than the FOR."[99]

For all his admiration for the Edwardses, and his goodwill toward the Louisville Fellowship, Cunningham believed the organization could do more to reach out to African-Americans. He had what he gently described as "a little problem" in the early 1990s with the fact that FOR, nationally, "[wasn't] attracting very many black folk, and others." He reflected, "I don't think that was anything that was intentional, I just think

---

98. Robert Cunningham interview.
99. Ibid.

it was part of the culture that we're in." He felt his presence on the steering committee might improve the organization's credibility among African-Americans in Louisville, leading them to believe, in his words, "They must be OK, if Bob Cunningham is there."[100] Believing conversation and friendship could break down racism's barriers, Cunningham was fond of repeating a phrase he had used during the school desegregation crisis in Louisville in the mid-1970s: "There are only two names that black working people and poor white working people should be calling each other. It's not 'honky,' and it's not 'nigger.' It's brother and sister."[101] Cunningham saw his role with the Fellowship as creating goodwill and building closer relationships between Fellowship and Alliance activists, never proposing specific action plans but consistently reiterating his view that the first step for peace was for people "to first realize the kinship of all of us."[102]

The fact that the national FOR's membership did not reflect that kinship of all humanity, being overwhelmingly white and middle-class, had concerned some members for years. Pat McCullough, the leader of Louisville's Council on Peacemaking and Religion and a member of the LFOR's steering committee, reported from the National Council meeting in 1985 that "several people" had initiated a discussion at that meeting about their perception that "FOR is racist and sexist."[103] The national organization eventually acted on those critiques, seeking to diversify its staff and its board as the 1990s began. The Louisville chapter had long been known as one of FOR's most active chapters, and it was not surprising that the new position of racial and economic justice coordinator was filled from among the Louisville Fellowship's allies.

When the national FOR created that position in early 1991, George Edwards encouraged Mattie Jones, chair of the Kentucky Alliance Against Racist and Political Repression, to apply for it. Jones was a longtime activist for racial justice, moving from the Black Workers' Coalition to the Kentucky Alliance when it was founded in 1975. Jones immediately felt "very comfortable" with longtime civil rights activist Anne Braden, her fellow parishioner at the mostly black St. George's Episcopal Church, and was impressed with the Alliance's commitment to "direct action" rather

100. Ibid.
101. Cunningham was quoted as making that comment in "Angela Davis Speaks," *Courier-Journal*, July 14, 1976, and again in "No Easy Task" (interview with Robert Cunningham), *FORsooth*, May 1992, LFOR.
102. "No Easy Task."
103. Steering committee minutes, June 3, 1985, LFOR.

than "paperwork": "They were demonstrating, they were protesting and all. So I liked that."[104] Like her Kentucky Alliance colleague Bob Cunningham, Jones got to know and respect Jean and George Edwards through her work with the Alliance. At first, she remembered, "I thought they were *strange* white folks! Very strange to put their life and their name, and with him being Dr. Edwards from out to the seminary and everything—just put everything on the line for what [they] believed in. And I couldn't do nothing but admire the two of them, man and wife."[105] Jones knew something about spouses working as a team to achieve a common purpose. She and her husband, Turner Jones, had fostered more than one hundred children, as well as raising their own eight.[106] From the 1960s on, the Joneses worked out an arrangement whereby Mattie became the activist in the family, while her husband supported her political work at home. Given the two spouses' different temperaments, Mattie Jones recalled, "He wasn't going to get out and do the marching and all that I was doing, but he was very supportive with the babies." Turner "would work in the day" and come home in time for Mattie to attend her meetings, so that "wherever, whatever was going on: I had to be there, he made sure I got there."[107]

When Mattie Jones started her new job with national FOR in the spring of 1991, she continued to live in Louisville where her family was rooted, traveling frequently to FOR headquarters in Nyack, New York, and to various points South, where FOR wanted her to focus. Jones undertook several ambitious projects in her time with national FOR, organizing two conferences on women of color in the workplace to focus on issues facing low-wage women workers in the South, from poultry workers in North Carolina to public housing residents in Louisville. She soon found, however, that her chief—if unanticipated—role at the national office was to educate the white staff about racism within their society, the organization, and themselves. Jean Edwards later remembered that the national office had looked to their new staff member to give them "direction" in matters of race, but as far as Jean knew—or was willing to say publicly—the FOR's white membership was open to change. When Jones was introduced to the FOR National Council, of which Jean was

104. Mattie Jones interview with Lee.
105. Ibid.
106. "Mattie Jones, Civil Rights Activist from Louisville, Kentucky, Has Joined the FOR National Staff," *Fellowship*, June 1991.
107. Jones interview with Lee.

a member, "You could have heard a leaf drop. She faced a large circle of almost all white faces. But they were not hostile white faces, such as she has encountered on numerous occasions. They were eager faces, cheering her on, seeking direction. They were not disappointed."[108]

Mattie Jones soon found, however, that she and those eager white pacifists had serious disagreements about what constituted reconciliation. She later reflected, "I went, I guess, blindfolded . . . [thinking] I will not meet racism there with peace-loving and peace-seeking and justice-seeking people." Jones believed she and her white colleagues had different operative definitions of peace: "They thought keeping peace was [working with] other people that were different in nationality but the same skin color as they were."[109] Jones pushed them to expand their concept of violence: "They know war is violent. But what is more violent than a police officer that shoots down a black young man? What is more violent than to hire me on my job and let me stay a few days and then you fire me or make me so unwanted that I can't stay any longer? What is more violent than when you walk into the courtroom and you see all those black men being shunted off to the penitentiary?" She summarized, "They only think that you can bring peace to the world by ending the war."[110] For Jones, however, embracing reconciliation meant "that I'm my brother and sister's keeper, that an injury to one is an injury to all."[111] Jones consistently reminded white colleagues of the need to work as equal partners with African-American activists and to remain open to the prospect of change: "Don't put yourself out first with 'Hey, I come to help you,'" she warned.[112] Jones found FOR's executive director, Mennonite pastor and lifelong peace activist Doug Hostetter, uninformed about racism but receptive to her critiques of the Fellowship. Although Jones described her early relationship with Hostetter as "almost a mixture of day and night," she found him eager to deepen his understanding of racism and reconciliation. "One thing I loved about Doug," she recalled, "he said 'Please, work with me to help me understand,'" so the two began "to work very closely, closely together."[113]

108. Jean Edwards, "An Appreciation of Mattie Jones" (written upon Jones's retirement in 1997), *Fellowship*, September/October 1997.

109. Mattie Jones interview with Betsy Brinson.

110. Jones interview with Lee.

111. Ibid.

112. "Jones Anxious to See FOR Be Multi-racial," *FORsooth*, May 1991, LFOR.

113. Jones interview with Lee.

Jones spoke of the Louisville chapter as something of an exception within the Fellowship of Reconciliation: although the LFOR had few African-American members, Jones believed that "they reach out," creating "that bonding between the civil rights movement and the peace movement."[114] Years before Jones joined the national FOR staff, she had praised George Edwards for his witness, calling him "truly a very unselfish person" as he retired from Louisville Seminary. "He gave his whole young life and continues to struggle for freedom and justice for mankind" because, Jones believed, "he really believes he is his brother's keeper."[115] She knew she could count on George to be present to witness to racial justice, especially in a crisis, such as the aftermath of police violence. Still, her ally was conscious of the tensions between his commitment to peace and his concern for racial liberation. George had long debated the issue of black Americans' involvement in the military with one of the few African-American members of the Fellowship, local activist Willie Gray, and other black friends. In the mid-1990s, George remarked that the LFOR's "efforts in racial justice" ran "parallel and then [also] contrary to our international commitments." The African-Americans he tried to convert to pacifism over the years had chided him for worrying more about the well-being of people abroad than about their need for job security. He described the arguments they had put to him: "'We don't live over there, we are right here. We are trying to put bread on our table, and when you attack our jobs'—which means in their case, many times, military jobs—'you're taking bread off our tables.'" George acknowledged, "And it is jobs. I'm not unaware of that."[116] He saw racist hypocrisy, however, in government policy that encouraged what many pacifists called an "economic draft" by investing in the military but not in civilian job creation. And ultimately, his primary commitment would always be to fight against war, as he remarked, "I think racial issues are certainly one of the top two or three issues in the present history of humanity, but I still think that war is the most serious threat of all."[117] Gray and George's debates, and the challenges Bob Cunningham and Mattie Jones faced in the local and national FOR, highlighted the intertwining of the heresies of racism and militarism and the need for the whole church to expose and resist them together.

114. Jones interview with Lee.
115. "Edwards Retiring from Seminary—But Not from Peace Work."
116. George and Jean Edwards interview with K'Meyer, April 23, 1996, 26.
117. Ibid., 27–28.

"Praying for Peace and Paying for War Are Inconsistent"

George and Jean's abhorrence of violence, and their belief in the possibility of reconciliation even in extreme situations, made them strong advocates for the abolition of the death penalty. As George reflected in 1996, "For me, there has never been any theological doubt about the immorality of the death penalty." He understood the desire to see murderers put to death, remarking that "people think that the pain of their losses... will be alleviated by the execution," but he believed that capital punishment and the provision for victims' families to witness executions "only really encourage the vengeance motive."[118] George and Jean saw racism, poverty, and the death penalty as inextricably linked, and under their leadership the Louisville Fellowship of Reconciliation spoke out against capital punishment in ways that emphasized its connection to white supremacy. The specific focus of the LFOR's actions changed along with national and state attitudes toward the death penalty. The state of Kentucky executed no prisoners between 1962 and 1997. Until 1977, the state was within the national norm: there were no executions in the country between 1967 and 1972, when the Supreme Court imposed a moratorium on the death penalty. After the moratorium ended in 1977, a few activists sought to convince the state to do away with the possibility of executions altogether.[119] The LFOR supported those efforts, offering financial support to state organizations fighting the death penalty as early as 1981.[120] In 1983 the Fellowship joined the campaign to win a new trial for Johnny Imani Harris, an African-American sentenced to death in 1975 by an all-white jury in Alabama for participating in an inmate protest in which a prison guard was stabbed to death.[121] Noting "the deep-seated prejudice" in Baldwin County, where Harris was tried, the Fellowship appealed to its mailing list in 1983 for funds to contribute to his defense, netting $500.[122] After several false starts, the informal alliance that gathered around such

---

118. Ibid., May 9, 1996, 3–4.

119. For a legal history of the death penalty in the United States, see Foley, *Arbitrary and Capricious*.

120. Steering committee minutes, July 27, 1981, LFOR. The minutes from May, July, and September 1981 note attempts to "revive" or "reactivate" the KCADP. It is described as "newly active" in March 1984 and "continu[ing] to meet monthly" in November 1985.

121. Gardner, "Johnny 'Imani' Harris and the Alabama Death Sentence." Harris was eventually released in 1993.

122. Steering committee minutes, October 17, 1983, LFOR.

initiatives became the Kentucky Coalition to Abolish the Death Penalty (KCADP) in 1984.

George and Jean Edwards supported the KCADP, which often met at their house, while devoting their primary energies to the peace movement. Catholic priest Patrick Delahanty, who became the chair of the KCADP in 1988, first met George and Jean Edwards at the potluck suppers held at their church, Central Presbyterian, to bring opponents of capital punishment together in the 1980s. Political agreement, however, did not always translate into effective action. Delahanty lost patience with those suppers mid-decade, believing that "these were important meetings, but those gathered there were all committed abolitionists and sitting around talking . . . would not get us to our ultimate goal." One evening Delahanty announced that "I would not be back and that I planned to go to Frankfort [the state capital] because lawmakers could do something about this." Delahanty started quietly lobbying legislators in 1987. When he became the chair of the Coalition a year later, he knew he could count on George and Jean to attend KCADP rallies and legislative sessions on death penalty issues. Delahanty later described the Edwardses as "much more movement persons than I am," prone to organize "demonstrations, get arrested, et cetera," while he favored pressuring lawmakers face to face, by legal means. George's statements at those rallies, however, moved him: "The theological content, the crafting of his comments, were eloquent and forceful and deeply moving. The depth of his love for others and his desire never to inflict violence on anyone was quite touching; and he would never take credit for anything."[123]

George and Jean's concern for justice made all the difference in the life of one man: William Thomas Gregory, sentenced in 1993 to seventy years' imprisonment for the rape and attempted rape of two Louisville women. Although George and Jean had never met Gregory, George was pen pals with a man, Cullen Ray, who befriended him at the Northpoint Training Center near Danville, Kentucky. Ray had been a student in the elementary New Testament Greek class that George taught on a volunteer basis, after he retired, at the Kentucky State Reformatory in LaGrange. Believing Gregory's protestations of innocence, Ray appealed to George for help. By 1995, new DNA testing methods, unavailable during the trial, had been developed, so George and Jean began raising the $5,000 necessary for the Innocence Project, an organization dedicated

---

123. Patrick Delahanty e-mail to Rhonda Mawhood Lee, March 7, 2007.

"Praying for Peace and Paying for War Are Inconsistent"

to freeing wrongfully convicted persons, to have the evidence against Gregory retested. "Not well-to-do people," as George described himself and his wife, it took the Edwardses five years to raise the funds, "five dollars here and five dollars there," with the help of Central Presbyterian Church and other congregations, until they had enough to send to the Innocence Project. Until the results came back in the summer of 2000, Jean and George had retained some skepticism; as Jean said, "We couldn't be reassured" about Gregory's innocence until they saw the test results. On the strength of those results, Gregory was exonerated and released, meeting his champions for the first time as they drove him to a series of media appearances on his first day of freedom.[124] Before and after his release, George and Jean acted as, in Gregory's words, "his second mom and dad," Jean sending him "letters of encouragement on recycled paper" as he waited in prison and then helping with his search for work and housing after he was freed.[125]

In the mid-1990s, as George and Jean were organizing support for William Gregory, the LFOR was feeling the aftershocks of a seismic shift at Southern Baptist Theological Seminary, a few blocks away from George's former employer. Faculty members like Glen Stassen and E. Glenn Hinson had long been members and allies of the Fellowship, and the group had occasionally used the seminary's facilities for its activities. Southern Seminary, known as the most intellectually rigorous and theologically diverse of the Southern Baptist Convention's six seminaries, was the last denominational institution to be incorporated into the inerrantist, or biblically fundamentalist, transformation that had started in 1979.[126] The six seminaries were targeted in the 1980s for fundamentalist control, which became a reality over the course of the 1990s. The changeover at Southern Seminary took place in 1993 as R. Albert Mohler Jr. replaced the moderate Roy L. Honeycutt.[127] Over the next three years, 60 percent of Southern Seminary's full-time faculty resigned or took early retirement under pressure. Three departments—Christian ethics,

124. "Presbyterians Split Hairs to Free Man Unjustly Convicted of Rape." Gregory's story is included in Garrett, *Convicting the Innocent*.
125. Quoted in "Outspoken Activist the Rev. George Edwards Dies," *Courier-Journal*, June 2, 2010.
126. On the transformation of the Southern Baptist Convention, see Leonard, *God's Last and Only Hope*.
127. "Baptist Seminary's Chief Says He Will Retire in '93," *Courier-Journal*, October 13, 1992.

153

preaching, and church history—underwent a complete faculty turnover by the spring of 1996, and one school, the Carver School of Church Social Work, closed. Stassen and Hinson were two of the last faculty members to leave, in 1996.

As it became clear that Stassen would be leaving Louisville after decades of "marching, organizing, vigilling, praying, building coalitions, [and] encouraging fellow strugglers for justice and peace," he collaborated with another professor of Christian ethics and a doctoral student at Southern Seminary on an essay for *Sojourners*.[128] Drawing upon their experiences both at Southern Seminary and with liberal Christians who lacked the passion that fundamentalists had in abundance, Stassen and his coauthors called upon Christians to take on "a spirituality of incarnational discipleship" in the tradition of Dietrich Bonhoeffer and Martin Luther King Jr. That spirituality would be distinct from mainline churches that "suffer from a crisis of identity or failure of conviction" and evangelical churches that "reduce Jesus to a personal savior and a name to be praised—without ... following Jesus' teachings and example." They reclaimed their religious heritage, critiquing what they believed their Southern Baptist churches had become. Although "Our heritage is to baptize believers who commit themselves to a life in Christ," they lamented, "our culture—and churches—have become addicted to secular ideologies of greed, self-indulgence, polite racism, patriarchal authoritarianism, militarism, and just plain apathy without compassion." They called for "a repentance that repudiates these addictions and includes the kind of community that helps us live lives of incarnational discipleship," and a church renewal movement that would "reject legalism, cheap grace, and sentimental love for a praxis of empowering grace and delivering love."[129]

While Stassen and his evangelical colleagues were calling for a new vision of Christian discipleship, the Louisville Fellowship of Reconciliation was taking stock of its own past so as to chart its course for the future. In late 1994, the Fellowship conducted a survey of its steering committee, which had grown to twenty-nine members, of whom twenty-two responded. Their responses showed that a significant portion of the LFOR's leadership was concerned about its involvement in a wide variety of issues and wanted to return to its focus on international peace and disarmament. A total of fourteen respondents expressed concern about

---

128. Glen Stassen letter, *FORsooth*, March 1996, LFOR.

129. Michael Westmoreland-White, Glen Stassen, and David P. Gushee, "Disciples of the Incarnation," *Sojourners*, May 1994.

the number of LFOR programs, or believed that the group "needed its own agenda" and "a sense of itself and its own mission." Four insisted on the need to ground programs in pacifism or coordinate "the peace movement," and one "said it had been a long time since members had talked about how they embody active non-violence in our community." Two long-standing programs were most widely considered "successful": annual commemorations of the nuclear attacks on Hiroshima and Nagasaki, and the LFOR's monthly newsletter, *FORsooth*. "Anti-government policy work such as Central America" also received favorable mentions. Developing new leadership was perhaps the most significant concern: "Several members were concerned about FOR's identity and future when George and Jean are no longer actively involved."[130]

A couple of years later, George and Jean Edwards themselves wondered out loud about the future of the organization they had founded. In 1996, the Louisville Fellowship of Reconciliation hired University of Louisville historian Tracy K'Meyer to conduct an extensive oral history of the couple, to honor their contribution to Louisville's peace movement and to learn from the insights they had gleaned from their lifetime of activism together. The final issue that K'Meyer asked George and Jean to consider was the LFOR's future without them. George was pessimistic, noting that "despite my great affection for many of the younger people who are in the FOR," he did not see in the group "a leadership that can do what we are doing." He added, "I'm not exaggerating what we're doing. I'm talking about who's going to have an office in their house?" The "younger people" to whom George referred were in their forties and fifties at the time; like other established peace groups, the LFOR faced the challenge of involving a new generation witnessing for peace. Jean acknowledged that the Louisville Fellowship's future was uncertain, remarking, "As an organization, who knows? It may not function as an organization." Ultimately, the two spouses agreed that, in George's words, "peace people were here before we came, and they'll be here when we've gone."[131]

The generations following George and Jean would have to face the same questions they had: what forms should their witness for peace take, and how would they build communities to support that witness? Over time, the LFOR had faced the challenge of living out its members' convictions that war was destructive and that issues of violence were intertwined,

---

130. "Fellowship of Reconciliation Summary of Surveys," November 1994, held with steering committee minutes, LFOR.

131. George and Jean Edwards interview with K'Meyer, June 18, 1996, Tape 2, 59.

without grounding itself in a shared faith beyond those affirmations. Its breadth allowed the LFOR to recruit more people to participate in its work—although none were as active as George and Jean—but left its members without a common theological or philosophical reference point from which to begin new initiatives and to sustain them once begun. That fact presented the LFOR with a dilemma: how could members support each other in their radical witness for peace while being primarily a collection of individuals working toward a shared goal rather than a community grounded in a shared identity? As a married couple whose life together had long been rooted in their faith in Jesus Christ, George and Jean Edwards faced personal and political risks together. For others who did not share that mutual vulnerability and support, a broader community of self-sacrificial companionship would be necessary, but the LFOR was not conceived to provide it.

EPILOGUE

"Through with Kings and Armies"

The Legacy of George and Jean Edwards

George Edwards died of congestive heart failure at the age of ninety on June 2, 2010. According to his wishes, in an act reminiscent of his wartime service on Welfare Island, his body was donated to the University of Louisville School of Medicine. A couple of weeks later, the chapel of Louisville Presbyterian Theological Seminary overflowed with hundreds of family members, friends, and colleagues who had come to offer thanks for his life. Many laughed in recognition when eulogist Bob Cunningham recalled first hearing of George during Louisville's school merger crisis of 1975. Intrigued by what his fellow activists had to say about "George Anjean's" commitment to racial justice, Cunningham had looked forward to meeting "this Mr. Anjean." Thirty-five years later, to honor both George and his widow, Cunningham spoke of his delight when he met the Edwardses and realized that "Mr. Anjean" was, in fact, two inseparable but distinct people.[1]

Bob Cunningham met George and Jean at a turning point in their lives, when Jean was about to come into her own as a witness for peace after decades of supporting George's teaching and activism. Twenty years later, the national Fellowship of Reconciliation recognized the complementary gifts each spouse brought to their shared work by declaring November 10,

---

1. Rhonda Mawhood Lee personal recollection.

1995, "George and Jean Edwards Day" at Shadowcliff. The FOR's proclamation celebrated the fact that George and Jean had "not only tirelessly worked for the FOR in Louisville, but have also spent many months working at the national office," that "many an FOR member has been recruited through Jean's irresistible efforts," that "Jean's bright voice and George's booming response are legendary at Shadowcliff," and that they "epitomize the image of FOR as a 'long-distance runner' for peace and justice."[2] Jean and George had run that race together, adapting their pace and handing off the baton of leadership as needed, so that each of them could grow as fully as possible into the vocations to which they had been called.

That growth required both personal discipline and the support of friends and allies. Interviewed in his seventies, after decades of taking unpopular stands, George echoed the FOR's use of the long-distance runner metaphor as he noted with satisfaction that he and Jean "still have some people that work with us . . . [who] say, 'We'll run this race with you.' There's nothing better."[3] His words evoked both the comment attributed to the elderly Apostle Paul, "I have fought the good fight, I have finished the race, I have kept the faith," and the African-American spiritual "Guide My Feet," the refrain of which is "for I don't want to run this race in vain." Neither he nor Jean, however, harbored illusions that they had won the fight against war. Around the same time, Jean used a martial metaphor to make it clear that the evils against which she and George had struggled remained strong: "I don't have any grand illusions about what we've accomplished. I think we have done some things here in Louisville that are very good, but, by and large, you have to realize that we're losing the war."[4] On another occasion, she phrased her assessment of the LFOR's work more positively, in terms that reflected her background as a Christian educator. "I think the main work that we've done and strived to do is educational," she remarked, noting that they had tried in that way "to overcome the evil in society" along with "some of the bias that people have."[5] Overall, as Jean judged her efforts, she declared that "I like to feel that I have taught a few things."[6]

---

2. National FOR proclamation, reprinted in *FORSooth*, December 1995–January 1996, LFOR.

3. George and Jean Edwards interview with K'Meyer, May 9, 1996, Tape 2, 51.

4. Ibid., June 18, 1996, Tape 2, 58.

5. Ibid., May 9, 1996, Tape 2, 48.

6. Ibid., Tape 2, 52.

"Through with Kings and Armies"

Neither Jean nor George was overly discouraged by their lack of measurable success in swaying either church or state. More than a decade into retirement they maintained that, in George's words, "with what energies we have left we want to work for . . . the abolition of war." Aware that the dispute over slavery had split their Presbyterian Church—and virtually all white American churches—in the nineteenth century, the Edwardses were not deterred by the fact that their abolitionist goal might seem unrealistic. The reliably contrarian George drew strength from history, noting that "the abolition of slavery, when it was first announced, was a totally utopian thought. It was ridiculous and it was uneconomical, and it was this and that and blah, blah, blah. You were fighting the churches, you were fighting government, you were fighting civilization, millenia of slavery, which has proven such a very valuable institution for those that weren't slaves." All those factors, George concluded, led him to believe that the goal of abolishing war was "comparable."[7] Even though he and Jean had no expectation of seeing that goal realized in their lifetimes, they held fast to the central tenet of their faith, which he restated succinctly at the age of eighty-five: "The confession of Christ, to me, means that you are through with kings and armies."[8]

That conviction kept Jean and George going despite the discouraging sense that they were, in Jean's military metaphor, "losing the war." Their commitment sustained friends like Jim Flynn, who called them "the glue for FOR in this area." Appreciating that the Edwardses were "willing to do the grunt work of mailings and that kind of thing," while maintaining "a vision of how putting stamps on [letters] . . . plays into the larger picture," Flynn summed up their mutual commitment in two words: "dogged faithfulness."[9] Mark Baridon saw that faithfulness in action when he returned to Central Presbyterian Church as its co-pastor in 2001, having stayed in touch with George and Jean while he served a Cleveland church for over a decade. Although Baridon continued to respect the Edwardses' witness for peace, pastoral experience had deepened his appreciation of their marriage and the ways in which, in their later years, "They just looked after and cared for each other so well." As George's back troubles worsened, Baridon recalled, he leaned increasingly on Jean because of her "stronger physical health." George's stooped posture and cardiac troubles, however, did not keep him from a task he

7. Ibid., March 12, 1996, Tape 1, 22.
8. George and Jean Edwards interview with Lee.
9. James Flynn interview, 29.

and Jean had taken on more than twenty years before his death: serving as dishwashers for Central Presbyterian Church's monthly dinner for persons living with HIV and AIDS. That commitment kept the church from using paper plates and plastic utensils, which George and Jean, long concerned with the well-being of all creatures, could not condone.[10]

Although Flynn, Baridon, and others recognized George and Jean as faithful fellow Christians who remained loyal, if dissident, church members their whole lives, the couple was deeply aware of the gap that had widened over the years between their beliefs and those of most Christians. In her seventies, Jean remarked that while her pacifist beliefs had originally been rooted in her Christian faith, after years of activism, "I see nothing but politics now" in the struggle for peace.[11] Even so, she remained an active church member, continuing to call Christians to account for their implicit or explicit support of violence even as she sought allies of all persuasions to join her in taking a personal stand against war. Her husband, the pastor, seminary professor, and Sunday school teacher, did not go as far as Jean in appropriating secular language, but he did note, "I'm not really very orthodox now, theologically, because, as I was saying to my adult [Sunday school] group . . . 'Jesus is not coming back again.'" In his final years, George's hopes for "the second coming" of Jesus Christ were limited to "the appropriation" of his mission "within the community that is identified as Christian."[12] In other words, Jesus would be present in the world to the extent that his followers committed themselves to his rebellious, nonviolent way. In George's experience, that manifestation of Christ remained all too infrequent, but it did become visible from time to time in the fellowship of witnesses for peace.

In George's later years, he drew inspiration for his ongoing struggle of faith from a source that appealed to his unconventional nature: the neo-Marxist philosopher Ernst Bloch. Bloch, an atheist Jew, had fled Nazi Germany, returned to East Germany after the Second World War, and later taught in Tübingen, where George became familiar with his work. Bloch was known for elaborating what he called a "secular eschatology," or theory of the ultimate goal of history, that emphasized the need to persist in hope while striving to build an equitable society on earth.[13] Despite

---

10. Baridon interview.

11. Jean Edwards interview with K'Meyer, 26.

12. Ibid., March 26, 1996, Tape 2, 66.

13. Bloch, *The Principle of Hope*. Bloch's work was appropriated into Christianity by the German theologian Jürgen Moltmann.

his atheism, Bloch rooted his hopeful view of the future in the book of Exodus, affirming the argument of Jewish and Christian scholars that the name of God spoken to Moses out of the burning bush was the future form of the Hebrew verb "to be." George found that argument "very persuasive," that God's name "is actually . . . 'I will be what I will be.'" George reclaimed Bloch's insight for his own Christian theology, arguing that "religion has to have this future note." As George paraphrased Bloch: "He said, 'You've got to do something every day that is futuristic. You've got to struggle for the thing that has not yet come into being.' I think that's a very important thing, and a very religious thing." That insight influenced George's commitment to carry on the struggle for peace even though he knew he was unlikely to see his vision of a church—much less an American nation—dedicated to nonviolence come to fruition. As he noted with a sigh, "I sometimes despair of trying to get these ideas over to religious people."[14]

George and Jean's ally Paula Jackson affirmed a similar faith in more orthodox Christian terms. When asked, twenty years after the height of her involvement with the LFOR, if she and her fellow peace activists had expected to win any of their struggles, she answered, "I knew we would win eventually." That faith was rooted, not in self-confidence, but in her understanding of God's nature. "Because God's not going to give up . . . how many times a day do we say, 'thy kingdom come, thy will be done on earth as in heaven'? And we don't say that because we wish it could happen, if only, but it won't. We say that because we already know it will. And by saying it ourselves, we're signing on. 'OK, God, I know this is going to happen, but *I* want to participate in it. Let me be part of it.' I don't know how long it will take. How much time has God got?"[15]

In making their common commitment to peace the foundation of their marriage, George and Jean Edwards affirmed their desire and their decision to inhabit God's kingdom, whether or not they saw its full establishment in their earthly lifetime. Living with urgency while trusting in eternity, they suspected that their warnings and their witness would never be heeded. They were right: while most Americans eventually came to believe that the war in Vietnam had been a mistake, only a minority of American Christians dared even to experiment with embracing nonviolence. But in the sixty-three years they ran their race together, George and Jean Edwards joined Paul, and everyone who had ever placed their trust in the Sermon on the Mount, in affirming two

14. George and Jean Edwards interview with K'Meyer, March 26, 1996, Tape 2, 61.
15. Paula Jackson interview.

things: that to commit to following Jesus Christ is already to finish the race he has set us; and that to witness to the gospel is already to share in his peaceful victory.

Questions and Topics for Discussion

1. How do you define Christian marriage? What elements must be present for a relationship to be considered a marriage? Does your concept of marriage differ in any way from your church's teaching about it? Are there any relationships that include the expression of sexual desire that you would not consider to be marriage, but that you believe the church should recognize and honor in some way? Why are they of value?

2. How might churches help members discern whether they might be called to marriage, or to singleness? How could they help a couple discern a possible call to marry each other?

3. If a couple goes to a pastor seeking to be married, what sorts of issues should be discussed? Should the couple be asked to commit to any kind of work, worship, or spiritual practices during their engagement? How might a pastor discern whether or not he or she is called to marry this couple? How might the pastor involve the church in that discernment?

4. If you are married or partnered, do you and your spouse agree on how to witness publicly to your Christian faith? How do you discern together which practices to take on? How do you involve other members of your church, and of the larger Christian community, in your discernment? If you and your spouse are of different faiths, how do you negotiate your individual and joint commitments, and what common ground have you found? (These questions also apply to engaged couples as you discuss your future life together.)

5. If you are single, but feel called to marriage or lifelong partnership, how important is it to you that a future spouse share your understanding of how to practice Christianity in your home, in your church community, and in the larger world? If you do not feel called to marriage or lifelong partnership, to whom do you look for support in your journey?

6. In what ways can spouses strengthen each other's ministry, and in what ways can the single life (or widowhood) free us for ministry? What sacrifices are inherent in each state of life (including singleness and marriage, as well as ordination, living as a layperson, or taking religious vows)?

7. What are your vocations? What are the vocations of members of your family, and your circle of close friends? How do you support each other in the commitments to which you have been called? Are there times when one of your vocations seems to conflict with another, or when the vocations of different people within your family or circle of friends conflict with each other?

8. How do you discern the sacrifices you may be called to make for the sake of your vocation or that of someone with whom you share a covenant or another bond? What sacrifices did George and Jean make, individually and jointly, for the sake of their shared commitment to pacifism? Who supported them in the risks they took? Who might support you in taking risks? Whom might you be called to support?

9. How can parents encourage their children's discernment of their own vocations? How can congregations help parents and young people with this process?

10. Are any occupations or activities incompatible with Christian faith? What criteria can one use to determine what they might be? What role does corporate discernment play in that determination, and how much weight should be given to personal conscience?

11. Can political protest be a spiritual discipline for Christians? Under what circumstances, and in what forms?

12. What kinds of support might the church be called to offer those who break the law for reasons of conscience? Are there acts that the church cannot condone, even if those who commit those acts

Questions and Topics for Discussion

believe they are taking a stand for conscience? What criteria can help the church decide whether to offer or withhold support? To what extent are Christians called to remain in dialogue with each other about our disagreements? What are some ways in which we might do that?

13. How does your church discern the ways in which it is called to witness publicly to the gospel? What kinds of support might your congregation (and its larger judicatory body) seek from other Christians in that discernment and witness?

14. Is it possible to make alliances with people of other faiths, and of no faith, for the sake of Christian witness? If so, what kinds of alliances might be possible? What might be gained from that cooperation? What might be lost?

15. How would you like to be remembered after your death? What faith practices might you begin, or continue, in order to shape your life accordingly?

Bibliography

Appelbaum, Patricia. *Kingdom to Commune: Protestant Pacifist Culture between World War I and the Vietnam Era*. Chapel Hill: University of North Carolina Press, 2009.

Arsenault, Raymond. *The Sound of Freedom: Marian Anderson, The Lincoln Memorial, and the Concert that Awakened America*. New York: Bloomsbury, 2009.

Baskir, Lawrence M., and William A. Strauss. *Chance and Circumstance: The Draft, the War, and the Vietnam Generation*. New York: Alfred A. Knopf, 1978.

Bechtel, Judith A., and Robert M. Coughlin. *Building the Beloved Community: Maurice McCrackin's Life for Peace and Civil Rights*. Philadelphia: Temple University Press, 1991.

Blackwell, Joyce. *No Peace without Freedom: Race and the Women's International League for Peace and Freedom*. Carbondale: Southern Illinois University Press, 2004.

Blair, John. "Return to Marble Hill: Indiana's Rusting Nuke." *The Bloomington Alternative*, July 27, 2003.

Bloch, Ernst. *The Principle of Hope*. 3 vols. Translated by Neville Plaice and Stephen Plaice. Cambridge: MIT Press, 1995.

Braden, Anne. *The Wall Between*. 1958. Reprint. Knoxville: University of Tennessee Press, 1999.

Brandon, S. G. F. *Jesus and the Zealots: A Study of the Political Factor in Primitive Christianity*. New York: Scribner, 1967.

Brody, Reed. *Contra Terror in Nicaragua: Report of a Fact-Finding Mission: September 1984–January 1985*. Boston: South End, 1985.

Bullock, Robert H., Jr. "A Critical Period: 1880–1940." In *The Diversity of Discipleship: Presbyterians and Twentieth-Century Christian Witness*, edited by Milton J. Coalter et al., 55–82. Louisville: Westminster John Knox, 1991.

Bultmann, Rudolph. "Theology for Freedom and Responsibility." *The Christian Century*, August 27, 1958.

Butigan, Ken, et al., editors. *¡Basta! No Mandate for War: A Pledge of Resistance Handbook*. Philadelphia: New Society, 1986.

Calvin, John, and John T. McNeill. *Institutes of the Christian Religion*. Translated by Ford Lewis Battles. Louisville: Westminster John Knox, 1960.

Carmichael, Omer, and Weldon James. *The Louisville Story*. New York: Simon & Schuster, 1957.

Bibliography

Cavanaugh, William T. *Torture and Eucharist: Theology, Politics, and the Body of Christ.* Oxford: Blackwell, 1998.

Chambers, John Whiteclay, II. "Conscientious Objectors and the American State from Colonial Times to the Present." In *The New Conscientious Objection: From Sacred to Secular Resistance*, edited by Charles C. Moskos and John Whiteclay Chambers II, 23-46. New York: Oxford University Press, 1993.

Clapp, Rodney. *Families at the Crossroads: Beyond Traditional and Modern Options.* Downers Grove, IL: InterVarsity, 1993.

———. "From Family Values to Family Virtues." In *Virtues and Practices in the Christian Tradition*, edited by Nancey Murphy et al., 185-201. Harrisburg, PA: Trinity, 1997.

Clotfelter, Charles T. *After Brown: The Rise and Retreat of School Desegregation.* Princeton: Princeton University Press, 2006.

Coontz, Stephanie. *Marriage, A History: How Love Conquered Marriage.* New York: Penguin, 2005.

Cortright, David. *Peace Works: The Citizen's Role in Ending the Cold War.* Boulder, CO: Westview, 1993.

Cott, Nancy F. *Public Vows: A History of Marriage and the Nation.* Cambridge: Harvard University Press, 2000.

Crews, Clyde F. "Hallowed Ground: The Cathedral of the Assumption in Louisville History." *Filson Club History Quarterly* 51 (1977) 249-61.

Crittenden, Ann. *Sanctuary: A Story of American Conscience and the Law in Collision.* New York: Weidenfeld & Nicolson, 1988.

DeBenedetti, Charles, with Charles Chatfield. *An American Ordeal: The Antiwar Movement of the Vietnam Era.* Syracuse: Syracuse University Press, 1990.

Dekar, Paul. *Creating the Beloved Community: A Journey with the Fellowship of Reconciliation.* Telford, PA: Cascadia, 2005.

D'Emilio, John. *Lost Prophet: The Life and Times of Bayard Rustin.* Chicago: University of Chicago Press, 2003.

Edwards, George R. "Biblical and Contemporary Aspects of War Tax Resistance." In *The Peacemaking Struggle: Militarism and Resistance*, edited by Ronald H. Stone and Dana Wilbanks, 111-22. Lanham, MD: University Press of America, 1985.

———. "Christology and Ethics." In *Biblical Realism Confronts the Nation: Ten Christian Scholars Summon the Church to the Discipleship of Peace*, edited by Paul Peachey, 89-102. New York: Fellowship, 1963.

———. *Gay/Lesbian Liberation: A Biblical Perspective.* New York: Pilgrim, 1984.

———. *Jesus and the Politics of Violence.* New York: Harper & Row, 1972.

———. "The Qumran Sect and the New Testament Church." PhD diss., Duke University, 1955.

Egerton, John. *Speak Now against the Day: The Generation before the Civil Rights Movement in the South.* New York: Knopf, 1994.

Ely, Carol. *Jewish Louisville: Portrait of a Community.* Louisville: Jewish Community Federation of Louisville, 2003.

Ericksen, Robert P., and Susannah Heschel, editors. *Betrayal: German Churches and the Holocaust.* Minneapolis: Augsburg Fortress, 1999.

Ernst, John. "Vietnam War." In *The Encyclopedia of Louisville*, edited by John E. Kleber, 912-13. Lexington: University Press of Kentucky, 2001.

Ernst, John, and Yvonne Baldwin. "The Not So Silent Minority: Louisville's Antiwar Movement, 1966-1975." *The Journal of Southern History* 73:1 (2007) 106-42.

Ferguson, Ron. *George MacLeod, Founder of the Iona Community: A Biography*. London: Collins, 1998.

First Presbyterian Church, Nashville, Tennessee. "The History of First Church." Online: http://fpcnashville.org/home/history/.

Foley, Michael A. *Arbitrary and Capricious: The Supreme Court, the Constitution, and the Death Penalty*. Westport, CT: Praeger, 2003.

Fosl, Catherine. *Subversive Southerner: Anne Braden and the Struggle for Racial Justice in the Cold War South*. Lexington: University Press of Kentucky, 2006.

Frazer, Heather T., and John O'Sullivan. *We Have Just Begun to Not Fight: An Oral History of Conscientious Objectors in Civilian Public Service in World War II*. New York: Twayne, 1996.

Freedman, Lawrence. "The First Two Generations of Nuclear Strategists." In *Makers of Modern Strategy: From Machiavelli to the Nuclear Age*, edited by Peter Paret, 735-78. Princeton: Princeton University Press, 1986.

Freire, Paulo. *Pedagogy of the Oppressed*. Translated by Myra Bergman Ramos. New York: Herder & Herder, 1970.

Gardner, Tom. "Johnny 'Imani' Harris and the Alabama Death Sentence." *Southern Changes* 1:5 (1979) 10-14.

Garrett, Brandon L. *Convicting the Innocent: When Criminal Prosecutions Go Wrong*. Cambridge: Harvard University Press, 2011.

Garrison, Dee. *Bracing for Armageddon: Why Civil Defense Never Worked*. Oxford: Oxford University Press, 2006.

Garrow, David. *Chicago 1966: Open Housing Marches, Summit Negotiations, and Operation Breadbasket*. Brooklyn: Carson, 1989.

Gerlach, Wolfgang. *And the Witnesses Were Silent: The Confessing Church and the Persecution of the Jews*. Translated by Victoria J. Barnett. Lincoln: University of Nebraska Press, 2000.

Goens, C. C. *Broken Churches, Broken Nation: Denominational Schisms and the Coming of the Civil War*. Macon, GA: Mercer University Press, 1985.

Goossen, Rachel Waltner. *Women against the Good War: Conscientious Objection and Gender on the American Home Front, 1941-1947*. Chapel Hill: University of North Carolina Press, 1997.

Greene, Christina. *Our Separate Ways: Women and the Black Freedom Movement in Durham, North Carolina*. Chapel Hill: University of North Carolina Press, 2005.

Grise-Owens, Erlene, et al. "Organizing for Change: One City's Journey toward Justice." *Journal of Gay and Lesbian Social Services* 16:3/4 (2004) 1-15.

Hall, Mitchell K. *Because of Their Faith: CALCAV and Religious Opposition to the Vietnam War*. New York: Columbia University Press, 1990.

Hallie, Philip. *Lest Innocent Blood Be Shed: The Story of the Village of Le Chambon and How Goodness Happened There*. New York: Harper Perennial, 1994.

Harrod, Mary Jo. "George and Jean Edwards: Living Peace." *Mosaic* 12:2 (2005). Online: http://www.lpts.edu/alumni/Edwards-MosaicSumo5-AlumTributes.pdf.

Hedeman, Ed. *War Tax Resistance: A Guide to Withholding Your Support from the Military*. Edited by Ruth Benn. 5th ed. New York: War Resisters League, 2003.

Herring, George C. *America's Longest War: The United States and Vietnam, 1950-1975*. 4th ed. New York: McGraw-Hill, 2002.

Bibliography

Horowitz, Daniel. *Jimmy Carter and the Energy Crisis of the 1970s: The "Crisis of Confidence" Speech of July 15, 1979: A Brief History with Documents*. Boston: Bedford/St. Martin's, 2005.

Johnson, James Turner. *Just War Tradition and the Restraint of War: A Moral and Historical Inquiry*. Princeton: Princeton University Press, 1981.

Käsemann, Ernst. *On Being a Disciple of the Crucified Nazarene: Unpublished Lectures and Sermons*. Translated by Roy A. Harrisville. Grand Rapids: Eerdmans, 2010.

Katz, Milton S. *Ban the Bomb: A History of SANE, The Committee for a Sane Nuclear Policy, 1957-1985*. New York: Greenwood, 1986.

Keim, Albert N. *The CPS Story: An Illustrated History of Civilian Public Service*. Intercourse, PA: Good Books, 1990.

Kiffmeyer, Thomas J. "From Self-Help to Sedition: The Appalachian Volunteers in Eastern Kentucky, 1964-1970." *The Journal of Southern History* 64:1 (1998) 65-94.

King, Martin Luther, Jr. "Beyond Vietnam: A Time to Break Silence." April 4, 1967. Online: http://www.americanrhetoric.com/speeches/mlkatimetobreaksilence.htm.

Kleber, John F. "Busing, Public School." In *The Encyclopedia of Louisville*, edited by John E. Kleber, 148-49. Lexington: University Press of Kentucky, 2001.

Klibaner, Irwin. *Conscience of a Troubled South: The Southern Conference Educational Fund, 1946-1966*. Brooklyn: Carlson, 1989.

K'Meyer, Tracy E. *Civil Rights in the Gateway to the South: Louisville, Kentucky, 1945-1980*. Lexington: University Press of Kentucky, 2009.

———. *Interracialism and Christian Community in the Postwar South: The Story of Koinonia Farm*. Charlottesville: University of Virginia Press, 1997.

Kornbluh, Peter. *Nicaragua: The Price of Intervention*. Washington, DC: Institute for Policy Studies, 1987.

Kornbluh, Peter, and Malcolm Byrne. *The Iran Contra Scandal: The Declassified History*. New York: New Press, 1993.

Kosek, Joseph Kip. *Acts of Conscience: Christian Nonviolence and Modern American Democracy*. New York: Columbia University Press, 2009.

Kotelanski, Jorge. "Prolonged and Patient Efforts: The Desegregation of Duke University, 1948-1963." Undergraduate honors thesis, Duke University, 1990.

Kotz, Nick. *Wild Blue Yonder: Money, Politics, and the B-1 Bomber*. Princeton: Princeton University Press, 1988.

LaFeber, Walter. *America, Russia, and the Cold War, 1945-2002*. 9th ed. New York: McGraw-Hill, 2002.

Laurence Lee Howe Papers, 1937-1978. University of Louisville archives. Online: http://louisville.libguides.com/content.php?pid=43752&sid=323532.

Lee, Rhonda Mawhood. "'Admit Guilt—And Tell the Truth': The Louisville Fellowship of Reconciliation's Struggle with Pacifism and Racial Justice, 1941-1945." *The Journal of Southern History* 76:2 (2010) 315-42.

———. "'God Alone Is Lord of the Conscience': Fellowship of Reconciliation Activists Confront Church and State in Louisville, Kentucky, 1975-1995." *Ohio Valley History* 7:3 (2007) 49-67.

Leithart, Peter J. *Defending Constantine: The Twilight of an Empire and the Dawn of Christendom*. Downers Grove, IL: InterVarsity, 2010.

Leonard, Bill. *God's Last and Only Hope: The Fragmentation of the Southern Baptist Convention*. Grand Rapids: Eerdmans, 1990.

Lester, Muriel. *It Occurred to Me*. New York: Harper & Brothers, 1938.

Bibliography

Lichter, Daniel T., et al. "Race and Poverty: Divergent Fortunes of America's Children?" *Focus* 24:3 (2006) 8–16.

Maisel, Albert Q. "Bedlam 1946." *Life*, May 6, 1946, 102–18.

Mather, Eleanor Price. *Pendle Hill: A Quaker Experiment in Education and Community*. Wallingford, PA: Pendle Hill, 1980.

McCarthy, David Matzko. *Sex and Love in the Home: A Theology of the Household*. Rev. ed. London: SCM, 2004.

Meyer, David S. *A Winter of Discontent: The Nuclear Freeze and American Politics*. New York: Praeger, 1990.

Milestones (yearbook of Ward-Belmont College).
   1939: http://www.archive.org/details/milestones1939ward.
   1940: http://www.archive.org/details/milestones1940ward.
   1941: http://www.archive.org/details/milestones1941ward.

Morse, Arthur D. *While Six Million Died*. New York: Random House, 1968.

Morton, Nelle. *The Journey Is Home*. Boston: Beacon, 1985.

National Interreligious Service Board for Conscientious Objectors. *1996 Directory of Civilian Public Service*. Scottdale, PA: Mennonite Publishing House, 1996.

Niebuhr, Reinhold. "Why the Christian Church Is Not Pacifist." In *Christianity and Power Politics*, 1–32. New York: Scribner's, 1940.

Nutt, Rick. *Many Lamps, One Light: Louisville Presbyterian Theological Seminary, A 150th Anniversary History*. Grand Rapids: Eerdmans, 2002.

———. *Toward Peacemaking: Presbyterians in the South and National Security, 1945–1983*. Tuscaloosa: University of Alabama Press, 1994.

Ogilvie, Sarah A., and Scott Miller. *Refuge Denied: The St. Louis Passengers and the Holocaust*. Madison: University of Wisconsin Press, 2006.

Orfield, Gary, and Susan E. Eaton. *Dismantling Desegregation: The Quiet Reversal of Brown v. Board of Education*. New York: New Press, 1997.

Otter, Elna, and Dorothy Pine, editors. *The Sanctuary Experience: Voices of the Community*. San Diego: Aventine, 2004.

Presbyterian Church USA. *Book of Confessions, Study Edition*. Louisville: Geneva Press, 1996.

———. *Definitive Guidance: The Church's Statements on Homosexuality*. Louisville: Geneva, 2004.

"Presbyterians Split Hairs to Free Man Unjustly Convicted of Rape." PCUSA News, July 11, 2000. Worldwide Faith News Archives. Online: http://www.wfn.org/2000/07/ms.00088.html.

Reagan, Ronald. "Address before a Joint Session of Congress on Central America." April 27, 1983. Online: http://www.reagan.utexas.edu/archives/speeches/1983/42783d.htm.

Reid, B. L. *First Acts: A Memoir*. Athens: University of Georgia Press, 1988.

Remnick, David. *King of the World*. New York: Vintage, 1998.

Sauvage, Pierre. *Weapons of the Spirit*. New York: First Run/Icarus Films, 1988.

Schoenwald, Jonathan M. "We Are an Action Group: The John Birch Society and the Conservative Movement in the 1960s." In *The Conservative Sixties*, edited by David Farber and Jeff Roche, 21–36. New York: Peter Lang, 2003.

Segal, David R., and Mady Wechsler Segal. "America's Military Population." *Population Bulletin* 59:4 (2004) 1–40.

Bibliography

Simmons, Paul D. "Personhood, the Bible, and the Abortion Debate." Religious Coalition for Reproductive Choice (March 2005). Online: http://rcrc.org/pdf/RCRC_EdSeries_Personhood.pdf

Smith, Christian. *The Emergence of Liberation Theology: Radical Religion and Social Movement Theory.* Chicago: University of Chicago Press, 1991.

———. *Resisting Reagan: The U.S. Central America Peace Movement.* Chicago: University of Chicago Press, 1996.

Stassen, Glen. *The Journey into Peacemaking.* Memphis: Southern Baptist Convention Brotherhood Commission, 1983.

Stassen, Glen H., and David P. Gushee. *Kingdom Ethics: Following Jesus in Contemporary Context.* Downers Grove, IL: InterVarsity, 2003.

Stevens, Daniel. "Public Opinion and Public Policy: The Case of Kennedy and Civil Rights." *Presidential Studies Quarterly* 32:1 (2002) 111–36.

Stone, Ronald H., and Dana W. Wilbanks, editors. *The Peacemaking Struggle: Militarism and Resistance: Essays Prepared for the Advisory Council on Church and Society of the Presbyterian Church (U.S.A.).* Lanham, MD: University Press of America, 1985.

Streit, Clarence K. *Union Now: A Proposal for a Federal Union of the Democracies of the North Atlantic.* New York: Harper, 1938.

Swerdlow, Amy. *Women Strike for Peace: Traditional Motherhood and Radical Politics in the 1960s.* Chicago: University of Chicago Press, 1993.

Taylor, Steven J. *Acts of Conscience: World War II, Mental Institutions, and Religious Objectors.* Syracuse: Syracuse University Press, 2009.

Tucker, Todd. *The Great Starvation Experiment: The Heroic Men Who Starved So That Millions Could Live.* New York: Free Press, 2006.

U.S. Census Bureau. "Health Insurance Coverage: Who Had a Lapse between 1990 and 1992?" Bureau of the Census Statistical Brief (1994). Online: www.census.gov/apsd/www/statbrief/sb94_6.pdf.

Van Wijk-Bos, Johanna W. H. "May the Beauty of His Life Shine Forevermore: Tribute to George Edwards (1920–2010)." *Mosaic* (Winter 2010) 25.

War Resisters League. "History of War Tax Resistance." Online: http://www.warresisters.org/node/328.

———. "IRS Seizure and Court Actions against War Tax Resisters." Online: http://www.warresisters.org/convicted_wtr.htm.

Warrior, Robert Allen. "Canaanites, Cowboys, and Indians: Deliverance, Conquest, and Liberation Theology Today." *Christianity and Crisis*, September 11, 1989, 261–65.

Weems, Ann. *Family Faith Stories.* Philadelphia: Westminster, 1985.

Weinberg, Gerhard L. *A World at Arms: A Global History of World War II.* Cambridge: Cambridge University Press, 1994.

Wette, Wolfram. *The Wehrmacht: History, Myth, Reality.* Translated by Deborah Lucas Schneider. Cambridge: Harvard University Press, 2006.

Williams, Daniel Day. *The Spirit and the Forms of Love.* New York: Harper & Row, 1968.

Williamson, Lamar, Jr. "Limits on a Christian's Obedience to the State." In *The Peacemaking Struggle: Militarism and Resistance*, edited by Ronald H. Stone and Dana Wilbanks, 103–10. Lanham, MD: University Press of America, 1985.

Winn, Albert C. *Ain't Gonna Study War No More.* Louisville: Westminster John Knox, 1993.

Winter, Gibson. *The Suburban Captivity of the Churches: An Analysis of Protestant Responsibility in the Expanding Metropolis.* New York: Doubleday, 1961.

Witte, John, Jr. *From Sacrament to Contract: Marriage, Religion, and Law in the Western Tradition.* Louisville: Westminster John Knox, 1997.
Wittner, Lawrence S. *Confronting the Bomb: A Short History of the World Nuclear Disarmament Movement.* Stanford: Stanford University Press, 2009.
———. *Toward Nuclear Abolition: A History of the World Nuclear Disarmament Movement, 1971–Present.* Stanford: Stanford University Press, 2003.
Wright, George C. *A History of Blacks in Kentucky.* Vol. 2, *In Pursuit of Equality, 1890–1980.* Frankfort, KY: Kentucky Historical Society, 1992.
———. *Life Behind a Veil: Blacks in Louisville, Kentucky, 1865–1930.* Baton Rouge: Louisiana State University Press, 1985.
Zahn, Gordon. *In Solitary Witness: The Life and Death of Franz Jägerstätter.* Rev. ed. Springfield, IL: Templegate, 1986.

Interviews

By Betsy Brinson:

Mattie Jones, February 5, 1999, Kentucky Civil Rights Oral History Project, Kentucky Oral History Commission, Kentucky Historical Society

By Tracy E. K'Meyer (all archived at Oral History Collection, University of Louisville Archives, Louisville, KY):

George Edwards, February 9, 1996
Jean Edwards, Feb. 29, 1996
George and Jean Edwards, March 12, 1996; March 26, 1996; April 23, 1996; May 9, 1996; and June 18, 1996
James Flynn, February 5, 1997

By Rhonda Mawhood Lee (all in author's possession):

Mark Baridon, January 18, 2011
Eileen Blanton, April 17, 2006
David Brown Kinloch, February 26, 2007
John Cumbler, March 22, 2006
Robert Cunningham, June 26, 2006
George and Jean Edwards, October 17, 2006
John Douglas (Johnny) Edwards, January 16, 2011

Bibliography

Pat Geier, December 21, 2005, and February 27, 2007
David Horvath, December 12, 2005
Paula Jackson, November 4, 2005
Mattie Jones, April 3, 2006
Glen Stassen, March 18, 2006
Terry Weiss, February 1, 2006

Organizational Records and Personal Papers (privately held unless otherwise indicated; for access, contact the organization)

Blacknall Presbyterian Church (BPC), Durham, NC
Central Presbyterian Church (CPC), Louisville, KY
Church of the Epiphany (CE), Louisville, KY
Church Peace Mission (CPM), Swarthmore College Peace Collection
Clergy and Laity Concerned of Kentuckiana (CALCK), University of Louisville archives
Council on Peacemaking and Religion (CPR), Louisville, KY
Jean Edwards papers
Kentucky Religious Coalition for Reproductive Choice (KRCRC), Kentucky Civil Liberties Union, Louisville
Louisville Fellowship of Reconciliation (LFOR)
Louisville Presbyterian Theological Seminary archives (LPTS)
Rabbi Martin M. Perley papers, The Temple–Congregation Adath Israel Brith Sholom archives, Louisville, KY
Pittsboro Presbyterian Church (PPC), Pittsboro, NC
Progress in Education (PIE), University of Louisville archives
The Virtual Vietnam Archive, Texas Tech University: http://www.vietnam.ttu.edu/star/images/1451/14511249020.pdf.

Newspapers and Magazines

The Christian Century
Courier-Journal (Louisville)
Kentucky Jewish Post and Opinion
Louisville Fellowship of Reconciliation newsletter (titled *FORSooth* from 1990 on)
Louisville Times
Nashville Tennessean
New York Times
Presbyterian Outlook
Presbyterian Survey
Sojourners
Southern Patriot (newspaper of the Southern Conference Educational Fund)
The Register (Louisville Presbyterian Theological Seminary)
The Sou'wester: Student Weekly Publication of Southwestern at Memphis. http://dlynx.rhodes.edu/jspui/bitstream/10267/5638/1/19411205_souwester.pdf.

"Buddy" Edwards at a Presbyterian youth gathering, June 1941 (Courtesy of Jean Edwards)

George and Jean Edwards in front of Louisville Presbyterian Theological Seminary, January 1948 (Courtesy of Jean Edwards)

Riley, Virginia, and Johnny Edwards with their Sunday school class, Peace Presbyterian Church, circa 1961 (Courtesy of Jean Edwards)

George Edwards in the classroom, circa 1975 (Courtesy of Louisville Presbyterian Theological Seminary)

Jim Flynn at the Louisville airport with Central American refugees, circa 1983 (Courtesy of the Louisville Fellowship of Reconciliation—LFOR)

Jean and George Edwards celebrating the twentieth anniversary of the Louisville Fellowship of Reconciliation, 1995 (Courtesy of the LFOR)

Fellowship of Reconciliation

MARCH, 1988

LOUISVILLE CHAPTER, Fellowship of Reconciliation

...STOP PAYING FOR WAR.

64%
OF YOUR INCOME TAXES
GOES TO THE MILITARY
(The Budget of the U.S. Government—FY 1986. The percentages are Federal Funds, calculated after removing Trust Funds.)

REASONS FOR RESISTING WAR TAXES:

Four basic reasons have been cited:

1. Tax resistance allows one to withdraw consent and support for the war-making machinery; it challenges and interferes with "business as usual", for the tax resister.
2. It allows tax money to be redirected to socially useful purposes. Frequently, tax resisters re-channel their money to other peace-related work.
3. Refusal of military taxes and their subsequent redirection can play a key role in building a strong movement for peace and justice. It contributes to wider process of questions and publicly challenging institutionalized preparations for war.
4. It helps to make one's life more consistent with one's value system.

TELEPHONE WAR TAX RESISTANCE:

Although the federal excise tax on each monthly phone bill is small, it provides nearly two billion dollars a year which is spent in the most part by the military. It has been imposed during World War I, World War II, the Korean War and again during the Vietnam War (10%). Although it was supposed be phased out, it was raised in 1983 from 1% to 3%.

If thousands of us stop paying our phone taxes and redirect them to life-affirming purposes, we will create a significant statement for peace, a protest which cannot be ignored. The IRS can collect unpaid phone taxes, but your phone service cannot legally be cut off. You should include a note each month explaining that you are paying the full bill, less this tax, to protest military spending.

SYMBOLIC TAX WITHHOLDING:

Withholding a nominal amoung ($5 or $10) enables a person to protest without involving a great risk. Most important is the letter explanation which go to Senators and Representatives as well as newspapers and clergy.
(cont. next page)

What is Security?

In March we celebrate Women's History. A special article on "Building Security for Women" can be found on page 2. 2 out of 3 poor adults are women and 80% of the poor in the U.S. are adult women and children. How can we call ourselves secure with worldwide military expenditures at $800 billion annually?

Cover page, LFOR newsletter, March 1988 (Courtesy of the LFOR)

www.ingramcontent.com/pod-product-compliance
Lightning Source LLC
Chambersburg PA
CBHW020850160426
43192CB00007B/865